Whose Welfare?

WHOSE WELFARE?

☆

EDITED BY
GWENDOLYN MINK

CORNELL UNIVERSITY PRESS

ITHACA AND LONDON

Introduction, Chapters 7 and 10, and Index copyright © 1999 by Cornell University
Chapters 1–6, 8, and 9 copyright © 1998 by *Social Justice*

Most of the contents of this book first appeared in volume 25, number 71 of the journal *Social Justice*.

This book first published 1999 by Cornell University Press.

Printed in the United States of America

Library of Congress Cataloging-in-Publication Data

Mink, Gwendolyn, 1952–
Whose welfare? / edited by Gwendolyn Mink.
p.   cm.
Includes bibliographical references and index.
ISBN 0-8014-8620-3 (pbk.)
1. Poor women—Government policy—United States.
2. Public welfare—United States.   3. Welfare recipients—
Employment—United States.   I. Title
362.83′8′0973—dc21   99-37636

Cornell University Press strives to use environmentally responsible suppliers and materials to the fullest extent possible in the publishing of its books. Such materials include vegetable-based, low-VOC inks, and acid-free papers that are recycled, totally chlorine-free, or partly composed of nonwood fibers. Books that bear the logo of the FSC (Forest Stewardship Council) use paper taken from forests that have been inspected and certified as meeting the highest standards for environmental and social responsibility. For further information, visit our website at www.cornellpress.cornell.edu.

Paperback printing   10 9 8 7 6 5 4 3 2 1

Contents

Introduction   I
Gwendolyn Mink

I   Historical Perspectives on Contemporary Welfare Politics

1   Dependency and Choice: The Two Faces of Eve   7
Rickie Solinger

2   When Work Is Slavery   36
Eileen Boris

3   From Maximum Feasible Participation to Disenfranchisement   56
Nancy A. Naples

II   Class, Race, and Gender in the New Welfare Regime

4   Welfare and Work   83
Frances Fox Piven

5   Asian Immigrant Communities and the Racial Politics
of Welfare Reform   100
Lynn H. Fujiwara

6   Women, Welfare, and Domestic Violence   132
Demie Kurz

7   Welfare's Ban on Poor Motherhood   152
Dorothy Roberts

III Toward a New Welfare Politics?

8 Aren't Poor Single Mothers Women? Feminists,
Welfare Reform, and Welfare Justice   171
Gwendolyn Mink

9 Welfare, Dependency, and a Public Ethic of Care   189
Eva Feder Kittay

10 Toward a Framework for Understanding Activism among
Poor and Working-Class Women in Twentieth-Century
America   214
Mimi Abramovitz

Contributors   249

Index   251

Whose Welfare?

Introduction

As the welfare regime established by the Personal Responsibility and Work Opportunity Act (PRA) of 1996 enters its fourth year, proponents crow that welfare reform has "worked." If we measure the law's success by the decline in the number of people receiving cash benefits, the aggregate data certainly support this claim. According to President Clinton, 900,000 people left the welfare rolls between September 1997 and May 1998—a precipitous decline. The National Governors' Association announced during the summer of 1998 that the average national decline in welfare caseloads under the PRA hovered near 30 percent, with caseloads reduced by as much as 40 percent in some states—a handsome achievement by any standards. In my home state of California, the percentage decline has been much more modest—around 12 percent, according to statistics released in July 1998—but because of the size of California's welfare population, it represents a staggering number of cases that have simply vanished from the rolls: 25,000 in Los Angeles County alone.

Although the people who championed welfare reform have been enjoying an "I-told-you-so" kind of moment, their focus on the reduction in caseloads obscures many worrisome trends. For example, some states have reduced caseloads by preventing or discouraging participation in welfare in the first place. "Diversion" programs urge applicants to pursue alternatives to public assistance—to complete a supervised job-search program, to persevere in noxious working conditions, or to exhaust family charity—before they can receive their first welfare check.[1] Another worrisome trend is the increasing racialization of welfare, as the decline in welfare participation has been greatest among whites, who were already less than 40 percent of the aggregate welfare caseload before welfare was "reformed".[2] Racism in employment decisions, the geography of jobs, and the effects of racially stratified educational opportunity all play a part in this outcome.

It is also fairly clear that families that leave welfare are not necessarily leaving poverty. For many, in fact, poverty may worsen, as the exchange of welfare for employment often is accompanied by the loss of food stamps and medicaid. More important, mere employment does not guarantee an above-poverty income. As the National Conference of State Legislatures observed in its 1998 report, although 40 to 60 percent of those who leave welfare obtain some kind of employment, they do so at wages below the poverty line ($13,650/year for a family of three).[3] A Government Accounting Office study released in August 1998 drove home this point, finding that mean wages for recipients who left welfare for employment ranged between $5.60 and $6.60 per hour. A year-round full-time job at $5.60 brings in an income well below the poverty line.[4]

Meanwhile, not all recipients even find jobs, let alone at decent wages. A 1998 study of adult recipients in New York showed that only one-fifth to one-third who left welfare found jobs. A 1997 study of what kinds of jobs might be available to low-skilled recipients living in the Midwest revealed that there are twenty-two workers for each job that pays at least a poverty wage; sixty-four workers for every job that pays 150 percent of poverty ($18,417); and ninety-seven workers for each job at a living wage ($25,907/year for a family of three).[5] Given the paucity of jobs at living wages, most people who leave welfare remain in poverty, even if they find employment. Moreover, according to one 1999 study, most former recipients who find employment do not have full-time, full-year

1. Barbara Vobejda and Judith Havemann, "States' Welfare Shift: Stop It Before It Starts," *Washington Post*, August 12, 1998; Jason DeParle, "What Welfare-to-Work Really Means," *New York Times Magazine*, December 20, 1998: 54–55.
2. Jason DeParle, "Shrinking Welfare Rolls Leave Record High Share of Minorities," *New York Times*, July 27, 1998, A1.
3. Children's Defense Fund, "Welfare in the States: CDF, New Studies Look at Status of Former Welfare Recipients" (May 8, 1998), http://www.childrensdefense.org/fairstart_status.html.
4. Government Accounting Office, *Welfare Reform: Child Support an Uncertain Income Supplement for Families Leaving Welfare* (Washington, D.C., August 1998).
5. Mark Weisbrot, "Welfare Reform: The Jobs Aren't There," http://www.rtk.net/preamble/welfjobs/fulltex2.html.

jobs. Hence, annual earnings are meager, averaging between $8,000 and $9,500.[6]

For recipients who can find jobs, the problem is not just that wages are low. It's also that child care, health care, and transportation are so expensive. So although many welfare recipients have moved into some form of employment, often they cannot really afford to be employed. According to one Washington-area welfare department, recipients need to earn at least $10 an hour in a full-time job to make ends meet; yet recipients average under $6 an hour.[7] The need for decent wages is particularly urgent in situations where recipients are parenting alone, because lone parents are the source of both income and care. If a single mother's job doesn't cover health care, she has to pay for it. If her kids aren't in school or if she works odd hours, she has to pay a surrogate to watch over them. If her job isn't nearby or if she needs to race to pick up her child from child care before the center closes at 5 P.M., she has to buy a car or hire an occasional taxi. After she pays for the services she and her children need so she can go to work, very little is left over to pay for other basics such as food, shelter, and clothing. And if she works an eight-hour day, she has no time to attend the job training classes that might get her better wages down the line—that is, unless she can afford to pay another surrogate to care for her children.

A Virginia mother captured the predicament of poor, single mothers with the question: "Who's giving me time to be a mother?"[8] The Temporary Assistance for Needy Families (TANF) program, the welfare regime set up by the Personal Responsibility Act, erases the care giving work of single mothers who need welfare. Requiring children's care givers to work outside the home and strictly limiting their lifetime eligibility for cash benefits, TANF ends a long-time policy commitment to the well-being of children in poor families. It is not really a *welfare* program at all.

The essays in this collection explore how we lost welfare and to what end. Three authors excavate the past, tying the trajectory of welfare politics since the 1960s to changing attitudes toward "working mothers" and

---

6. Maria Cancian, Robert Haveman, Thomas Kaplan, Daniel Meyer, and Barbara Wolfe, "Work, Earnings, and Well-Being after Welfare: What Do We Know?" paper presented at a congressional briefing sponsored by the Northwestern/University of Chicago Joint Center for Poverty Research, Washington, D.C., March 11, 1999.
7. Christina A. Samuels, "Nearly 3 Years Later, Welfare Reform Gets Mixed Grade; County Rolls Shrink; Many Still Lack Work," *Washington Post*, December 2, 1998, B1. Spencer S. Hsu, "Faring So-So after Leaving Welfare; Lifetimes of Problems Difficult to Surmount," *Washington Post*, October 11, 1998, B1.
8. Hsu, "Faring So-So After Leaving Welfare."

dependent ones (Solinger); to the repudiation of motherwork in the 1967 welfare amendments that established the Work Incentive Program (Boris); and to the dynamics of empowerment and backlash seeded by social policies that encouraged or permitted citizen participation by the poor, especially poor women (Naples). Four authors examine the various impacts of the Personal Responsibility Act: on employment and wages (Piven); on noncitizen immigrants (Fujiwara); on mothers coping with domestic violence (Kurz); and on poor women's right to be mothers (Roberts). In the penultimate essays, the authors address themes introduced early in the collection about dependency and care giving (Kittay) and about feminism's relationship to welfare reform (Mink). Both search for an alternative premise for welfare policy and find it in the need to support the care giving work mothers do. The collection concludes with a historical analysis of poor women's political agency (Abramovitz). Illuminating a legacy of activism that has sometimes enabled poor women to win claims and shape policy on their own behalf, Abramovitz challenges us to build our feminist, progressive agendas from the demands and actions of poor and working-class women.

Whose Welfare? is a critical response to welfare reform written by feminist scholars who are undauntable activists for welfare justice. Most of the authors participated in the Women's Committee of One Hundred, a feminist mobilization against punitive welfare reform that arose under Eva Kittay's leadership in the spring of 1995. All of us have struggled alongside welfare participants, squeezing politicians and agency officials to make changes in policy and rules that might make life under welfare a bit more manageable. Though it is a venue for our scholarship, this volume also presents perspectives developed from our political work and insights learned from mothers whose welfare the Personal Responsibility Act has put at risk.

Gwendolyn Mink

I

Historical Perspectives on Contemporary Welfare Politics

CHAPTER ONE

Dependency and Choice: The Two Faces of Eve

—Rickie Solinger

Beggars can't be choosers.
— Old saw
If people are willing to believe these lies [about welfare mothers], it's partly because they're just special versions of the lies that society tells about all women.
—Johnnie Tillmon, "Welfare Is a Women's Issue," 1972

Dependency—as in "the deep, dark pit of welfare dependency"[1]—is the dirtiest word in the United States today. *Choice*—as in the choice to get an abortion—is not so generally reviled as dependency, though it does spark more violent controversy. These two words—these groaningly laden concepts—*dependency* and *choice*—may be the two most powerful abstractions governing women's lives in the United States. As a matter of course, we use these words separately, to refer to apparently distinct issues: welfare and abortion. But it seems to me that these terms (both their official policy definitions and typical public usage) are actually *coupled*. Together they bind the lives of women in concrete ways and keep women vulnerable to censure and control.

Dependency and choice refer to each other, directly: they are antitheses that depend on each other for meaning—and for the shifting meanings that society has attached to them over time. One reason that it seems useful to clarify this relationship between dependency and choice now is that welfare reformers have very successfully named dependency as the

---

1. Senator Orrin Hatch, *Women in Transition*, Hearing Before the Committee on Labor and Human Resources, U.S. Senate, 98th Congress, 1st sess., An Examination of Problems Faced by Women in Transition from Work Without Pay to Economic Self-Sufficiency, November 8, 1983 (Washington, D.C.: U.S. Government Printing Office, 1984), 2.

disease of poor women. As a result, poor women are more than ever isolated in this country from others, most consequentially from other
women. In the interest of reconciling the history and the concerns of
middle-class women and poor women, I want to consider the relationship between these two key concepts and how these terms have been applied to the lives of women, especially mothers, in two different eras of
the twentieth century.

OVERVIEW: DEPENDENCY AND CHOICE IN THE 1950S AND 1980S

It is a well-known fact that in our recent past, dependency was considered a normative and positive attribute of some white American
women. In the 1950s cultural authorities, including psychiatrists, profes-
sors, and judges, insisted in every way they could that dependency was a
gender-appropriate status for white, middle-class wives, mothers, and
daughters. These authorities urged other authorities—teachers, parents,
employers—to enforce female dependency within the school, the family, the workplace. Along with psychologists and sexologists, parenting experts of that era described such women as dependent on men and
the family for self-definition and self-preservation. One popular parents' guide, referring to the family responsibilities of white, middle-class
women, explained, "A married woman only has two jobs, one to care for
her children, the other to keep a man happy."[2] Femininity indexes in the
1950s invited these women to determine whether they were *dependent
enough* to claim status as a "real woman."

Today, of course, the personal trait of dependency is roundly condemned in any adult, especially in poor women tagged as welfare dependents. But whether dependency is generally considered a good thing for
white women, as it was in the 1950s, or a bad thing for poor women and
many women of color, as it is today, *the core, essential attribute of a person
in the state of dependency is the absence of the capacity to make sensible
choices.*

Over time, social commentators have been consistent: dependent
women can't make good choices. When female dependency was good, in
the early postwar decades, Midge Decter wrote that young women were
"plagued with choices." And that was bad because "choice breeds rest-

2. David Goodman, *A Parent's Guide to the Emotional Needs of Children* (New York: Hawthorne, 1959), 35.

lessness." Choice also, she wrote, could create "a disruption of the natural order" of the lives of young women, cause "grave concern" and "domestic crises."[3] In the 1980s, when female dependency on welfare became the target of public vitriol, Gary Bauer described the source of the problem as women's "reckless choices." If women continued irresponsibly to choose divorce and illegitimacy, he observed, "there will either be no next generation, or [there will be] a next generation that is worse than none at all."[4]

Attaching the epithet "dependent" to womanhood, to groups of women, or to an individual woman has never been enough, of course, to stop women from trying in various ways to control their own lives by making choices. But women tagged as dependent, whether in the 1950s or the 1980s, who exhibited choice-like behavior, were accused of dangerous, pathological behavior. They were routinely described as mentally sick or scammers or both.

Perhaps the most frequently quoted book from the earlier period, *Modern Woman: The Lost Sex*, defined the "independent woman," that is, again, a white, middle-class woman who made choices for herself against the grain of culturally prescribed femininity, as "a contradiction in terms." This woman debased her essential nature by attempting to rival men.[5] Predictably, instead of improving women's lot, this "masculinization" led women into discontent, frustration, hostility, destructiveness, frigidity, and child rejection. The authors of *Modern Woman* argued that when women attempted to exercise independent judgment and choice, they became neurotic feminists. In the era of glorified and mandated female dependence, the desire to exercise choice was said to reflect and intensify women's mental illness. The authors suggested mass psychotherapy for women in the United States. Only professional treatment, they argued, could revitalize the natural dependency of American women and their femininity.

Many nominally dependent girls and women in the 1950s made decisions for themselves, of course. For example, many made choices when they found themselves pregnant in difficult circumstances.[6] Millions

3. Midge Decter, "Women at Work," *Commentary Magazine*, March 1961: 243–250.
4. Gary L. Bauer, *The Family: Preserving America's Future* (Washington, D.C.: U.S. Department of Education, December 12, 1986), 1.
5. Ferdinand Lundberg and Marynia Farnham, *Modern Woman: The Lost Sex* (New York: Grosset and Dunlap, 1947).
6. In this era, unwanted pregnancy itself was often considered a sick choice. See, for example, Stephen Fleck, "Pregnancy as a Symptom of Adolescent Maladjustment," *International Journal of Social Psychiatry* 2 (Autumn, 1956): 118–131.

throughout the decade sought and got illegal abortions or "therapeutic" hospital abortions.[7] But Mary Romm, a psychoanalyst, sounding much like the authors of *Modern Woman: The Lost Sex*, claimed in a 1954 book on therapeutic abortion that "the very fact that a pregnant woman cannot tolerate a pregnancy is an indication that the pre-pregnant personality of this woman was immature and in that sense can be labeled as psychopathological. The problem centers around unresolved oedipal situations. Exaggerated narcissism is present in all cases."[8] In short, any woman who chose to have an abortion demonstrated by that choice that she was sick.

Smaller numbers of white, mostly middle-class, unmarried girls and women found ways to have and keep their children, resisting the intense pressure in those days for this group to relinquish their babies for adoption.[9] Such a person was sure to be condemned for that choice and found, because of it, to be mentally unstable.[10] Many experts on unwed pregnancy in the 1950s believed that all white, unmarried women who got pregnant suffered from neurosis. But they held apart a special classification for the ones who chose to keep their babies: psychosis. Again, a dependent female who exercised what looked like reproductive choice revealed the mark of bad sense, bad choice, and pathology. None of these females escaped the censure of experts — physicians, psychologists, and social workers, often lawyers and judges, frequently journalists — who expressed their discomfort with the specter of dependent women making choices.

In the 1950s, work was another area in which white women who made choices were marked as ill or abnormal. In fact, in the 1950s, women defined specifically as working "by choice," instead of from necessity, were "empirically associated" with causing serious social problems, such as juvenile delinquency and divorce. One of many studies designed to measure the (bad) effects of mothers working in the postwar era was called, "Employment Status of Mothers and Some Aspects of Mental Illness." The author's findings were complicated, but in the end he concluded, "if women become employed [that is, choose to work] in order

7. Rickie Solinger, "A Complete Disaster: Abortion and the Politics of Hospital Abortion Committees, 1950 –1970," *Feminist Studies* 19 (Summer 1993): 241–268.

8. Mary Romm, in Harold Rosen, *Therapeutic Abortion* (New York: The Julian Press, 1954).

9. Rickie Solinger, *Wake Up Little Susie: Single Pregnancy and Race before* Roe v. Wade (New York: Routledge, 1993), chap. 5.

10. See, for example, Henry Meyer, Wyatt Jones, and Edgar F. Borgatta, "The Decision by Unmarried Mothers to Keep or Surrender Their Babies," *Marriage and Family Living* 18 (April 1956): 5–6.

to express neurotic pressures from within their own personalities, then employment of the mother may lead to a breakdown in the quality of family interaction."[11]

Today the choice to get an abortion, to become a single mother, or to take a job has become so normal for so many women in the United States that the association of choice and mental illness in our recent past may seem outlandish, or simply quaint. But many women who confronted difficult reproductive or employment issues personally in the 1950s remember how inconsistent and even dangerous it was to mix "choice" with "dependency" in those days.

By the 1980s, the capacity of many women to make sensible reproductive and employment choices was recognized, as dependency ceased to modify the life status of every female. Women who were poor in the Reagan era, however, were not generally considered able to make sensible choices or to choose without opprobrium, particularly if they were welfare recipients and therefore *dependent*. When this kind of woman exhibited choice-like behavior (for example, getting pregnant, staying pregnant, staying home to take care of her children), she was accused of irresponsible behavior or worse.[12]

Stereotypes associated with the behavior of "welfare mothers" are based on a belief in the incompatibility of dependency and sensible or good choices. More pointedly, the stereotypes explicitly connect dependency and bad choices or scamming. For example, women who receive welfare benefits have been accused of having babies for the sole purpose of making themselves eligible for benefits or for additional benefits. This charge clearly reflects a judgment that such women don't—and can't— make good choices. The same is true for claims that welfare dependents spend their checks on luxuries while letting their children go hungry, or that they typically stay on welfare for generations, or that they prefer to laze about rather than get a job. By the middle 1970s, many middle-class women may have achieved the status of choice makers, but poor women generally remained trapped by a label of dependency that, by definition, excluded them from that status.

Ironically, as many middle-class women sloughed off a number of the trappings of "dependency," most of them did not look back to consider the situation of other women still entrapped. But whether a woman

---

11. Lawrence J. Sharp, "Employment Statuses of Mothers and Some Aspects of Mental Illness," *American Sociological Review* 25 (October 1960): 714–717.

12. Rickie Solinger, "Poisonous Choice," in Molly Ladd Taylor and Lauri Umansky, eds., *Bad Mothers* (New York: New York University Press, 1997).

was "privately" dependent on her husband in the 1950s or "publicly" dependent on welfare in the 1980s—and exercised what looked like choice —her behavior stimulated cultural judgments and public policies designed to stamp out choice and legislation enabling the state to punish her for making choices. In the earlier period, when the behavior of white, middle-class women was at issue, sanctions took forms such as antiabortion statutes and prosecutions, the adoption mandate, and misogynistic psychiatric diagnoses and treatment. Later, as poor women of color were targeted, "family caps," welfare time limits, and public denouncements were sanctions of choice.

Many women who attained the status of choice makers in the 1970s and 1980s experienced this achievement as an individual accomplishment. They ignored or slighted the impact of mass movements and economic shifts that relieved them of full dependency status. Women who felt they chose, or personally earned, this new status had some reasonable grounds for defining themselves as independent actors. If a person recognized as having the capacity to make sensible choices cannot be classified as a dependent, then many women who began to make important choices for themselves in the 1970s and 1980s could justifiably claim independence. After all, the experience of making choices in the life-defining realms of sex and employment supported many women's belief that they were operating in the world on a basis more like men. In addition, the consumerist notion of "choice"—that which individuals may exercise freely and independently in the marketplace, when they have the resources to do so—supported many women's belief that being able to make choices about their own lives was a hallmark and proof of independence.[13] This last rang especially true as larger numbers of women, both married and single, took on paying jobs and began to earn the money that made their choices possible.[14]

Many men and women in the United States today are so focused on the association of dependency and welfare—and on the assumptions about dependent women making bad choices that characterize welfare reform rhetoric and law—that it is difficult to remember how radically definitions and valuations of female dependency have changed since the early postwar decades. So it must be stressed that between 1950 and 1980,

13. See Solinger, "Poisonous Choice."
14. By 1972, among white married women who lived with their husbands, 40.5 percent were employed; among black women in the same situation, 51.9 percent worked. Just a generation earlier, in 1941, only about one of ten married women were in the workforce. *Economic Problems of Women*, Part 3, Hearings before the Joint Economic Committee, Congress of the United States, 93d Congress, 1st sess. (Washington, D.C.: U.S. Government Printing Office, 1973), 548.

Americans did dramatically alter their attitudes regarding the nature of dependency, regarding who we define as dependent, whose dependency we find acceptable, and who in our society has the capacity to make sensible choices in their own behalf.

In this chapter, I consider the case of shifting attitudes toward working mothers to demonstrate the nature of these changes and to raise questions about the consequences. This case shows clearly that in our recent past, female dependency was widely considered normative and healthy, and female choice was pathologized. By the 1980s, dependency was associated with pathology, while choice was considerably normalized, though restricted to women defined by some measure as independent. It is important to note that whichever model of dependency and choice was ascendant, dependency and choice were in a fixed, antithetical relation to each other. And this relationship between dependency and choice created fertile grounds for justifying the regulation of women's behavior, including the punishment of women who resisted regulation or could not meet its conditions.

Dependency and Choice in the 1950s: Pathology at Work

Defining women's roles in the 1950s has been a special challenge for writers of women's history in the United States, partly because so many people—including many historians themselves—"remember" the decade through the great, iconic women of that time: TV matrons. And the television moms, such as June Cleaver and Harriet Nelson, were always the same, always at home, always lovingly available to their children and husbands. Recently historians have gone some distance toward showing that, for real women, the 1950s were a much more complicated era.[15] They have asked questions about which women actually were housewives and only housewives after World War II. They have considered the ways in which real women experienced their domestic roles and meshed them with roles outside their homes. Historians have questioned why cultural authorities then exhorted women so often and so threateningly to be first and foremost "good mothers" and "good wives." They have documented the lives of women whose experiences in the 1950s were "nonconforming," for example, the women who streamed into the paid workforce, joined unions, organized and marched for civil rights and against the

---

15. Most important, see Joanne Meyerowitz, ed., *Not June Cleaver: Women and Gender in Postwar America, 1945–1960* (Philadelphia: Temple University Press, 1994).

bomb, and got illegal abortions. They have uncovered aspects of American culture in the 1950s that encouraged women to resist culturally mandated feminine roles and supported the idea that women could make—and ought to make—significant contributions to society as mothers and as workers, at the same time.

Two very striking features of the 1950s especially stand out. First, the number of married women, with children living at home, who took paying jobs escalated rapidly in the 1950s. By the end of the decade, 39 percent of all women with school-aged children were in the labor force. Second, the responses to this phenomenon—white mothers at work—were deeply ambivalent and often hostile.[16] Americans had just recently experienced crisis-driven, "artificially high" levels of female workforce participation during World War II. The number of working mothers with children under the age of eighteen doubled between 1941 and 1945. But when it became clear that lots of white mothers were in the workforce to stay, Americans did not simply embrace wage-earning for this group. Early in the postwar era, the results of one large poll measuring attitudes toward women working revealed the public's resistance: three-quarters of the sample believed that "an employer should fire a competent woman whose husband could support her, in preference to an inefficient man who had a family to maintain." [17]

Social commentators and ordinary people talked endlessly about the meaning and the impact of white mothers working. Most were especially worried about the dangers that might befall children, husbands, whole families, and communities if these mothers continued to slight or abandon their domestic stations for paying work. In 1955, for example, *Ladies Home Journal* warned "the American woman" that "her children will hate her if she works." [18]

Articles in the popular press, academic studies, cocktail conversation, cartoons, and books devoted to the subject of white mothers working often had at their heart a concern about preserving the traditional and antithetical relationship between female dependency and choice. Typically and meaningfully, these various discussions distinguished mothers who *chose to work* from women who had *no choice* but to work. The first group

---

16. Susan M. Hartmann in "Women's Employment and the Domestic Ideal in the Early Cold War Years," and Joanne Meyerowitz in "Beyond the Feminine Mystique: A Reassessment of Postwar Mass Culture, 1946–1958," both in *Not June Cleaver*, demonstrate that hostility toward working mothers was not ubiquitous. Nevertheless, responses to the swell of mothers in the workforce *were* often hostile.

17. *Womanpower: A Statement by the National Manpower Council with Chapters by the Council Staff* (New York: Columbia University Press, 1957).

18. Agnes Meyer, "Children in Trouble," *Ladies Home Journal*, 72 (March 1955), 205.

got almost all of the attention. Commentators usually ignored the lives of poor and minority mothers who were much more likely to be employed than the white, middle-class mothers whose jobs caused so much concern.

Discussion about white mothers working took place, of course, in an era when psychiatrists, psychologists, child-rearing experts, and others were intent on educating the public about the pathologies associated with womanhood and motherhood *generally*. White, middle-class mothers who seemed to have pushed aside their dependent role came in for harsh evaluations. The influential family therapist Nathan Ackerman described the modern family as under the sway of the "dramatized" mother, a woman whose aggressiveness masked the sadness and fear she felt now that it seemed she could no longer "depend safely on the man" of the family.[19] Other therapists observed "hostile onslaughts of these aggressive women" in their offices, often dragging along their "confused, tense," and disturbed children for treatment.[20] Such bad mothers were "ambitious and controlling"[21] and "dominated by a vengeful competitive attitude toward males and by a strong wish to be a man."[22]

Employed white mothers were widely considered a subgroup of this reviled category of aggressive women. This was so despite—and because of—the fact that during the 1950s so many mothers with children between six and seventeen years old were working outside their houses. As *The Saturday Evening Post* editorialized, "With one woman of three in the United States working full or part time outside the home, you'd think the public would accept this as a necessary part of our modern, superproductive life." But, the editorial went on, "a lot of people don't accept" working mothers.[23] "The Tangled Case of the Working Mother," a 1961 essay in the *New York Times Magazine*, classified this type as "so suspect in our culture that any new study appearing to link her working with delinquency, school failure, or emotional disturbance in her young, is almost certain . . . to make headlines."[24] Studies also regularly associated

19. Nathan W. Ackerman, *The Psychodynamics of Family Life: Diagnosis and Treatment of Family Relationships* (New York: Basic Books, 1958), 178–179.
20. Dorothy McGriff, "Working with a Group of Authoritative Mothers," *Social Work* 5 (January 1960): 63–68.
21. Charles Wener, Marion W. Handlon, and Ann M. Garner, "Patterns of Mothering in Psychosomatic Disorders," *Merrill Palmer Quarterly* 6 (April 1960): 165–170.
22. Herbert S. Strean, "Treatment of Mothers and Sons in the Absence of the Father," *Social Work* 6 (July 1961): 29–35.
23. "Is It Too Late to Send Working Mothers Back to the Kitchen?" editorial in the *Saturday Evening Post*, January 24, 1959, 10.
24. Dorothy Barclay, "The Tangled Case of the Working Mother," *New York Times Magazine*, May 14, 1961, 75. Also see, for example, *Womanpower*, "The impact of married women's working

these employed mothers with fathers dethroned and pushed, as Ackerman put it, into the shadows—and with feminine dependency denied.

Given this climate, white mothers—especially those associated with the engrossing category of "middle class" in the postwar years—who were deciding whether to take jobs were counseled to make that choice very carefully. They were urged to plumb their motivations with virtually impossible thoroughness. A *New York Times* feature called "Mother's Dilemma: To Work or Not?"[25] listed the questions such a mother should ask herself before seeking employment: "Do I need the money and for what? Do I make my decisions as a team member of the family? Do I consider husband and children too? Have I balanced the possible cost of financing, training, the physical exertion, and the time factor against the end result of a work experience that may or may not be satisfying and stimulating?" The implication here and elsewhere was that most of these mothers jumped into jobs willy-nilly, and many ended up making poor, selfish, and damaging choices.

In the late 1940s and into the 1950s, academic researchers took up the task of proving that too many women were, indeed, making bad choices when they went out to work. The dozens of studies designed to measure the impact of mothers' employment were constructed on a racially specific base of doubt. Over and over, researchers reflected public skepticism as they fielded studies aiming to uncover the contradictions that resulted when natural dependents (that is, white mothers) chose to work. Studies tested whether mothers who worked, and their daughters, ended up with diminished femininity, whether the woman's mothering skills were weakened by working, and whether children whose mothers worked were more likely to get in trouble or do poorly in school.

These postwar studies, based on the responses of white, middle-class samples, with all other demographic groups carefully screened out, often yielded uncertain results. No matter what the data appeared to show, however, the researchers underscored continuing worries about the relationship between white maternal employment, juvenile delinquency, and other forms of personal and family "functional disorganization." Many of the studies did pinpoint trouble spots. A sympathetic researcher who

---

on the welfare of their children has probably received more widespread attention than any other issue growing out of the increasing employment of women. . . . Many observers have been quick to attribute the reported rise in juvenile delinquency to the absence of working mothers from the home," 54.

25. Helen F. Southard, "Mother's Dilemma: To Work or Not?" *New York Times Magazine*, July 17, 1960, 39.

believed that daughters of white working mothers could be inspired by their mothers' efforts, admitted that all the girls with working mothers in her study scored below normal on the Index of Traditional Femininity.[26] Another study examined the "adjustment" to family of 302 Missouri girls between the ages of thirteen and eighteen. It found that "girls whose mothers are employed are, on the average, more poorly adjusted to family life than are those whose mothers do not work and . . . there is greater feeling of lack of love, understanding, and interest between many parents and their daughters if the mother works . . . [and] also . . . greater lack of cooperation and appreciation on the part of the girls in the homes of employed mothers."

In the late 1950s, the Harvard-based researchers Eleanor and Sheldon Glueck looked at how one influential profession assessed working mothers and family problems. In "Working Mothers and Delinquency," the Gluecks observed, "Psychiatrists . . . view with alarm the growing excursions of young [white] mothers into factory and shop. They are convinced that the economic gain to the family is far too high a price to pay for the loss of emotional stability of the children. They point to the child's repeated traumatic experiences when again and again his mother, the major source and symbol of his security and love, goes off and leaves him yearningly unsatisfied. . . . They speculate that beneath the ostensible economic reason for the mother's leaving the family roof there may be in many cases the deeper motivation of a wish to escape maternal responsibility or a pathologic drive to compete with men."[27] Like others, psychiatrists linked the harm that befell children of white working mothers to the sick or bad wishes/drives/*choices* of these women. The implication of this and many of the postwar studies was that white mothers, children, and whole families would be healthier, albeit a bit less economically flush, if the mother accepted dependency and eschewed choice.

To be sure, other prominent experts in the postwar era spoke up in defense of white, working mothers and tried valiantly to uncouple the subjects of maternal employment and women's pathological choices. But even the defenders of women's choice to work often ended up cautioning women about the dangers or disappointments of choice. A prominent guidebook for modern middle-class women explained, "We are con-

26. Elizabeth Douvan, "Employment and the Adolescent," in F. Ivan Nye and Lois Wladis Hoffman, eds., *The Employed Mother in America* (Chicago: Rand McNally, 1963), 142–164.
27. Sheldon Glueck and Eleanor Glueck, "Working Mothers and Delinquency," *Mental Hygiene* 41 (1957): 327–352.

cerned mainly with the woman who has been brought up to feel that she is free, that she has a choice, yet who becomes discouraged and baffled by her actual life . . . because it often seems as though she had no real choice, as though in the end it always boiled down to the one bitter choice: do you want to be an aggressive careerist or a dull housewife."[28]

Psychologist Stella Chess was one of the few mental health experts of the era who attempted to rehabilitate all mothers, in part by downplaying the problematic, choice, and by suggesting that families exist in complex contexts. Mothers, Chess argued, are only one element of this context. They can't be saddled with the responsibility for everything that goes wrong in the family, whether they are employed or not. "In analyzing child behavior problems," Chess wrote in a 1964 response to the hundreds of mother-blaming books and articles published in the postwar period, "diagnosticians must refrain from automatically assuming that the child's problems stem from the mother's attitude and behavior toward him, and explore other possible influences such as developmental history, socio-economic circumstances, family and health and educational background."[29]

But between 1945 and 1965, the most high-profile pronouncements about the wages of previously fully dependent, white mothers going to work were censorious. In this vein, Psychiatrist Leo Bartemeier announced in a 1955 McCall's article, "Is a Working Mother a Threat to the Home?": "Until children are at least six, motherhood is a 24-hour job and one that no one can do for you. A mother who runs out on her children to work—except in cases of absolute necessity—betrays a deep dissatisfaction with motherhood or with her marriage. Chances are, she is driven by sick, competitive feelings toward men, or some other personality problem. She does a grave disservice to her children, although the harm may not show up for years."[30]

Other experts, however, were most concerned about the harm that showed up immediately, in the form of juvenile delinquency. Harvard's Eleanor Maccoby referred to "the positive correlation assumed [to exist] between mothers' employment and juvenile delinquency," and remarked that "it is not uncommon to find a judge in a juvenile court delivering a strong reprimand to a working mother and urging her to stay at home."[31]

28. Sidonie M. Gruenberg and Hilda Sidney Krech, The Many Lives of Modern Woman: A Guide to Happiness in Her Complex Roles (Garden City, N.Y.: Doubleday, 1952), 30.
29. Stella Chess, "Mal de Mere," American Journal of Orthopsychiatry 34 (July 1964): 613–614.
30. Elizabeth Pope, "Is a Working Mother a Threat to the Home?" McCall's (July 1955): 29.
31. Eleanor E. Maccoby, "Children and Working Mothers," Children 5(1958): 83–89.

James H. B. Brossard, the author of one of the most influential child development texts of the era, told this vivid story about child neglect in his widely used and cited volume: "Ernestine had a part in her school play. Her working mother rushed there in time to see her daughter appear on the stage displaying an atrocious color combination and stockings with two holes showing. Shortly afterwards, the mother withdrew from employment. In her letter to her employer, she wrote that 'every growing child needs a mother in the home.'"[32]

The author of the 1955 *McCall's* article, Elizabeth Pope, began her consideration of the threat posed by white, working mothers by naming the force that led many mothers into the workforce: "the seduction of a weekly pay check."[33] The Gluecks used related language in 1957, similarly associating the "choice" to work with illicit temptation and will-less women lacking the capacity to exercise good judgment: "Basically," they wrote, "the time is ripe for a reassessment of the entire situation. As more and more *enticements* in the way of financial gain, *excitement*, and independence from the husband are offered married women to *lure* them from their domestic duties, the problem is becoming more widespread and acute"[34] (italics added).

Susan Hartmann is undoubtedly correct in labeling the postwar decades a period of transition regarding women's employment.[35] And periods of transition are often marked by a surgence of conservatism, that is, aggressive resistance to change. Between 1945 and 1965, while millions of mothers of school age children in the United States were accepting paid employment, many Americans did not adjust gracefully to the change. During these postwar decades, hefty cultural resources were devoted to disseminating and enforcing messages about the natural dependency of Mother and the pathological essence of her efforts to undermine or slough off that status.

Considerable cultural resources were also—wittingly or unwittingly —devoted to foregrounding the mostly white, mostly middle-income women who went to work "by choice" against other women, often poor and African American, who were defined, when they were noticed at all, as having *no choice* but to work. The work lives of these two groups were often dependent on each other, of course. As Mirra Komarovsky put it,

32. James H. B. Brossard, *The Sociology of Child Development* (New York: Harper and Brothers, 1948), 383.
33. Pope, "Is a Working Mother a Threat?" 29.
34. Glueck and Glueck, "Working Mothers and Delinquency," 350.
35. Hartmann, "Women's Employment and the Domestic Ideal," 84.

"Back of a career mother, there often stands another woman," one she described as "a person of inferior skills."[36]

DEPENDENCY, NO CHOICE, AND BAD CHOICE:
SHIFTING THE FOREGROUND

The almost exclusive focus in the mass media and academic studies on the white mother's work dilemma came close to eclipsing the situation of "the mother [who] is compelled to work."[37] This was the mother "forced by grim economic necessity to go to the factory or to clean offices while leaving young children in the care of an adolescent daughter. . . ." This was the mother "whose every earned penny must be spent in the corner grocery and who returns from her job to do the washing and the cooking and the cleaning for the family."[38] As one researcher put it in 1955, "The overwhelming majority of [such mothers] can't afford to choose."[39] For these women, work was a given. And so was their dependency, defined by their race, gender, and class "inferiority" and by their typical status as low-paid domestic service workers. These women were defined as dependents even though they worked day in and day out to support their families.[40] While the bad choices of white, economically better-off mothers justified public excoriation, the choiceless status of poor mothers of color justified workplace and other forms of exploitation. White women were perceived as thrusting themselves into the workforce because they were psychologically disturbed, while African American and other women of color were described as fully alienated from the civilized complexities of psychology. For a poor woman, survival issues, some claimed, "superseded attention to her own psychological dilemmas," if, indeed, she had such dilemmas at all.[41]

This perspective was, of course, congruent with prevailing racial dis-

---

36. Mirra Komarovsky, *Women in the Modern World: Their Education and Their Dilemmas* (Boston: Little, Brown, 1953), 191.
37. *Womanpower*, 340.
38. Komarovsky, *Women in the Modern World*, 189.
39. Pope, "Is a Working Mother a Threat?" quoting Marie Jahoda, Associate Director of the New York University Research Center for Human Relations, 73.
40. In 1960, 39.3 percent of African American women workers were employed in domestic service jobs; 23 percent worked in service jobs outside private households. Teresa Amott and Julie Matthaei, *Race, Gender and Work: A Multi-Cultural Economic History of Women in the United States* (Boston: South End Press, 1996), table 6–1, 158.
41. Alva Myrdal and Viola Klein, *Women's Two Roles: Home and Work* (London: Routledge and Paul, 1956), 151.

tinctions in the realm of sexual misbehavior. Sexually misbehaving white females in the postwar era were diagnosed as psychologically disturbed (because they made the bad choice to engage in nonmarital sexual relations), while African American females were described as sexually impelled by earthy, biologically determined forces that overtook them in the absence of psyche.[42]

Until the Moynihan Report[43] was published in 1965, the employment behavior of African American women was not usually associated with pathology.[44] Social commentators did not believe that poor minority women were capable of making the bad choices that were the hallmark of pathology in that era. (It is possible that it wasn't until after 1960 — when the rates of domestic service jobs held by African American women began to decline dramatically as other employment opportunities opened up,[45] and white employers had less absolute control over these women — that mainstream commentators began to associate African American women's work lives with bad choices and pathology.) But even before the Moynihan Report, experts *were* worried about the social consequences, if not the psychological causes, of maternal employment for minorities. Experts' concern about what would happen to small African American children whose mothers worked rarely included references to toddlers developing unhealthy anxiety levels and separation traumas.[46] Concerns were more likely to center on the substitute care that relatives could give to these youngsters with working mothers, which was "not likely to be adequate."[47]

After approximately 1965, the *choicelessness* associated with the work and other life experiences of women of color began a process of mutation. Academics and social commentators in the popular media referred less often to these women as having no choice. Now African American

---

42. See Solinger, *Wake Up Little Susie.*
43. Daniel Patrick Moynihan, *The Negro Family: The Case for National Action* (Washington, D.C.: Government Printing Office, 1965).
44. See Franklin E. Frazier, *The Negro Family in the United States* (Chicago: University of Chicago Press, 1939) for an earlier and equally influential treatment of Black family dilemmas and "pathologies." This study, in fact, provided the basis of Moynihan's later work.
45. Amott and Matthaei show that "between 1930 and 1960 the share of Black women employed in manufacturing jobs almost doubled, while the share in clerical and sales jobs grew eightfold. These changes finally allowed Black women to move out of private household service, which employed 42 percent of Black women workers in 1950, 39 percent in 1960, and 18 percent in 1970." *Race, Gender and Work,* 173.
46. See, for example, Lois Meek Stolz, "Effects of Maternal Employment: Evidence from Research," *Child Development* 31 (December 1960): 749–782.
47. "Conference Discussion: Working Mothers and the Development of Children," in *Work in the Lives of Married Women* (New York: Columbia University Press, 1958), 186.

women—poor women of color, generally—were accused, as white women had been, of making bad choices. This shift from "no choice" to "bad choices" in the case of women of color was occurring, in zero-sum fashion, as middle-class, white women were beginning to win rights to make sensible and depathologized choices for themselves about work, contraception, and abortion. Now poor women of color replaced middle-class working mothers in the foreground of public discussion and concern.

When policymakers and commentators accused poor women of color of making bad choices, the charge was complex. Often it referred to the fact that these women were unemployed. Just as often, it referred to the fact that they had jobs while African American men did not. But once women of color were associated with making bad choices, the charges spread to cover all the important areas of their lives: work, sex, marriage, family, and motherhood. In 1965, the Moynihan Report enumerated the consequences of these bad choices: African American women were making a mistake by taking jobs and status from black men; they were making a consequential mistake by presiding over families constructed, non-normatively, as matriarchies. They were making bad choices when they didn't marry and had babies anyway. All these mistakes and bad choices inexorably led African American women (and other poor women of color) deep into welfare dependency.

"Culture of poverty" theory, introduced most prominently by anthropologist Oscar Lewis in *La Vida: A Puerto Rican Family in the Culture of Poverty, San Juan and New York*, a book published one year after Moynihan's report on the black family, provided a richly narrative and decidedly unpsychological explanation for the charge that poor women made bad choices.[48] In the somewhat liberalized political climate of the 1960s, Lewis intended to render "the poor" as legitimate, interesting subjects whose lives were battered by poverty. He wanted to show that poverty itself generated a way of life that constituted a unique culture of poverty. This was a liberal, innovative perspective because "the poor" had previously been constructed as lacking culture.

Despite this intention, however, policy analysts and others read accounts of the culture of poverty as evidence that the folkways of the poor were crude and irresponsibly self-indulgent. The inescapable moral of culture of poverty analysis was that the poor became economically disadvantaged because they misbehaved perpetually. Their disorganized hedonism—constructed of bad choices—was both a mark of poverty

48. Oscar Lewis, *La Vida: A Puerto Rican Family in the Culture of Poverty, San Juan and New York* (New York: Random House, 1966).

and what chained them to poverty, generation after generation. Analysts denied or diminished the roles of racism, colonialism, substandard housing, education, medical care, and job opportunities in creating and sustaining poverty. Poverty and the culture it allegedly spawned—the culture of dependency—were seen as the offspring of individual and group irresponsibility or poor choices.

This interpretation of culture of poverty theory was successfully popularized at the height of the civil rights movement. For some, culture of poverty theory functioned as a justification for resisting institutionalized, racial equality. Many politicians, policymakers, academics, and others used Lewis's work to justify the position that it was deeply problematic to mount public policy initiatives to ameliorate the lives of the poor. After all, the culturally determined bad choices of poor people themselves caused their lives of endemic, enduring poverty and dependency. This adaptation and application of culture of poverty theory was particularly unfair in the case of African American women, who by the mid-1960s were, in very large numbers, making significant and sensible choices in their own interests, even within the context of a violently racist society. These choices included a mass exodus from domestic service jobs as soon as they had other opportunities (in 1960, 39.3 percent of African American women workers were domestics; in 1990, 2.2 percent[49]) and a mass participation in the civil rights movement.[50] Nevertheless, the fact that so many African American mothers remained poor in the United States sustained the popularity of culture of poverty theory, locking it into the heart of conservative politics for the rest of the twentieth century. It helped consign poor women of color to a status defined by the combination of "bad choices" and "dependency."

In the first two postwar decades, the lives of most mothers were constrained by the culturally mandated association of mothers and dependency and by the related alienation of women from sensible decision making. But the different experiences of white, middle-class women and poor women of color within these constraints demonstrate a key aspect of the relationship between sexism, racism, and class oppression. When cultural, political, and legal authorities have taken the right to deny all women independence and access to self-determining decision making, these authorities have also been able to treat different groups of women differently, depending on the variables of race and class.

In the earlier period, white, middle-class women were excoriated for

49. See note 44.
50. See Paula Giddings, *When and Where I Enter: The Impact of Black Women on Race and Sex in America* (New York: William Morrow, 1984), part III.

violating the conditions of dependency when they "chose" to work for wages. But those with jobs were more likely to achieve diagnoses of "deviance" as bad choice makers than they were to achieve "independence" in the 1950s. On the other hand, social commentators rendered the work lives of mothers of color invisible. Although these mothers were much more likely than white mothers to work for wages, they did not achieve the status of "independence" either. Social commentators claimed that these mothers worked because their poverty gave them "no choice." This claim obscured the racist and sexist standpoint of commentators. It also justified the proposition that mothers of color were essentially dependent, no matter whether or how much they worked outside the home. This was so because, in the United States, the woman constrained from making choices is the same woman who cannot make a good choice. In either case, forced alienation from choice is the fundamental condition of adult "dependency."

The Death of Republican Motherhood: Disconnecting Dependency and Choice

Between the late 1960s and 1980, American culture experienced a phenomenon that can be called "the death of Republican Motherhood."[51] During this period, the United States underwent a traumatic and very public shattering of what had been widely considered a relatively stable, if racialized, set of concepts defining "mother." Over the course of this scant decade and a half, the landscape became littered with new kinds of mothers. Many mothers in new roles made strong claims that they defined their motherhood status for themselves by virtue of newly normalized choice. Many others, though, were defined by cultural commentators as occupying a status shaped by the older category: bad choice. All of these mothers' statuses, however, were associated with mothers making choices, often about the relationship between motherhood and work. The American public struggled in this period to reconcile or reject the validity of this association.

During the 1970s, formerly disgraced unwed mothers became simply "single mothers." Legions aimed to become supermoms, with high-powered careers and a passel of kids. Mothers became murderers of unborn babies, welfare dependents with too many kids, welfare queens, and

---

51. I deal with this subject in depth in the final chapter of a manuscript in progress, "The Cost of Choice: How Choice Trumped Women's Rights after *Roe v. Wade.*"

heads of households in unprecedented numbers. They became mommy track mothers, American mothers of third world babies, earthmothers, militant stay-at-home moms, technologically assisted mothers, feminist mothers, lesbian mothers. They became mothers who should put their children in daycare because, experts warned, they were unequipped to be good mothers. Alternatively, they were tagged as mothers who selfishly and neglectfully stuck their children in daycare.

Not too far into this period, motherhood had become "a very uncertain assignment" in the United States, with no single language or set of criteria to describe its status or to evaluate women who held it.[52] In 1977, one young woman attending a meeting on the family at Tulane University was reported in the *New York Times* as plaintively asking the panel of experts before her, "I just want to get married and have a child. Is that still okay?" At the same time, other women were deeply engaged in "the fight . . . to win agreement that working women can also be mothers."[53] Still others, of course, were becoming poor, single mothers and facing the charge that nonworking, poor women could not afford to be mothers and should refrain from having children. But most important, all of these mothers were associated with making choices—often called *lifestyle choices*—whether they were rich or poor, white or not. Now choice seemed normalized for mothers; in fact it was an integral part of becoming a mother in the first place. This was an early and powerful impression created by *Roe v. Wade* and by the liberatory promises of the civil rights movement and women's movement.[54]

By the early 1970s, in fact, many women appeared to be choosing their motherhood circumstances from a menu of options. Contraception and abortion were available to millions of women. Single mothers became heads of households in explosive numbers.[55] Welfare eligibility and benefits expanded, stimulating the claim that, in response, poor mothers were illegitimately "choosing" motherhood.[56] And mothers entered the labor force in unprecedented numbers. During the 1970s, three of five

52. C. Christian Beels, "The Case of the Vanishing Mommy," *New York Times*, July 4, 1976, VI, 28.
53. Jon Nordheimer, "The Family in Transition: A Challenge from Within," *New York Times*, November 27, 1977, 1.
54. See Solinger, "Poisonous Choice."
55. Between 1960 and 1977, the number of one-parent families grew twice as fast as the number of two-parent families. Jean Y. Jones, *The American Family: Problems and Federal Policies* (Washington, D.C.: Congressional Research Service, Library of Congress, 1977), 6.
56. Between 1960 and 1970, the value of welfare benefits increased 75 percent. Harriet Ross and Isabel Sawhill, *Time of Transition: The Growth of Families Headed by Women* (Washington, D.C.: Urban Institute, 1975), 98.

people entering the workforce were women. And just as dramatic, between 1950 and 1980, the labor force participation of women went from 35 percent to 52 percent.[57] Many Americans watched the behavior of mothers with alarm. While most would not have put it this way at the time, in retrospect it seems as though some of that alarm had to do with the ways in which women were constructing lives for themselves that ignored or denied the 1950s relationship between dependency and choice. Gary Bauer described the great problem these women represented for policymakers as a matter of figuring out "how to get the genie of personal indulgence back into the bottle of legal restraints."[58]

Many Americans in the late 1970s and 1980s expressed their disapproval of women submitting to personal indulgences by supporting "dependency advocates"—spokespersons who repudiated the "rights" and "choice" gains of the 1960s and early 1970s and advocated overturning them. Others remained silent as these advocates attacked women for behaving as if they were no longer dependents. "Dependency advocates" focused efforts in many policy arenas that affected the lives of girls and women. Some focused on recriminalizing and repathologizing abortion. Others were interested in constraining and punishing teenagers who got pregnant. Still others stressed the importance of defeating the Equal Rights Amendment. Perhaps the most extensive and ultimately most successful effort of "dependency advocates" was in the area of women and work.

In 1978, Sheila Kammerman of the Columbia University School of Social Work remarked that "underlying all United States policy today affecting families . . . is a pervasive ambivalence about women working. . . ."[59] Politicians, policymakers, and conservative commentators in the Reagan era drew on that ambivalence to blunt the impact of feminist- and civil rights–driven guarantees for women workers. They also focused on reforging the link between dependency and pathologized choices that many women had recently broken. This part was a cynical effort. Many who worked hardest to resuscitate the definition of unemployed, poor mothers as dependents making bad choices had generally been hostile to the needs of employed mothers and had participated in efforts to limit their achievements. During Reagan's presidency, these efforts included failing to insist that employers comply with Title VII of the Civil Rights Act of 1964 and providing only weak enforcement of the

57. *Economic Problems of Women*, 1982, 4.
58. Gary Bauer, *The Family: Preserving America's Future*, 4.
59. White House Conference on the Family, 1978, 182.

affirmative action order that prohibited federal contract funds from going to employers who discriminated in employment policies and practices. Yet even as they withheld support for women workers in the 1980s, conservatives used the burgeoning rates of employment among mothers with young children to make the case that the poverty and unemployment of mothers on welfare were their own fault.

REVITALIZING DEPENDENCY, REPATHOLOGIZING CHOICE

Politicians and policymakers used two key strategies in the 1980s to revitalize dependency, this time as a degraded, not normative, condition of (some) women. First, policymakers set about repathologizing "choice-like behavior" for poor, unemployed, single mothers. Second, policymakers constructed an effective policy apparatus to punish poor, unemployed mothers whose receipt of welfare "proved" that they had made bad choices.

Efforts to repathologize choice were central to redefining dependency as a degraded status. But the argument was different now from what it had been thirty years before. In the 1950s, (white) women were supposed to be dependent. Their independent choices were inconsistent with dependency and therefore were very likely to reflect poor decision making and carry bad consequences. In the 1980s, politicians and others claimed that dependent women (of color) got that way, not because of their gender, but because of their bad choices in the face of "opportunity" and "guaranteed equal rights." Those engaged in revitalizing dependency insisted that the choices a woman made while she was dependent were likely to be bad, as well, because dependency was still inconsistent with sensible choices.

By 1980, poor, unemployed, single mothers of young children were extremely vulnerable to the charge that they were welfare dependents because they had made bad choices. Few Americans who were not on welfare calculated the impact of factors beyond the control of these women that pushed them to accept public assistance. These factors included the lack of appropriate jobs that paid a living wage for women in their situation and the lack of affordable day care, coupled with the fact that welfare benefits grew in the early 1970s faster than wages.[60]

60. In 1975, the prospects looked good for poor women. Two policy analysts found, "Overall, the picture is one of more favorable income and benefit status for female-headed families in many jurisdictions, and of increasing favor for those families as (1) welfare benefits grow faster than earn-

Nevertheless, in the 1980s, after the real value of the welfare check began to plummet, conservative politicians and public policy experts attacked poor mothers with vigor, claiming that their receipt of welfare benefits—their welfare dependency—was built on choices that reflected irresponsibility, even depravity. Lawrence Mead, a politics professor at New York University and a major spokesman for this position drew a thick bottom line in defining "welfare mothers" during a Congressional hearing in the mid-1980s. "I wanted to comment," he said, "on the presumption that the poor are like the rest of us." This, Mead argued, was a misconception. Unlike "us," the poor are "remarkably unresponsive to . . . economic incentives." He found their behavior "a mystery," but suggested an interpretive key: welfare recipients were "semi-socialized." Unable to make sensible choices, they became wholly dependent on welfare.[61]

The purpose of policy, Mead argued, is "not to expand the freedom of . . . recipients. It is, in fact, to constrict their freedom in necessary ways."[62] In other words, poor women could not and should not exercise choice. Mead and others in the policy arena were emphatic: when poor, unemployed women made unconstrained choices for themselves, the consequences were awful. Gary Bauer admitted in a 1986 report to President Reagan that he could cite no statistical evidence to prove that these unemployed women decided to have babies in order to collect welfare. "[A]nd yet," he claimed, even the "most casual observer of public assistance programs" could perceive this motivation.[63] Revitalizing this thirty-year-old charge—that dependent women were schemers who debased their bodies and degraded motherhood for public money—depended on convincing the citizenry that dependent women were deliberate malfeasants or compulsive miscreants. Either way, their choice to have babies and to stay home with them was constructed as pathological. Many argued that compounding this bad choice was another, though

---

ings, and (2) female-headed families continue to experience broader categorical eligibility for cash and in-kind programs, and lower tax rates in those programs than husband-wife families." Ross and Sawhill, *Time of Transition*, 101. Mimi Abramovitz notes that "between 1960 and 1970, the average earnings of workers rose by 48 percent, while the average AFDC benefits jumped 78 percent. In the early 1970s, the AFDC grant exceeded the minimum wage in many high-benefit states." *Under Attack, Fighting Back: Women and Welfare in the United States* (New York: Monthly Review Press, 1996), 76.

61. *Workfare vs. Welfare*, Hearing before the Subcommittee on Trade, Productivity, and Economic Growth of the Joint Economic Committee, U.S. Congress, 99th Congress, 2d Session, April 23, 1986 (Washington, DC: Government Printing Office), 98.

62. Ibid., 39.

63. Bauer, *The Family*, 24.

lesser bad choice: the unnatural decision to give birth to babies who would not have proper fathers.[64]

Basically, these charges against poor, unemployed mothers made sense to many Americans because these women did not have paying jobs.[65] After all, following the legalization of abortion, *the single motherhood of women with decent jobs was far less morally or otherwise problematic for most Americans.*[66] Economic dependency, caused by bad choices and leading to more of the same, was now seen as the core problem of poor, unemployed mothers, not racism or sexism or the effects of deindustrialization, or even the absence of a husband, all of which exercised powerful constraints on the opportunities of poor women.[67] Lawrence Mead, Gary Bauer, and Charles Murray met a warm reception in Washington after 1980, when they claimed that eradicating dependency involved aborting the bad choices of poor women, including their choices to have too many children.

While increasing the military budget, granting corporate tax relief, and investing in the private sector, the Reagan administration aimed to "break the cycle of dependency" by reducing the number of choices a poor, unemployed mother could make. For example, the administration eliminated CETA and diminished appropriations for the Vocational Education Act, which had provided jobs and training options for poor mothers. The U.S. Civil Rights Commission noted early in the Reagan era that "Federal support for employment and training programs has decreased dramatically, and therefore, special efforts will be needed to provide alternate sources of skills training for poor women unable to gain access to currently available resources. If not, they may find themselves trapped in poverty in spite of their best efforts to avoid or overcome their dependency."[68]

The administration also crafted policies that eliminated a significant amount of public housing stock, raised rents, and reduced federal subsidies for new construction and rehabilitation of dilapidated housing

---

64. See, for example, Anthony Brandt, "The Right to Be a Mother," *McCall's* (March 1984), 146.
65. In "The Patriarchal Welfare State," Carol Pateman argues that paid employment has replaced military service as "the key to [male] citizenship." In the 1980s, employment—or economic solvency—was becoming key to female citizenship as well. In *Democracy and the Welfare State*, ed. Amy Gutmann (Princeton: Princeton University Press, 1988), 237.
66. See Solinger, "Poisonous Choice."
67. The U.S. Civil Rights Commission asserted in 1983 that "Poor women do participate in the laborforce. . . . The problem is they are often unable to find work, must work part-time, or the jobs do not pay a wage adequate to support a family." *A Growing Crisis: Disadvantaged Women and Their Children* (Washington, D.C.: U.S. Civil Rights Commission, May, 1983).
68. Ibid., 35.

stock. It slashed fuel assistance programs for low-income households and made obtaining free legal representation much more difficult for poor women. Very significantly, the administration cut allocations for child care programs at the same time that 36 percent of low-income women and 45 percent of single mothers said they would work if child care were available. For example, Title XX of the Social Services block grant, a major source of child care funding, was cut 21 percent in 1981.[69] Finally, Reagan's policies continued the process of reducing the real value of the average AFDC check—between 1970 and 1985, the real value of these benefits declined 33 percent—and began aggressively pushing mothers with young and younger children into the workforce.[70]

As housing, employment and training options, and day care programs were liquidated or hobbled in the 1980s, the administration also focused on policy initiatives that would directly punish unemployed, poor mothers for the double-barreled bad choice they were accused of making: having a baby and not having a job. (In this climate, Lawrence Mead suggested that "Congress might wish to consider differentiating between married and unmarried mothers, the latter to face more immediate work obligations."[71]) Typically, punishments targeted the reproductive capacity of these mothers and aimed to make any additional bad choices (babies) impossible, at least until the woman got a job, and maybe forever.

Hilmar G. Moore, the Chairman of the Texas Human Resources Board and the mayor of Richmond pushed in 1980 for a policy in Texas mandating sterilization of mothers on welfare.[72] Policymakers in other states designed programs for paying indigent women to put their babies up for adoption, for establishing "family caps," and then for paying recipients to use Norplant, a long-acting contraceptive.[73] All of these proposals were predicated on the belief that the dependency of an unemployed, poor woman canceled out her right to have a baby. Because so many women made the "bad choice" to have a baby despite these stric-

69. *Problems of Working Women*, Hearing before the Joint Economic Committee, U.S. Congress, 98th Congress, 2d Session, April 3, 1984 (Washington, D.C: Government Printing Office), 97; *Barriers to Self-Sufficiency for Single Female Heads of Families*, Hearings before a Subcommittee of the Committee on Governmental Operations, U.S. House of Representatives, 99th Congress, 1st Session, July 9–10, 1985 (Washington, DC: Government Printing Office), 179.

70. *Poverty and Hunger in the Black Family*, Hearing before the Select Committee on Hunger, U.S. House of Representatives, 99th Congress, 1st Session, September 26, 1985 (Washington, DC: Government Printing Office), 6.

71. *Barriers to Self-Sufficiency*, 509.

72. *New York Times*, February 28, 1980, 16.

73. See, for example, Isabel Wilkerson, Wisconsin Welfare Plan: To Reward the Married, *New York Times*, February 12, 1991, 16; also see Carol Sanger, "M is for the Many Things," *Southern California Review of Law and Women's Studies* 1 (1992).

tures (Mead and others were calling this phenomenon "the plague of illegitimacy"), public policies were needed to constrain their fertility effectively. The point was not only to reduce the number of welfare dependents, but also to punish women who persisted in behaving as if pregnancy were a legitimate choice for poor women without jobs.

The results of Reagan era policies were very quickly grim. Between 1980 and 1984, the incomes of the bottom one-fifth of American families, a quintile that included 43 percent of African American families, dropped by 9 percent. At the same time, income rose 9 percent for the top quintile, a segment that took in only 7 percent of African American families.[74] The Congressional Research Service reported that 557,000 people became poor because of cutbacks in social programs that Congress approved at the request of President Reagan during the first years of his administration. This was in addition to the 1.6 million people who became poor in 1982 due to the economic recession.[75] In these same years, the percentage of children who were living in poverty rose from 16 percent to 20 percent, a development that brought the number of children in the United States living in households subsisting at or near poverty levels to one in four.[76]

Colorado Representative Patricia Schroeder reflected on the Reagan administration's cruel treatment of the mothers of these poor children. "I think," she said, "one of the toughest things that's gone on [recently] . . . was the cutting off of the life raft we had thrown to those kind [sic] of women." Poor mothers had been "so excited," according to Schroeder, to have educational and occupational training options available to them. Now those were gone. "And I don't think there's anything crueler or more dangerous in a society than to say, 'Here is the life raft,' they climb up and, just as they're ready to enjoy it, you push them back off and say, 'Whoops, not yet. We decided we don't have room for you this time.'"[77]

This politics of reviling and punishing poor mothers for being unemployed, while at the same time making it more difficult for them to receive the education and training necessary to secure family-sustaining jobs, was a hallmark of the Reagan years. President Reagan, himself, complained that people unhappy with this policy paradox were simply "sob sisters" unwilling to face reality.[78]

President Reagan's epithet—"sob sisters"—perfectly captured the con-

---

74. *Poverty and Hunger in the Black Family*, 15.
75. *New York Times*, July 26, 1984, 19.
76. *New York Times*, April 29, 1983, 12.
77. *Economic Status of Women*, 1982, 33.
78. *New York Times*, March 3, 1982, 26.

servatives' firm determination in the 1980s to clarify welfare as an issue associated with weak women. Opponents of tough (masculine) Reagan policy were cast as emotional, irrational partisans, wallowing in expensive and destructive sentimentality. Also, Reagan administration attacks on "sob sisters" (welfare mothers and others who spoke out in support of these women's needs) were calculated to salvage traditional gender and race ideologies that had been battered by a generation of liberatory legislative, judicial, and policy innovations and mass movements.[79]

Having lost significant battles in the effort to maintain male supremacy and white supremacy in the generation between 1954 and 1980, Reagan-aligned politicians and policymakers were waging one of their fiercest battles over considerably diminished terrain: the definition of poor women. Many entered this battle as though the fight to constrain the misbehavior of unemployed, poor mothers was the last great legitimate effort of government and as though winning this battle was crucial to restoring the health of American society.

The conservatives' struggle to define and constrain poor, unemployed mothers was characterized throughout the 1980s by desperate determination and distortion, not unlike what characterized the reactionary struggles in the United States against school integration and legal abortion. This determination stemmed in part from so many traditional features of women's roles having already been effaced.[80] Between 1960 and 1970, for example, the number of female-headed families increased ten times as rapidly as the number of two-parent families. In 1971, 2.1 million single mothers were employed outside the home; twenty years later, 5.8 million were. By 1980, mothers going out to work, full- or part-time, had become so normative for women of every class, married and single, that President Carter designated the day before Labor Day as Working Mother's Day.[81] Still, conservatives such as Gary Bauer held out hope that the phenomenon of white mothers working for pay was a temporary aberration caused by "bad economic policy in Washington." He imagined that "with the breaking of inflation, a gradual decline of interest rates, and the return of stability and predictability to the economy," many of these mothers might go back home.

Reagan era policies defining and constraining poor, unemployed mothers effectively masked the role of large economic forces in creating

79. See Gwendolyn Mink, "Welfare Reform in Historical Perspective," *Connecticut Law Review* (Spring 1994), 882.
80. See Ross and Sawhill, 5.
81. "Single Mothers Struggle with Tiny Paychecks and Little Help," *New York Times*, March 31, 1992, 1; *New York Times*, August 30, 1980, 44; Economic Status of Women, 1982, 4.

and sustaining the poverty of these women. Conservative policy advocates ignored problems such as that a minimum wage–no benefits service job could not support a mother and child above the poverty level and that real wages had been declining for American workers since 1973. They did not link the decline in high-paying manufacturing jobs, the increase in low-paying service jobs, poverty policies that forbade poor people to accumulate savings, or the sharp increase in uneven income distribution to the hard time that many mothers had escaping poverty. The only significant cause of women's poverty, now called with a nasty edge *dependency*, was the bad choices of women whose choice making needed to be proscribed.

DEPENDENCY AND CHOICE: UNDERWRITING PARADOXES WE CAN LIVE WITH

The extraordinary success of welfare "reformers" in the 1980s and 1990s—culminating with President Clinton and Congressional Democrats and Republicans all joining to enact the Personal Responsibility Act in August 1996—reflects the completion of the process of reinstitutionalizing "female dependency" and reaffirming the relationship between dependency and women making bad choices. In addition to welfare "reform," another measure of the long-term success of policymakers in this domain is how effective dependency and choice have been in resolving potentially very troubling policy paradoxes regarding the lives of resourceless women.

For the past two decades, many congressional and state politicians have worked hard to ensure that few poor women would have abortions paid for with public funds. At the same time, many of the same politicians have overseen cuts in welfare benefits, including child care subsidies, and have worked to impose "family caps" and stimulate public censure of "excessively fertile" women. Many Americans have had a hard time understanding how these apparently contradictory policy initiatives can simultaneously serve our national interests. Some feminists and others have adopted the slogan "Life begins at conception and ends at birth" to express their frustration with the impact of these contradictory policies. But for an *explanation* of how politicians—and a large segment of the American public—resolve the apparent contradiction or live comfortably with the paradox, one may look at the revitalized relationship between dependency and choice. Today many Americans are convinced that poor women as dependents do not and cannot make good choices.

This conviction tends to be applied categorically, whether a poor woman chooses to get an abortion that she does not have the money to pay for herself or whether she chooses to have a baby while she is poor. Adapting the perspective of Mary Romm, the 1950s psychoanalyst, policymakers insist that these pregnancy and motherhood choices of poor, dependent women, *whatever the choices are*, "are immature and in that sense can be labeled as pathological." In short, when poor women appear to exercise choice regarding pregnancy and motherhood, they are blamed and blocked and finally excoriated as bad mothers.

Pregnant teenagers, of course, face similar policy paradoxes. Many of the same politicians and policymakers determined to block this group's access to sex education and safe, effective contraception also champion parental consent laws to constrain the abortion choices of teenagers. And these are often the same folks who lament teenage pregnancy and lambaste poor, teenage mothers. Again, many Americans live comfortably with apparently contradictory policies that are resolved not by a real belief that dependent girls will stop having sex, but by the conviction that they can be stopped from making choices.

The role that the dependency/choice antithesis plays in making sense of these paradoxical policies illustrates the powerful relationship between welfare politics and reproductive politics today. Far from simply referring to the separate arenas of welfare and abortion, dependency and choice vibrantly interact with each other, depend on each other for meaning, and together shape and justify punitive and constraining public policies, including eugenically based definitions of motherhood.

Dependency, and its association with bad choices, shapes dangerous terrain for women today, just as these concepts did in the past. Today the foregrounded target is the poor, unemployed mother, rather than the white, middle-class mother of the postwar years, but both groups of mothers have suffered substantially because of the kinds of policies these terms have always mandated. We must remember that the protracted struggle for women's rights in this country had at its heart women's determination to disassociate themselves from "dependency" and establish their right to make motherhood and employment decisions on their own behalf. Women struggled for these goals because of the ways in which they had been constrained and tainted by "dependency" and "bad choice." Remembering women's efforts to change these conditions of their lives may stimulate contemporary, female choice makers to feel less comfortable with the slurs regarding dependency and bad choices that are attached to vulnerable women today.

But if women, particularly poor women, are finally to be disass from "dependency" and "bad choices," the task will require mor sharpening the memories of female choice makers. The task will re..uire, at least, the emergence of a vibrant justice movement that unrelentingly demands the conditions of human dignity and independence for all women, including all mothers, in this country. These claims might be made using the same language, and with the same intentions, that the "founding fathers" used in behalf of "free white men" in 1776.

CHAPTER TWO

When Work Is Slavery

—Eileen Boris

Unable to find another job after being laid off in 1992, Hattie Hargrove, a Long Island custodial worker, labored in July 1997 for her old supervisor at her old tasks for the Mineola County Department of Social Services—but in place of wages she ended up each month with a $53.50 welfare check, $263 in food stamps, and no employee protections. Hargrove was participating in New York's Work Experience Program (WEP), one of the state-level workfare initiatives developed presumably to teach those on public assistance how to labor. As an employee, she explained, "I'd be making more money, and I'd have benefits instead of Medicaid. I know I would feel better because I'd be getting a paycheck and people wouldn't look down at me like I was crazy anymore." Hargrove was a double casuality of a budget-cutting mania that had led to the downsizing of government employment, while forcing welfare recipients to "work" for their benefits by undertaking jobs previously performed by public employees. "I don't mind doing the work," similarly reported street cleaner Geneva Moore, a 45-year-old Bronx mother of three, "but we are just like a piece of waste material the way the state program treats us. They feel like we're slaves or something, having to work off our check." Complaining of dangerous conditions, sexual harassment, racial discrimination, and arbitrary treatment, those enrolled in WEP spoke of their labor as "slavery" or "indentured servitude." [1]

Requiring welfare participants to work for their benefits is not new, nor is the identification of workfare with "slavery." Beginning with 1967 amendments to the Social Security Act, which established the Work In-

I would like to thank Gwendolyn Mink, the staff of the Moorland-Spingarn Research Center, Howard University, and participants at the August 1997 American Studies Seminar, University of Melbourne, "The American Working Class Today," especially Diane Kirkby.

1. These women quoted in Melissa Healy, "N.Y. 'Workfare' Not So Fair After All, Some Say," *Los Angeles Times*, July 5, 1997, A1.

centive Program (WIN) that allowed mothers of even small children to participate in employment or training if child care was available, welfare reform has fought "welfare dependence," and poor single mothers have opposed "forced work" at less than the minimum wage.[2] Linking welfare—income maintenance or assistance to those in need—with dependency, and mandating work—public labor usually performed for a wage—as its antidote, welfare reform in the last decades of the twentieth century transformed the meanings of "work" and "welfare" and the relationship between the two. Nowhere is this more apparent than with the politics surrounding the now-defunct Aid to Families with Dependent Children (AFDC) program. We need to understand reform in the 1990s as the triumph of a thirty-year reaction against the gains of the 1960s, after African American women finally shared in AFDC and welfare finally became a right or entitlement. Here I explore contested understandings of "work" and its relation to "welfare." The voices of poor, single mothers, organized in the National Welfare Rights Organization (NWRO) from 1966 until 1975, offer an alternative vantage point from which to evaluate current welfare "reform." They recognized the necessity of not merely expanding the definition of work to embrace the unpaid labor of care giving or motherwork, but of refocusing the debate from work to income. Such a standpoint shifts the policy question from "Are you working?" to "Are you earning enough to raise your children in dignity?"[3]

THE HISTORICAL SHAPE OF WELFARE

Before the New Deal, the recipient of mothers' pensions was to be the white, worthy widow, the object of Congressional paeans when such programs found a federal niche in Title IV of the 1935 Social Security Act. (In theory, the 1935 law served all single mothers; though there was no mention of race, labor market segmentation and local administration led to discriminatory implementation.) The first major amendments in 1939 separated the widowed mother, deserving because her deceased husband qualified for social insurance, from the never-married or divorced

2. Nancy E. Rose, *Workfare or Fair Work: Women, Welfare, and Government Work Programs* (New Brunswick: Rutgers University Press, 1995), 93; Milwaukee County Welfare Rights Organization, *Welfare Mothers Speak Out* (New York: Norton, 1972), 109.
3. The best history of NWRO is Guida West, *The National Welfare Rights Movement: The Social Protest of Poor Women* (New York: Praeger, 1981). See also Premilla Nadasen, "Expanding the Boundaries of the Women's Movement: Feminism and the Struggle for Welfare Rights," unpublished paper, American Historical Association, January 1997.

mother, judged undeserving because she was a woman without a man mediating her relation to the state even from the grave. Where widows and their children received survivors' insurance after 1939, poor, single mothers received Aid to Dependent Children (ADC; changed to Aid to Families with Dependent Children, or AFDC, in 1962). Unlike the federally set survivors' insurance, ADC consisted of federal funds matched by the states, which ran their own programs with minimal federal supervision. Initially, funds covered only children, not care givers. In 1949, Congress authorized a care giver grant out of the belief that "it was 'necessary for the mother or another adult to be in the home full time to provide proper care and supervision.'"[4] State regulations could be parochial, discriminatory, and arbitrary as states gave different amounts of benefits, excluded "employable mothers," demanded "suitable homes," and policed sexual behavior, cutting off women with "men in the house." Southern states refused to qualify Black women for welfare or disqualified them when the cotton crop needed picking.[5]

With the post-WWII migration of African Americans from the South, more Black women were able to obtain welfare in northern and western cities throughout the 1950s.[6] The "welfare explosion" of the 1960s developed from a newly rights-conscious group demanding access to resources often withheld by bureaucracies. (From 588,000 families applying for AFDC in 1960, the numbers grew by more than half to 903,000 in 1966, then jumped threefold from 1965 to 1976, so that millions were obtaining aid.) Legal services and civil rights lawyers overturned "man in the house" rules and established a right to a fair hearing to obtain or maintain benefits.[7] As part of the civil rights movement, welfare rights orga-

---

4. H. Rep. No. 1300, 81st Cong., 1st Sess. (1949) at 46 quoted in *Brief Amici Curiae of the National Welfare Rights Organization, Citywide Coordinating Committee of Welfare Organizations and the Upstate Welfare Rights Organization, New York State Department of Social Services v. Dublino*, Supreme Court of the United States, Oct. Term, 1972, Nos. 72–792, 72–802, 7.

5. Joanne L. Goodwin, *Gender and the Politics of Welfare Reform: Mothers' Pensions in Chicago, 1911–1929* (Chicago: University of Chicago Press, 1997); Linda Gordon, *Pitied But Not Entitled: Single Mothers and the History of Welfare* (New York: Free Press, 1994); Gwendolyn Mink, *The Wages of Motherhood: Inequality in the Welfare State, 1917–1942* (Ithaca: Cornell University Press, 1995); Joanne Goodwin, "'Employable Mothers' and 'Suitable Work': A Re-evaluation of Welfare and Wage-earning for Women in the Twentieth-Century United States," *Journal of Social History* 29 (Winter 1995): 253–74; Blanche D. Coll, *Safety Net: Welfare and Social Security, 1929–1979* (New Brunswick: Rutgers University Press, 1995).

6. Michael Brown, "The Ghetto in the Welfare State: Race and Gender after the Great Society," unpublished paper, Social Science History Association, Washington, D.C., October 1997, in author's possession.

7. For numbers, Francis Fox Piven and Richard Cloward, *Poor People's Movements: Why They Succeed, How They Fail* (New York: Vintage, 1979), 274–75; Dorothy C. Miller, *Women and Social Welfare: A Feminist Analysis* (New York: Praeger, 1990), 54; for legal actions, Martha Davis, *Brutal Need: Lawyers and the Welfare Rights Movement, 1960–1973* (New Haven: Yale University Press,

nizing took on a Black face, even though the majority of women on welfare remained white.[8]

Politicians responded by lambasting welfare "queens" as "lazy parasites" and "pigs at the trough," as did California's governor Ronald Reagan.[9] In the public mind, those on welfare were unmarried mothers, sometimes teenagers, and always Black. Politicians and pundits scorned Black welfare mothers as unworthy, because they were stepping outside what society meant for Black women to do: they cared for their own children rather than the children of others; they were mothers, rather than workers.[10]

From the early 1960s, numerous proposals sought to encourage work by allowing welfare recipients to earn wages without losing all benefits. AFDC-UP included unemployed parents, especially fathers who became obligated "to accept job referrals in order to remain eligible since in those families the mother would be able to remain home to care for her child." The 1962 Community Work and Training Programs were developed primarily for the unemployed fathers.[11] WIN encouraged welfare participants to work for wages through an income disregard; amendments in 1971 "mandated" participation and encouraged states to develop their own programs. For example, in New York Work Rules—upheld by the Supreme Court in *New York State Department of Social Services v. Dublino* (1973)—"employables" not only had to travel to the State Employment Service to obtain their welfare check but also had "to make a 'diligent' search for day care for their young children, to follow up on each and every job 'referral' . . . and . . . accept any job offer."[12] This program and others like it varied in their mix of carrots and sticks but pushed jobs over education or training; mandatory work programs became institutionalized in the Family Support Act of 1988. Motivational and job search sessions often constituted the extent of training, child care

1993); Elizabeth Bussiere, *(Dis)Entitling the Poor: The Warren Court, Welfare Rights, and the American Political Tradition* (University Park: Pennsylvania State University Press, 1997).

8. Rickie Solinger, *Wake Up Little Susie: Single Pregnancy and Race Before* Roe v. Wade (New York: Routledge, 1992).

9. Johnnie Tillmon, "Welfare," reprinted in *Ms.* (July/August 1995), 52.

10. On stereotypes of Black women, Deborah Gray White, *Ar'n't I a Woman? Female Slaves in the Plantation South* (New York: Norton, 1985), 27–61; K. Sue Jewell, *From Mammy to Miss America and Beyond: Cultural Images and the Shaping of U.S. Social Policy* (London: Routledge University Press, 1993); on African American women as mothers, Patricia Hill Collins, "Shifting the Center: Race, Class, and Feminist Theorizing About Motherhood," in *Mothering: Ideology, Experience, and Agency*, Evelyn Nakano Glenn, Grace Chang, and Linda Rennie Forcey, eds. (New York: Routledge, 1994), 45–65.

11. *Amicus Brief of NWRO*, 7, 26.

12. 93 S.Ct. 2507; *Amicus Brief of NWRO*, 11.

funding never matched need, and the wages of welfare lagged behind rises in the cost of living.[13]

Public discussion over the Personal Responsibility and Work Opportunity Act of 1996 (PRA) reiterated the racialist rhetoric that disparaged Black women, but had an impact on all needy single mothers. This act ended any entitlement to welfare by replacing AFDC with Temporary Assistance for Needy Families (TANF), with time limits and work rules. Under its rules, states needed to have a quarter of caseloads "working" by fall 1997 or face loss of federal funds. Recipients are eligible for federal benefits for a lifetime maximum of five years. Block grants allow the states to create their own programs and devise more restrictions. Many states actually adopted shorter time limits and stricter work requirements than the federal law allowed; some refused to treat new migrants to their state the same as long-time residents; some instituted a family cap—no additional monies can go to a child born to a mother already receiving welfare. States need not provide all eligible families with child care; federal child care funding remains inadequate to cover all who must go on workfare to meet federal work participation timetables. (Crowded out by welfare recipients, low-waged women in 1997 began to find it impossible to receive state child care subsidies.[14]) States that lower illegitimate birth rates without increasing abortion rates will receive a monetary bonus. Teenagers have to live with parents or relatives or in a designated facility and attend school.[15] This social engineering from the political right intervenes in the lives of the poor as much as did the therapeutic regimes of the Charity Organization Societies and welfare caseworkers of the past.[16]

The act also increases work requirements without more funds to implement them. Within two months, the law requires community service unless a state asks to be removed from this requirement; within two years, a parent or care giver has to engage in work twenty hours per week in 1998 and thirty hours a week in 2000. The law is unclear about whether failure to find work counts as refusing work, which would reduce a family's benefits and the care giving adult's Medicare coverage. In practice, community service substitutes for paid work for those unable to find

13. For a summary of developments, Rose, *Workfare or Fair Work*, 76–149.
14. Sara Rimer, "Children of Working Poor Are Day Care's Forgotten," *New York Times*, November 25, 1997, A1, 22.
15. Children's Defense Fund, "Summary of the New Welfare Legislation," updated October 23, 1996, on-line; Robert Pear, "Rewards and Penalties Vary in States' Welfare Program," *New York Times*, February 23, 1997, 1.
16. Andrew J. Polsky, *The Rise of the Therapeutic State* (Princeton: Princeton University Press, 1991); for how clients transformed attempts at social control, Linda Gordon, *Heroes of Their Own Lives: The Politics and History of Family Violence* (New York: Viking, 1988).

jobs. "Work" seems to consist of a range of activities, from unsubsidized and subsidized private-sector employment to subsidized public-sector jobs, community service programs, child care services, one year of education and vocational training, job search and readiness programs, and on-the-job training. But the number of adult recipients who may receive education while satisfying their states' work participation requirement remains questionable. Some states insist that welfare recipients take any job rather than stay in school to train for better-paying work that could lift them out of poverty.[17]

Anecdotal evidence suggests that the welfare-induced growth of the low-skilled, low-waged labor force already has generated downward pressure on wages. Such an influx is just what employers needed to relieve a tight labor market and stymie burgeoning unionization of the service sector.[18] Trade unions responded by defining for the first time those on workfare as "workers." "Everyone who works should enjoy the same rights and have an opportunity to join a union," the AFL-CIO declared at its 1997 convention. The federation pledged "to organize former welfare recipients by integrating them into bargaining units, organizing new units, and defending the living standards and working conditions of all employee(s), whether engaged in work programs through welfare or otherwise."[19]

New York's District Council 37 joined with grassroots activists, including ACORN (Association of Community Organizations for Reform Now), to organize those on workfare who feel that "a union might make them treat us with respect." Social service and religious groups, who participated in New York's workfare program, cried, "Rudy, we will not be your slave drivers."[20] The city negotiated with the public employee union "not to use welfare workers to do jobs that otherwise would be done by public employees." However, it failed to extend workplace rights to "welfare workers," thus recreating the division worker/welfare worker.[21] Nine

17. Institute for Women's Policy Research, "Work and Welfare Reform," *Welfare Reform Network News*, January 24, 1997, no. 2; "No Ivory Tower: Poverty Comes to Campus," *Women's Review of Books* 14 (February 1997): 14–33; Judith Havemann, "Welfare Law's Lingering Issue: Whether School is 'Work,'" *Washington Post*, July 8, 1997, A4. In late 1998 a joint House-Senate conference committee debated whether to extend the number of years of education from one to two.
18. "Welfare Reform's Other Victims," *New York Times*, April 6, 1997, 18.
19. E-mail from Harry Kelber, "Labor Talk: Organizing Workfare," February 24, 1997; Steven Greenhouse, "Labor Leaders Seek to Unionize Welfare Recipients Who Must Go to Work," *New York Times*, February 19, 1997, 18.
20. Barbara Crossette, "Belabored: What Modern Slavery Is, and Isn't," *New York Times*, July 27, 1997, sect. 4, 1.
21. Steven Greenhouse, "City Labor Head Backs Effort to Organize Workfare Participants," *New York Times*, February 9, 1997, 39, 42; "Don't Unionize Workfare," *New York Times*, February 21, 1997, 36. Within a year, ACORN had stimulated welfare organizing in Los Angeles, Wisconsin,

months later, 17,000 WEP workers voted ACORN their representative in a "union" election under the auspices of the New York Workers' Rights Board and Jobs with Justice. On the second anniversary of "welfare reform," in August 1998, New York City welfare recipients, trade unionists, and supporters again protested for "real jobs and an end to workfare slavery."[22]

Unions and community activists likewise pressured Maryland's governor to bar workfare replacement of existing employees after Baltimore's largest hotel substituted welfare recipients for unionized housekeepers "embroiled for a year in an acrimonious labor dispute over wages." Activists feared that subsidized low-waged laborers would undermine Baltimore's "living wage" ordinance, which requires companies performing "services for the city to pay the employees who actually did the work a wage . . . set at $7.10 an hour," when the minimum wage stood at only $4.75. Maryland became the third state, after Illinois and Minnesota, to limit use of workfare. In contrast, New York City officials and Congressional Republicans differentiated workfare from employment by defining it as either "preparation . . . to get work" or payback by the able-bodied "in exchange for . . . benefits."[23]

States differ in workfare compensation rates: most pay less than $3 an hour and Mississippi, a mere 89 cents. Countering such rates, the president extended the minimum wage to workfare. Republican leaders in Congress pledged to negate this ruling. During the 105th Congress, Democrats further demanded that recipients who labor come under health, safety, and fair labor protections. But, as one Georgia representative contended, welfare recipients by definition were not "hard-working people just trying to raise a family." Those "who could not find work do not deserve the same treatment as others."[24] In contrast, others believed, "anyone who doesn't see this as a way of sidestepping laws that interfere with the greed of the 'haves,' and creating a virtual slave labor force, isn't

New Jersey, Arkansas, Dallas, and New Mexico, as well as in New York. See Ruth Wielgosz, "Organizing Welfare Workers," March 17, 1998, Welfare-L@American.edu.

22. Amanda Ream, "New York Workfare Workers Vote Union," *Labor Notes*, 225, December 1997, 1; "Workfare Protest on Anniversary of Welfare," Sunday August 30, 1998, Welfare-L, foreword of Greg Butterfield, "Workfare Workers Tell Clinton: Money for Jobs, Not for Missiles."

23. Jon Jeter, "Md. Shields Jobs from Welfare Law," *Washington Post*, May 4, 1997, A1, A11; Louis Uchitelle, "Maryland Order Limits Hiring of People in Workfare Programs," *New York Times*, July 1, 1997, A15.

24. Letter to the Editor from Kevin Ryan, "Workfare Wages," *Washington Post*, July 3, 1997, A18; Judith Havemann and Barbara Vobejda, "Congressional Panels Reject Clinton Rulings on Welfare," *Washington Post*, June 14, 1997, A7; Eric Pianin, "Medicare Eligibility-Age Rise Rejected," *Washington Post*, July 11, 1997, A4.

looking too closely." Or, as one Ohio woman—who is a welfare recipient, a student, and a veteran—declared, "We aren't slave labor! . . . We
all live under the same constitution. We did not agree to give up our
rights to the same fair treatment as anyone else in this country when we
signed welfare applications."[25]

CONTESTING WORK: TRADE UNIONISTS AND FEMINISTS

A quarter century ago, beliefs about women and work lagged behind
the growth in female employment. Trade unionists agreed with welfare
activists that lone mothers should remain at home. Their understanding
of women's proper labor derived from economic concerns, but ones that
reflected organized workers' long reliance on the male breadwinner ideal.
In rejecting this relegation of women to motherwork, feminists in essence dismissed the citizenship claims that NWRO women derived from
their life experience as mothers.[26]

Organized labor protested workfare schemes to protect union jobs and
wages. In the late 1960s, the AFL-CIO feared that resulting community
service jobs would undermine wage rates and the labor standards of public employees, both those who administered welfare programs and those
whose jobs might be jeopardized by workfare hires. (Current attempts at
privatization, as by the state of Texas, again threaten caseworkers.) It preferred to restrict welfare to those unable to work, a category that then still
included mothers.[27]

As one top spokesman put it in 1972, "welfare should concern itself
primarily with the needs of the children dependent on it and not on
the work or non-work of their mothers. This will be possible if it is recognized that most mothers on welfare should not be expected or even
encouraged—and certainly not be required—to work." Only when
there were adequate day care centers and child welfare services, as well as
"meaningful and appropriate training and employment opportunities,"
should solo mothers engage in paid labor. Moreover, forcing only the
poor, single mother "who is the only parent of her children to "'work' or

25. Nancy C. Bernardi-Baker, "Re: Welfare-L Digest-24 Oct 1997 to 25 Oct 1997," October 26,
1997; Julie Star, "Re: Community Service," Oct. 23, 1997, both available on Welfare-L@Ameri-
can.edu.
26. For women's citizenship claims, Gwendolyn Mink, *Welfare's End* (Ithaca: Cornell University
Press, 1998).
27. Jill Quadagno, *The Color of Welfare: How Racism Undermined the War on Poverty* (New York:
Oxford University Press, 1994).

both she and her children will starve" was immoral. Compared to the mother in a two-parent family, whom no one was forcing to leave the home to earn wages, the poor, single mother had "heavier parental and household responsibilities": demanding her labor market participation meant interfering with the needs of her children.[28]

Putting children first, this argument replicated the maternalist arguments developed earlier in the century by the Children's Bureau coalition of women reformers, who had rejected the equal rights feminism of their day to support women's work as caretakers of children. Maternalist reformers had focused on child welfare; through children they had hoped to improve the laboring conditions of mothers as well. The women's reform position had persisted among influential labor union women and their supporters in government, manifesting itself in policy debates throughout the late 1960s and early 1970s.[29]

Unlike Nixon, who killed the Comprehensive Child Development Act of 1971, labor recognized the need for child care if mothers were to become waged workers. While the AFL-CIO preferred legislation that removed all mothers from the welfare work requirement, it accepted proposals that exempted those of "school aged children from all job or training requirements" and established "day care centers with adequate standards to enable mothers who choose to accept employment to do so."[30] Instead of Nixon's Family Assistance Plan (FAP), labor desired that the federal government provide a poverty-level income, protect work standards, and exempt mothers. But in the 1970s the trade union federation still clung to a breadwinner ideal that placed mothers in another social category, lobbying for amendments to Nixon's plan that treated mothers differently.[31]

FAP was Nixon's failed attempt at welfare reform (authored by Daniel

28. Bert Seidman, "The Work Ethic and Welfare Reform," paper presented to the Annual Meeting of the Industrial Relations Research Association, Toronto, Ontario, December 29, 1972, 6–7, collection 1, box 54, folder 63, Records of the AFL-CIO, George Meany Center and Archives, Silver Spring, Md.

29. Johnson's head of the Women's Bureau, Mary Dublin Keyserling, for example, had led the National Consumers' League in the late 1930s. See Eileen Boris, *Home to Work: Motherhood and the Politics of Industrial Homework in the United States* (New York: Cambridge University Press, 1994), 246. On the women's reform network, see Mink, *The Wages of Motherhood*; Gordon, *Pitied But Not Entitled*.

30. Telegram to Andrew Biemiller from Arnold Aronson, April 6, 1971, collection 1, box 54, folder 63, Meany Archives.

31. Memorandum to Andy Biemiller from Bert Seidman on Possible Senate Amendments to Welfare Bill, March 18, 1970, 2, with attached Elizabeth Wickenden, "Progress Report on Welfare Legislation" (Confidential), February 4, 1970, collection 1, box 54, folder 63, Meany Archives; on Nixon and day care, Quadagno, *The Color of Welfare*, 149–53.

Patrick Moynihan). The plan would have bolstered the two-parent family by extending benefits more generally to working poor families with fathers present. As Jill Quadagno has shown, it also would have had women who were on welfare spend more hours earning wages. Thus, a mother could improve her situation best by marrying a wage-earning man. In this way, FAP would have enforced the traditional values of the work ethic and nuclear family.[32]

Liberal feminists rejected the assumptions of organized labor. Since the early sixties, they had pushed their own version of the work ethic. They embraced child care and waged labor, equating women's equality with labor market employment. Their demand for women's entrance into waged work ideologically undermined the association of women with mothers and mothers with the home at the very time that economic forces led greater numbers of women into the labor market. But economic conditions, rather than feminism, undoubtedly had more to do with the entrance of mothers into the paid labor force between World War II and the late 1960s and early 1970s, when Congress debated FAP. Women's labor force participation did not resolve central questions: Was motherwork a legitimate work activity for women? for which women?

In attempting to escape what they called the mother trap, liberal feminists devalued the work of mothering and suggested, as Betty Friedan did in *The Feminine Mystique*, that women needed to earn wages—to work—to be liberated or self-fulfilled. In her critique of "The Happy Housewife Heroine," Friedan argued that a woman lost her separate identity when tied to home and family; she was denied self-actualization through creative labor or work, here really understood as a career, that Friedan promoted as solving "the problem that has no name." Such liberal feminist thought emphasized equality of opportunity, speaking of choice as if all women had a choice whether to work in the home or for wages outside it or whether or not to have children. *The Feminine Mystique*, as now widely recognized, projected the situation of some white, middle-class suburban women onto all women, including poor women forced to earn wages and especially working-class African American women, few of whose men earned a family wage. Classical liberalism depended on a differentiation between the political and the family. Though liberal feminism actually questioned this separation, its solutions tended to facilitate participation in the world of paid labor

32. Quadagno, *The Color of Welfare*, 117–34; see also Gareth Davies, *From Opportunity to Entitlement: The Transformation and Decline of Great Society Liberalism* (Lawrence: University Press of Kansas, 1996), 211–33.

(through enforcement of the ban on discrimination under Title VII of the 1964 Civil Rights Act, affirmative action, maternity leave rights, nondiscriminatory Social Security benefits, child care, equal job training, and abortion rights) at the expense of improving the conditions of motherwork. Equality meant rejection of female difference, most symbolized by motherhood.[33]

Liberal feminism's prescriptions contrasted with early twentieth-century images of worthy widows, which still dominated the discourse of workfare opponents into the 1970s. Reverend Norman P. Thomas of the Detroit-based Citizens for Welfare Reform, for one, argued in 1971: "the overwhelming majority of welfare recipients are unemployable or the victims of unemployment. Only one percent of Michigan's categorical welfare recipients are employable fathers. The rest are old, disabled, blind, mothers and children." Debating FAP in 1972, Rhode Island Senator John Pastore reminded the nation of the original intent of AFDC: "Is it not going to be cheaper and better to keep that home intact by keeping the mother home with the children, rather than putting the children in a day-care center, which is going to be much more expensive, and have the mother go to work? That was the whole principle of aid to dependent children."[34]

IN DEFENSE OF MOTHERWORK

The NWRO embraced a similar understanding of AFDC when it argued before the Supreme Court in 1971 that Congress had intended "to help such mothers stay at home full-time in order to rear their children."[35] Unlike the AFL-CIO or its allies, though, it framed its defense of motherhood in terms that advanced women's agency, as had activist African American women a half century before.[36] Organized welfare recipients in NWRO resisted the liberal feminist paradigm that employ-

33. Betty Friedan, *The Feminine Mystique* (New York: Dell, 1963); Joanne Meyerowitz, "Beyond the Feminine Mystique: A Reassessment of Postwar Mass Culture, 1946–1958," in *Not June Cleaver: Women and Gender in Postwar America, 1945–1960* (Philadelphia: Temple University Press, 1994), 229–62; but Friedan today recognizes welfare as a women's issue; Felicia Kornbluh, "Welfare and the Women's Vanguard," *In These Times*, December 11, 1995, 40, 39.
34. Rev. Norman P. Thomas to Mr. George Meany, May 14, 1971, Legislative Records of the AFL-CIO, collection 1, box 54, folder 57, George Meany Archives, Silver Spring, Md.; *Congressional Record*, October 3, 1972, Senate, 16695.
35. *Amicus Brief*, 21.
36. Eileen Boris, "The Power of Motherhood: Black and White Activist Women Redefine the 'Political,'" in *Mothers of a New World: Maternalist Politics and the Origins of Welfare States*, Seth Koven and Sonya Michel, eds. (New York: Routledge, 1993), 213–45.

ment meant freedom. Yet neither did they accept the male breadwinner ideal or trade union definitions of them as outside the laboring class.

NWRO emerged from the ferment of the mid-1960s to mobilize poor people to demand their rights and gain an adequate guaranteed income for all, a strategy associated with social work professor Richard Cloward and political scientist Frances Fox Piven. Founded by George Wiley, a professor of chemistry and activist in the direct action Congress for Racial Equality, NWRO set about organizing welfare recipients to overload the system in order to transform it. Local groups undertook campaigns for furniture and winter clothing allowances, for credit cards at retail stores, and for monetary payments over vouchers. NWRO became a movement of poor, single, mostly Black mothers on AFDC, who demanded dignity and income rather than jobs. If a mother wanted to engage in paid labor, she should earn the minimum wage, they argued. But mothers need not be wage laborers because they already were performing essential work. After 1972, when recipients gained organizational control, NWRO became identified with Black feminism. Even earlier, leaders embraced a feminism of difference that derived from their experiences as poor Black women.[37]

NWRO chair Johnnie Tillmon, organizer of the Aid to Needy Children (ANC) mothers in Watts, understood the contradictions inherent in "the work ethic": "The president keeps repeating the 'dignity of work' idea. What dignity? Wages are the measure of dignity that society puts on a job. Wages. Nothing else. There is no dignity in starvation."[38] NWRO members insisted on their right to social services and a guaranteed living income, not the inadequate amount proposed by the Nixon administration that was pegged 40 percent below the poverty line. They called FAP "a multi-headed repression falling most heavily on the children of the poor" that would "legislate a separate class of poor children who are abandoned in custodial care as a means of coercing their mothers to work."[39] They vehemently rejected "forced work requirements" that "will only be used to harass, intimidate, and coerce recipients." They ob-

---

37. For this history, see West, *The National Welfare Rights Movement*; Fox Piven and Cloward, *Poor People's Movements*, 264–361. For the most perceptive analysis of welfare rights philosophy, Felicia Kornbluh, "To Fulfill Their 'Rightly Needs': Consumerism and the National Welfare Rights Movement," *Radical History Review*, no. 69 (Fall 1997), 76–113; Kornbluh, "Researching Welfare Rights and Organizing with the Women's Committee of 100," *Feminist Studies* 24 (Spring 1998), 65–78.

38. On Tillmon, see West, *The National Welfare Rights Movement*, 39, 83, 447–48 (index entries); Interview with Johnnie Tillmon, *The African World*, June 24, 1972, 12, box 2239, NWRO Papers, Moorland-Spingarn Research Center, Howard University.

39. Leaflet, Mrs. Johnnie Tillmon and George A. Wiley to All Local WRO groups, staff and friends, February 7, 1972, box 2061, NWRO Papers.

jected to requirements that mothers and pregnant women under nineteen "work" and those with children over three "register for and accept jobs" for which they need not be paid minimum wage.[40]

Charges of nonfreedom dominated this oppositional discourse. Welfare rights mothers angrily rejected FAP and its workfare requirements; those in Washington, DC, asserted: "we *will not* accept slave jobs and our kids *are not* going to starve!"[41] Workfare offered women "very little hope of breaking out of the slave labor market," Tillmon and organizer Faith Evans declared.[42] Civil Rights leaders concurred. National Urban League director Vernon E. Jordan Jr. in 1972 viewed FAP as "an instrument of control and coercion with respect to employment, child rearing, family relationships, health care, drug use, and other behavioral patterns."[43] Columbia University poverty lawyers labeled proposed New York requirements "a primitive form of coercion . . . to compel a parent to take certain actions by the manipulation of her child's basic means of survival."[44] As Rochester Action for Welfare Rights announced, "Experimental projects have started in New York state to force welfare mothers into slavery. Some working for no wages. Others babysitting for other recipients."[45] The 1971 Talmadge amendments to AFDC, which required women with children over the age of six to participate in WIN, became known as "the slave labor law."[46]

Since WIN, welfare rights organizations had informed recipients what constituted a suitable job. In Delaware, for example, recipients could reject jobs that took them too far from home (more than an hour commute each way), were unsafe, for which they were untrained, or that prevented them from taking care of their children. Other guides further emphasized labor standards: wages that matched either the federal or state minimum, even for piecework; a workplace not subject to a strike or lockout at the time of the job offer; no requirement to join or resign from a

---

40. NWRO, "Some Reasons Why NWRO is Opposed to H.R. 1—Nixon's Family Assistance Plan (FAP)," box 2061, NWRO Papers.
41. Elizabeth Perry to Mrs. Cavenaugh, December 10, 1971, box 2061, NWRO Papers.
42. Johnnie Tillmon and Faith Evans, *National Welfare Rights Organization Prospectus, 1974,* box 2239, NWRO Papers.
43. Jordan quoted in Dona Cooper Hamilton and Charles V. Hamilton, *The Dual Agenda: The African-American Struggle for Civil and Economic Equality* (New York: Columbia University Press, 1997), 190.
44. Nick Kotz, "Incentive Keyed to Welfare," *Washington Post,* A1, 6, clipping file c. August 1971, box 2061, NWRO Papers.
45. Flyer, "Attention Everyone!" Rochester Action for Welfare Rights, box 2061, NWRO Papers.
46. R[ita]. Gross, "The Kind of Child Care That Is Being Proposed by H.E.W. Office of Child Development," unpublished story for *Welfare Fighter,* NWRO Papers, box 2243 on Talmadge Amendments; Rose, *Workfare or Fair Work,* 102–4.

union; and no risk to occupational health or safety.[47] Contending that "everyone has the right to work," the NWRO argued for the right "to choose an occupation in line with their ability and ambition, be it plumber, mother, engineer, or artist."[48]

By including mother as an occupation, the NWRO defied the devaluation of care giving. National officer Beulah Sanders argued, "a mother should have the right to stay home with her children rather than be forced to work. She should have the right to say if she wants to work or she should have the right to say whether her children should be put into a Government-run center."[49]

Welfare rights activists felt "the belief that welfare mothers can work assumes that they are not working now." "Women's work is *real* work," Tillmon declared in 1972. Such a recognition "would solve this so-called welfare crisis . . . and go a long way toward liberating every woman." She would "start paying women a living wage for doing the work we are already doing—child-raising and housekeeping. Housewives would be getting wages—a legally determined percentage of their husband's salary—instead of having to ask for and account for money they've already earned."[50] Bessie Moore of Milwaukee proposed: "If the government was smart, it would start calling AFDC 'Day and Night Care,' create a new agency, pay us a decent wage for the service work we are now doing, and say that the welfare crisis has been solved because welfare mothers have been put to work."[51]

At a time when organized feminism concentrated on the Equal Rights Amendment,[52] welfare activists insisted on their right to the resources necessary to mother. They demanded, as a New Jersey activist put it, "help in the areas of emergency food, furniture, moving monies or help

47. Cray Smith, William Wlesch, and Mark Zola, *Welfare Rights in Delaware*, September 20, 1967, 10; for one such guide, Community Welfare Rights Organization, *Food Stamp Rules and Rights*, October 1972, both in box 2239, NWRO Papers.

48. Tillmon and Evans, *National Welfare Rights Organization: Prospectus*, box 2239, NWRO Papers.

49. Testimony of Beulah Sanders, October 27, 1969, House Ways and Means Committee, *Social Security and Welfare Proposals* (pt. 3), 91st Cong., 1st sess. (Washington, D.C.: GPO, 1970), 1017.

50. Tillmon, "Welfare," 55.

51. *Welfare Mothers Speak Out*, 77–79.

52. Still for Mother's Day, 1968, the Board of the National Organization for Women (NOW) voted to support the Poor People's Campaign and its Welfare Mothers March, which Mrs. Coretta Scott King was to lead. It also made May 18 a day to "Fast to Free Women from Poverty." "Memorandum to NOW Chapters" from Kathryn F. Clarenbach, box 10, folder 2, Dorothy Haener Collection, UAW Women's Department, UAW Papers, archives of Labor and Urban Affairs, Wayne State University, Detroit. Local chapters decided, however, their extent of participation. UAW activists in NOW strongly supported local welfare rights groups.

with other normal problems confronting welfare families, given their inadequate income and circumstances." She exclaimed: "We are not unfit mothers, but neither are we magicians, we do not get adequate monies or supportive services to begin with, in order to have a budget at all."[53] They submitted grants for federal monies to subsidize child care centers, to enable "some women who have been forced to go on the welfare rolls . . . to become self-supporting."[54] They supported national health care, legal services, child care, family planning, and an adequate national guaranteed income. The goal was not employment but an adequate income to support their duties as mothers.[55] This emphasis on social services contrasted with reform, which would shift the location of aid from the welfare office to the employment bureau and from the social worker to the job counselor.

Some wage-earning women, including those paid inadequately (like waitresses), rejected this stand. A California woman complained to the House Ways and Means Committee in 1969, "I'm getting fed up with having to work, taking my child to a baby-sitter's so some other mother can sit home and not do a blankety blank thing!" She would remove children from people on welfare to raise them with "the idea you don't get something for nothing" and sterilize such lazy men and women to prevent more babies. Buying into what NWRO named the "myths of welfare," this mother clung to the work ethic as a marker of respectability.[56]

Maternalism distinguished women welfare activists from the men of their own movement, who sought universal entitlements rather than rights based on motherhood and the labor of mothering. But all embraced the slogan, "Bread and Justice." By 1973, Black women of the NWRO gained control of the organization from Executive Director Wiley, whose dictatorial style and substance differed from their own. He had wanted a movement that encompassed all poor people and not only AFDC mothers.[57]

While defending the decision of welfare mothers to stay at home, Wiley emphasized male responsibilities for work and family. In 1967 tes-

53. Letter to Rev. John T. Asch from (Mrs.) Ruth Welfield, May 13, 1972, in box 2061, NWRO Papers. She was a white woman; communication from Guida West to Eileen Boris.
54. "Phoenix Day Care Center Hopes to Open Soon," newsletter of Christ Church (Episcopal), Collingswood, N.J., c. May 1972, box 2061, NWRO Papers.
55. "Democratic National Platform Position: Welfare and Unemployment," Western Regional Report, NWRO, 1972, n.p., box 2061, NWRO Papers.
56. *Social Security and Welfare Proposals*, 1042. See also the widowed waitress who complained that welfare recipients were cheaters but failed to report her tips. *Welfare Mothers Speak Out*, 88–89.
57. On conflict with Wiley and the NWRO as a woman's movement, West, *The National Welfare Rights Movement*, 120–23.

timony against WIN, he claimed that "for the government to try to force [mothers] into the job market when there are not enough jobs for the men in the ghetto, is to add insult to absurdity." He would provide training or work to able-bodied men in two-parent poor families, but "mothers should be protected against the brutality of a society that says that a mother can be forced to leave her children in some institutional care and go and accept work."[58] An exchange between Michigan Representative Martha Griffiths (Dem.) and Wiley at 1969 hearings highlights how distant his emphasis on adequate income was from her liberal feminist insistence on women's self-reliance through wage labor. Griffiths insisted that the young single mother "should be given training, then a chance to work," but charged that Wiley's disagreement came "because you are a man." Arguing that women members backed his position, Wiley distinguished the feminist fight against discrimination, which he supported, from "seek[ing] to deal with [women's special] problems while penalizing all people who are poor by giving them inadequate income and not providing adequate income for all poor people, is really, to my way of thinking, criminal."[59]

Beulah Sanders actually agreed with Griffiths' proposal. Unlike most white feminists, this African American woman had no problem in holding out for women's self-sufficiency through either adequate jobs or income and promoting men's employment. Such had been the double fight of Black communities since emancipation. As the Milwaukee County Welfare Rights Organization explained, "welfare mothers realize full well the burden on their men, who are considered failures because they are not able to provide for their families."[60]

Tillmon, who succeeded Wiley as executive director, differed with him when it came to the role of women, announcing "NWRO views the major welfare problems as women's issues and itself as strictly a women's organization."[61] But she agreed with his class analysis of differences among women. A June 1972 interview in *The African World*, at the height of the struggle to defeat FAP, reveals the dominant understanding of work held by NWRO women: "The work ethic is a double standard. It's applied to men and women on welfare. It doesn't apply if you're a society lady from Scarsdale and you spend all your time sitting on your prosperity pairing

58. Testimony of George Wiley, September 22, 1967, Senate Finance Committee, *Social Security Amendments of 1967* (pt. 3), on H.R. 12080, 90th Cong., 1st sess., 1921.
59. Testimony of Wiley, *Social Security and Welfare Proposals* (pt. 3), 1027–28, 1031–32.
60. On Black women's support of their men, Jacqueline Jones, *Labor of Love, Labor of Sorrow: Black Women, Work, and the Family* (New York: Basic Books, 1985); *Welfare Mothers Speak Out*, 85.
61. West, *The National Welfare Rights Movement*, 122.

your nails." [62] That was because "women aren't supposed to work. They're supposed to be married," she explained in the feminist magazine *Ms*.[63] A Minnesota activist contended, "when a mother lives in the suburbs and has two children, that's just ideal. But when you're on welfare and got two children you're supposed to be out working and farm those kids out . . . if you're on welfare you're trash." Only women on welfare had their performance of motherwork questioned—by caseworkers, usually other women.[64]

NWRO activists understood the connections between lack of child care and welfare. They established child care centers, sometimes staffed with recipients.[65] Before the establishment of the Children's Defense Fund, they framed analysis around the needs of children to argue against poverty and inequality, to improve conditions in African American communities. In March 1972, NWRO participated in the Children's March for Survival in support of comprehensive and quality child care. They protested federal standards for child care attached to workfare programs that would warehouse the children of recipients. They objected to adult-child ratios that created "babysitting situations . . . depriving the children of a developmental, educational program and . . . adults of a meaningful work experience," [66] attributing such defects to the target population: welfare mothers and their children. NWRO recognized class distinctions both in child care programs and tax deductions. Echoing the demands of the early War on Poverty, they called for parent participation. According to Rita Gross, editor of *The Welfare Fighter*, proposed child care standards under WIN meant that

1. Poor parents do not have the right to meaningful employment—reasonable working conditions, or decent wages.
2. Poor children do not have the right to a nutritious diet.
3. Child-life is not important enough to warrant quality child care.

---

62. Interview with Johnnie Tillmon, *The African World*.
63. Tillmon, "Welfare," 52.
64. Quoted in Susan Handley Hertz, *The Welfare Mothers Movement: A Decade of Change for Poor Women?* (Washington, D.C.: University Press of America, 1981), 104, 116.
65. There is an entire box (2243) in the NWRO papers with materials on child care, including "Proposal for Funding a Sample Outline Child Care Training Center for Low-Income and Welfare Families"; "Setting Up a Child Care Training Program with a University in Your Community"; "Children's Rights"; Robert L. Bender, Day Care and Child Development Council of America to Deborah Vajda, August 20, 1971; "History of Milwaukee County Welfare Rights Day Care Training Program."
66. NWRO, "Repressive Welfare Legislation Exploits Welfare Children—Provides Tax Deductions for Middle and Upper Income Families," 10/13/72, NWRO Papers, box 2243.

4. The compulsory school age level for poor children will eventually be three years of age, while the compulsory school age level for children of middle-and upper-income families is age six in most states.[67]

NWRO joined with child care advocates, such as the Day Care and Child Development Council of America, the National Organization for Women, and the National Committee on Household Workers, for a "National Working Mothers Day" to decry state and federal child care budget cuts. With similar advocacy groups, it questioned the creation of dead-end, low-wage "child development associate" jobs slated for welfare recipients that would fail to pay a living wage. Welfare activists rejected not work, for they saw themselves as hard workers, but demeaning labor that was hurtful to children.[68] As one Detroit woman testified in protesting inadequate clothing grants for their children, "We are not lazy—we have concern for our children—we want the same things that you want out of life—we have the same drive and ambitions. We just cannot make it as easy as you did and we have been driven into a condition over which we have no control. We did not create the conditions of poverty in which we find ourselves."[69]

Indeed, women on welfare were interchangeable with low-waged workers and even in the late 1960s and early 1970s moved in and out of the labor market. One Michigan study found that a quarter of recipients were already working full-time, earning wages so low that they qualified for welfare.[70]

Black Women and the Domestic

The slavery metaphor loomed large because welfare reform in the late sixties and early seventies attempted to push back civil rights gains and continue the exploitation of African American women's labor. Welfare

67. Gross, "The Kind of Child Care," NWRO Papers, box 2243.
68. Draft letter Johnnie Tillmon to Secretary Elliot Richardson, July 24, 1972; "Working Mothers Need Quality Day Care NOW," flyer for April 10, 1972, rally; Rita Gross, "Child Development Associates"; "Workfare for Welfare Recipients," September 18, 1972, all in NWRO Papers, box 2243.
69. "Adequacy of the Michigan Welfare Grant: Testimony of Mary Clavon," October 3, 1968, 7, box 10, folder 2, Haener Papers.
70. Rone Tempest, "Welfare Not Used to Avoid Working, U-M Study Claims," *Detroit Free Press*, July 2, 1973, A-3.

reform would reinscribe Black women as workers, not mothers, relegated to household labor as maids, nannies, and day care providers for other women's children.[71] In 1969 hearings on unemployment insurance, Georgia Representative Philip Landrum declared, "I find many people can't get domestic help. Couldn't domestics be taken off welfare?"[72] Senator Russell Long and others, it appeared, created workfare "to force lots of welfare mothers who are the sole parents in their families into cleaning the houses of more fortunate two-parent families," an opponent charged at the time.[73] At the NWRO alternative hearings on FAP, one woman testified: "We only want the kind of jobs that will pay $10,000 or $20,000. . . . We aren't ready to do anybody's laundry or baby-sitting except for ourselves." Others yelled, "Senator Long should get his wife or mother to do his shirts."[74]

Domestic work, those who performed it understood, left one poor. "I have had to work as a domestic since high school at poor wages and advancing loss of hearing," one nearly sixty-year-old woman wrote, as she sent a dollar dues to join a welfare rights organization.[75] The fledgling National Committee on Household Employment feared that FAP would undermine its efforts to organize "your present-day house slave or house darkie, your Aunt Jemima," as one organizer chided.[76] The domestic was interchangeable with the woman on welfare; both were poor and Black and dismissed by the larger society. Until 1974, household workers stood outside labor law, unprotected by social security.[77] We may never know how many domestics also received welfare to supplement their meager earnings. Recent studies reveal that most women on AFDC go in and out of employment, which they combine with welfare. That is, they "are *already* working, but cannot earn enough or find enough work to lift their families out of poverty."[78] NWRO activists also knew that education hardly guaranteed women "jobs that would pay enough to get them

71. For African American women and household labor, Tera Hunter, *To 'Joy My Freedom: Southern Black Women's Lives and Labor After the Civil War* (Cambridge: Harvard University Press, 1997).

72. Memorandum from Clint Fair to Andy Biemiller on Social Insurance and Welfare Hearings, October 9, 1969, collection 1, box 54, folder 62, Meany Archives.

73. Seidman, "The Work Ethic and Welfare Reform," 3–4.

74. Quoted in Cooper Hamilton and Hamilton, *The Dual Agenda*, 188.

75. Letter from Miss Mildred Coon in box 2039, NWRO Papers.

76. *Welfare Mothers Speak Out*, 110–12.

77. Phyllis Palmer, "Outside the Law: Agricultural and Domestic Workers Under the Fair Labor Standards Act," *Journal of Policy History* 7 (Fall 1995), 416–40.

78. Institute for Women's Policy Research, "Welfare to Work: The Job Opportunities of AFDC Recipients," *Research-in-Brief*, March 1995.

off welfare" for they were "grossly underpaid for doing the same things men do."[79]

From WIN onward, welfare reform has envisioned compensating some women to care for the children of other recipients who would participate in workfare or employment. It would create, as NWRO activists insisted, "a new form of slavery: institutionalized, partially self-employed nannies. And these nannies would get only three-quarters of the minimum wage."[80] This certainly was not what the AFL-CIO in 1969 meant by adequately funding child care and job training; nor is it what true welfare reform would mean.

We are left with an overdetermined identification, deeply rooted in American politics, economy, and culture, that signifies degradation, disparagement, and disgust, a low status that prefigures low income: the association of welfare with African American women and Black women with domestic labor. The maternalism of the NWRO was oppositional in this context because it demanded that poor women, regardless of race, be allowed to perform motherwork, even if that meant providing them with an adequate income in lieu of a breadwinner's wage and dependence on a man.

Motherwork finds few adherents today when 60 percent of mothers of preschoolers earn wages.[81] Newspapers feature women on welfare eager to enter the labor market—when not emphasizing dysfunctional traits in stories that transform social into individual pathology. Social policy refuses to support poor women's motherwork by insisting on work outside the home no matter the needs of children or their ability to handle both sides of the double day. Meanwhile, workfare threatens the livelihoods of all low-waged laborers and their efforts to unionize. A revitalized labor movement that organizes workfare participants as workers promises a first step toward ending poverty as we know it. But a second step is necessary: redefining care work as labor and rewarding it through minimum income or tax relief. Substituting work outside the home for family labor, workfare denies value to the labor that poor, single mothers already perform for their families and demands that they leave their children as a condition of welfare. Though a new world of employment beckons, poor, single mothers still recognize when work is slavery.

79. *Welfare Mothers Speak Out*, 79–80.
80. *Welfare Mothers Speak Out*, 116.
81. Diane E. Herz and Barbara H. Wootton, "Women in the Workforce: An Overview," in *The American Woman, 1996–97: Where We Stand, Women and Work*, eds. Cynthia Costello and Barbara Kivimae Krimgold (New York: Norton, 1996), Table I-1, p. 49.

From Maximum Feasible Participation to Disenfranchisement

—Nancy A. Naples

As a consequence of a unique confluence of political, economic, and social factors, the Great Society programs established by President Lyndon B. Johnson helped broaden the basis for citizen participation in poor urban communities across the United States. In the context of the Civil Rights Movement and an apparently strong and growing economy, Johnson declared a War on Poverty in his State of the Union address in January 1964.[1] The Economic Opportunity Act (EOA) of 1964 became the legislative linchpin. It called for maximum feasible participation of residents living in the poor neighborhoods served by newly established community action programs.[2] In his State of the Union message, Johnson explained: "I propose a program which relies on the traditional time-tested American methods of organized local community action to help individuals, families, and communities to help themselves."[3] Yet the designers of community action were unprepared for the political challenge

The author wishes to thank Gwendolyn Mink for insightful editorial suggestions and Wendy Sarvasy for helpful comments on an earlier draft. A version of this article was presented at the American Studies Association meetings in Washington, D.C., October 30, 1997.

1. James L. Sundquist, "Origins of the War on Poverty," in *On Fighting Poverty: Perspectives from Experience*, ed. James L. Sundquist (New York: Basic Books, 1969), 20, quoting Theodore Sorensen, *Kennedy* (New York: Harper and Row, 1965), 753, notes that Kennedy had his staff "working on a 'comprehensive, coordinated attack on poverty' more than a month before he went to Dallas—or sometime in October." He credits Assistant Budget Director Charles L. Schultze with suggesting that the antipoverty programs be renamed "action program," preferring this to the term under consideration by William B. Cannon of the Budget Bureau, "development corporation." Sundquist reports that some unidentified staff added the word "community" to the phrase.

2. Four different forms of citizen participation were included in the implementation of the EOA: policymaking, social service utilization, social action, and job experience [Ralph M. Kramer, *Participation of the Poor: Comparative Community Case Studies in the War on Poverty* (Englewood Cliffs, N.J.: Prentice-Hall, 1969)].

3. Quoted in Sundquist, "Origins of the War on Poverty," 23.

that participants would pose to the established political regimes in different locales.[4] City officials from across the United States responded to the challenge by pressuring the president to limit the poor's policymaking role.[5]

Nevertheless, the War on Poverty expanded local citizenship, albeit for a short time. This contrasts sharply with the disenfranchisement and urban disinvestment that characterizes the contemporary policy context. Commitment to maximum feasible participation of the poor has disappeared from the welfare policies of the 1980s and 1990s. Emphasis on community action and comprehensive, multiservice, community-based approaches to fighting poverty has receded from public discourse. So have calls for local community control over the assessment of community needs and the design and implementation of antipoverty programs. Contemporary welfare reform shifts control over funds for social support to the individual states, but it does not require or invite the active participation of community residents and welfare recipients in program design, resource allocation, and implementation. However, certain features that were prominent in the Community Action title of the EOA have gained renewed popularity in the contemporary conservative political climate, namely, community service and decentralization. In this chapter, I demonstrate how certain progressive aspects of community action shifted to serve conservative ends in the 1990s. Contemporary welfare policy reform embodies this shift, which narrows rather than expands the citizenship of the poor.[6]

Feminists who focus attention on the welfare state are particularly interested in expanding "women's access to social and political citizenship."[7] According to Wendy Sarvasy and Birte Siim, "The feminist no-

4. See, for example, Mitchell Sviridoff, "The Local Initiatives Support Corporation: A Private Initiative for a Public Problem," in *Privatization and the Welfare State*, eds. Sheila B. Kamerman and Alfred J. Kahn (Princeton, Princeton University Press, 1989), 207–234; Adam Yarmolinsky, "The Beginnings of OEO" in *On Fighting Poverty: Perspectives from Experience*, ed. James L. Sundquist (New York: Basic Books, 1969), 34–51.
5. See Barbara Cruikshank, "The Will to Power: Technologies of Citizenship and the War on Poverty," *Socialist Review* 23, no. 4 (1995): 29–55; Kramer, *Participation of the Poor*; Peter Marris and Martin Rein, eds., *Dilemma of Social Reform: Poverty and Community Action in the United States* (London: Routledge and Kegan Paul, 1972); Allen J. Matusow, *Unraveling of America: American Liberalism During the 1960s* (New York: Harper and Row, 1984); James A. Morone, *The Democratic Wish: Popular Participation and the Limits of American Government* (New York: Basic Books, 1990); and Frances Fox Piven and Richard Cloward, *Regulating the Poor: The Functions of Public Welfare* (New York: Vintage Books, 1971/1993).
6. Also see Gwendolyn Mink, *Welfare's End* (Ithaca: Cornell University Press, 1998).
7. Wendy Sarvasy and Birte Siim, "Gender, Transitions to Democracy, and Citizenship," *Social Politics* 1, no. 3 (1994): 250.

tion of 'access' requires expansion of formal rights, multiplication of participatory arenas of empowerment, and challenges to the asymmetries of institutional power relations."[8] Revising T. H. Marshall's[9] "evolutionary argument about the development of civil, political, and social citizenship,"[10] feminist welfare state theorists demonstrate the interdependency of all forms of citizenship.[11] The brief expansion of social and political citizenship for low-income residents that resulted from the War on Poverty has been turned back in the contemporary policy arena. In this regard, I use the term "disenfranchisement" to capture the narrowing of citizenship that results from the following: the devolution of the welfare state from the federal to the local level with decreased resources, privatization of welfare services, use of coercive welfare-to-work strategies, curtailment of legal protections for welfare recipients both as workers and as targets of state policies, exclusion of immigrants and those with certain disabilities from public assistance, and the loss of participatory strategies in the design and implementation of contemporary welfare programs. Although the specific mechanisms contributing to the process of disenfranchisement involve complex, often subtle strategies of exclusion that may differ by region and change over time, my discussion is designed to focus attention on aspects of the policy framework that contribute to the narrowing of citizenship more generally. Featured in my discussion are the shifts away from participatory democracy and social citizenship through the depoliticization and class differentiation of community-based service and strategies of decentralization.

8. Ibid.
9. T. H. Marshall, *Citizenship and Social Class and Other Essays* (Cambridge: Cambridge University Press, 1950).
10. Ann Shola Orloff, "Gender and the Social Rights of Citizenship: The Comparative Analysis of Gender Relations and Welfare States," *American Sociological Review* 58, no. 3 (1993): 306.
11. Sarvasy and Siim, "Gender, Transitions to Democracy, and Citizenship," 251; also see Suad Joseph, "Problematizing Gender and Relational Rights: Experiences from Lebanon," *Social Politics* 1, no. 3 (1994): 271–285. Furthermore, analyses of citizenship as limited to the nation-state and individual citizen have been challenged by processes of globalization and international migration. For example, Rina Benmayor and Rosa M. Torruellas, "Education, Cultural Rights, and Citizenship," in *Women Transforming Politics: An Alternative Reader*, eds. Cathy J. Cohen, Kathleen B. Jones, and Joan C. Tronto (New York: New York University Press, 1997) argue that constructions of citizenship need to incorporate a sensitivity to cultural rights, which may be defined as collective and transnational. They explain that "Cultural citizenship implies that citizenship is defined not simply by law but also by culturally specific understandings and practices" (188). Their critique of the notion of "empowerment" reflects my own analysis. Namely, that "Within mainstream discourse empowerment is often used to describe authorization" (189) rather than collective action. This usage contrasts with the more radical understanding of empowerment, which "expresses *collective processes* of resistance to social disenfranchisement and claims to entitlement and rights not acknowledged in preexisting institutions and definitions" (189).

I begin my discussion with a description of the research that forms the basis for my analysis. Next, I summarize the features of contemporary welfare policy that mark an end to the "safety net" for low-income families in this country. Ironically, although the 1996 welfare legislation called for the termination of Aid to Families with Dependent Children, the Community Action Agencies (currently funded through the Community Services Block Grant) were not targeted for extinction.[12] The second half of the chapter explores this apparent contradiction.

LOW-INCOME WOMEN IN THE WAR ON POVERTY

Community action programs (CAPs) funded under the Economic Opportunity Act provided the opportunity for women from low-income communities, particularly women of color, to gain leadership experience and to be paid for much of the work they already were doing for their communities for free.[13] Symbolically, if not also in practice, CAPs merged antipoverty policy with the expansion of citizenship rights.[14] During the War on Poverty, CAPs provided resources to low-income communities and offered sites designed to expand poor residents' political participation. In particular, the CAPs created a context for women with no training in community work to develop their political skills and for those with previous experiences to share their political analyses and develop their political networks. As a consequence of the War on Poverty, many community workers deepened their political perspectives and organized much more broadly than they did when they first began as community workers.

12. The Community Services Block Grant (CSBG) funds the antipoverty programs that were previously administered under the Office of Economic Opportunity. CSBG funds are managed under the Office of Community Affairs at the Department of Health and Human Services. CSBG is authorized through fiscal year 2002, with $500 million appropriated for 1999. The Republican-dominated Congress (over President Bill Clinton's opposition) appropriated $489.6 million for 1997, a 26 percent increase ($100 million) over fiscal year 1996 and $95 million more than the appropriation for 1981, when the CSBG was first established. According to David Bradley, Legislative Director of the National Community Action Foundation, in 1997, almost 99 percent of all U.S. counties were served by community action agencies funded through the CSBG, an increase of almost 9 percent from 1981 (personal interview, October 10, 1997).
13. See Nancy A. Naples, *Grassroots Warriors: Activist Mothering, Community Work, and the War on Poverty* (New York: Routledge, 1998).
14. See also Wendy Sarvasy, "From Man and Philanthropic Service to Feminist Social Citizenship" *Social Politics* 1, no. 3 (1994): 306–325; Birte Siim, "Engendering Democracy: Social Citizenship and Political Participation for Women in Scandinavia" *Social Politics* 1, no. 3 (1994): 286–305.

Analysts disagree over the extent to which designers of the EOA actually intended for the CAPs to organize the poor. In fact, in a 1966 study of how twenty cities implemented community action, Stephen Rose reports that less than three percent of the CAPs "were in any way designed to organize the poor, to transfer power, or to change the institutional structure."[15] Moreover, political pressures from mayors and other public officials and traditional social service organizations circumscribed the federal government's commitment to maximum feasible participation of the poor. The pressure to control the political behaviors of CAPs and their staffs frequently led to a return to the traditional social service approach that community action had been designed to replace.

In an effort to understand the experiences of women from low-income communities who were hired by CAPs during the late 1960s and early 1970s, I gathered focused life histories from women community workers in New York City and Philadelphia during the mid-1980s. Of the sixty-four activists I interviewed, forty-two lived in low-income neighborhoods where they were hired as community workers in community action programs, ten were nonresident community workers, and twelve of the community workers were not employed by the CAPs but worked in other community-based programs. I reinterviewed sixteen of the community workers in 1995.[16] I also interviewed in-depth four city, state, and federal officials who were responsible for designing and overseeing CAPs to gather additional information about the organizational structure and history of the CAPs in New York City and Philadelphia. I draw on this research and on diverse archival and secondary data for the discussion that follows.

Recent federal proposals to prohibit organizations that apply for or receive government funds from engaging in political activities reveal a complete abandonment of the principle of maximum feasible participation provided for in the EOA. In April 1995, Jeff Shear reported in the *National Journal* that conservative House Republicans were "aiming

15. Stephen M. Rose, *The Betrayal of the Poor: The Transformation of Community Action* (Cambridge, Mass.: Scherkman Publishing, 1972).

16. The sampling technique led to a sample that underrepresents those community workers who left for other occupations, who were laid off, or who for any other reason did not continue in community-based employment. The result is that those interviewed most likely held a more positive view of community work and the Community Action Agencies than others who were not interviewed for this study. However, their assessment of the programs offers another vantage point from which to explore the contributions of these programs to certain women's lives. Unfortunately, previous studies of the War on Poverty rarely incorporated the perspectives of low-income women of color hired by the Community Action Agencies. For a more complete discussion of the methodology and analysis of the interview data, see Naples, *Grassroots Warriors*.

to 'Defund the Left' by stopping the flow of federal money to not-for-profit organizations that have been associated with liberal causes."[17] Organizations identified as the target of this campaign included the Association of Head Start Grantees, the Child Welfare League, the Children's Defense Fund, the NAACP Legal Defense and Education Fund Inc., the National Council of La Raza, and the National Council of Senior Citizens.[18]

Set up to respond to local community needs, CAPs and other community-based organizations cannot avoid their role as advocates for residents in poor neighborhoods. All the women I interviewed emphasized that political activism is essential to their community work. Indeed, they believe that advocacy and other forms of political activism should be expanded rather than curtailed. According to Nina Reyes, a Puerto Rican community worker from the Lower East Side of Manhattan, community agencies must take more initiative to help organize residents in poor neighborhoods, to improve housing and other services, and to enhance the political participation of the poor. She complained that most social service agencies have a narrow definition of their role in organizing the local community. However, because agencies situated in low-income neighborhoods are vulnerable to funding cuts, those working in these organizations often find themselves fighting intense political battles to ensure their continued existence. Nina described how she successfully involved residents in her neighborhood in an effort to prevent funding cuts to her program for the elderly in 1995. Recognizing the need for ongoing organizing to prevent further cuts in subsequent years, Nina and her co-organizers established a coalition of different groups who would be affected by funding cuts in the future. As she explained, "People are getting older, people are getting sicker, so we have to keep our faith. We have to because we can't let the government run us."

CONTRACTION OF THE DEMOCRATIC STATE

Ignoring the documented economic need of low-income families and the dearth of above-poverty-level jobs for welfare recipients, Congress passed and President Bill Clinton signed the Personal Responsibility and Work Opportunity Reconciliation Act (henceforth, PRA) in August 1996, thus ending the Aid to Families with Dependent Children

17. Jeff Shear, "The Ax Files," *National Journal* (April 15, 1995): 924.
18. Ibid.

(AFDC) program established by the Social Security Act in 1935.[19] Although the inadequacies of AFDC are widely known, it provided an essential economic "safety net" for low-income families, especially those headed by single mothers. Beyond the withdrawal of the safety net, the PRA includes no federal oversight to protect the poor against arbitrary bureaucratic decisions and other problems with implementation. Other legislation now prohibits legal services attorneys from filing class action suits on behalf of groups such as children with disabilities or welfare recipients, so the ability of poor residents to defend their rights is further constrained.[20]

A 1996 study by Joe Volk, chair of Milwaukee's Task Force on Emergency Shelter and Relocation Services, reported that over three-fourths of the 500 people who attempted to find shelter in the 400 beds located in that city's five family shelters in late December 1996 lost welfare benefits in error.[21] This highlights the significance of the loss of legal services and procedural guarantees. Sanford Schram explains that the process of cutting eligible clients off public assistance, a process known as churning, is justified by the charge of bureaucratic "noncompliance," which includes, for example, failure to respond to letters requesting the client to appear for recertification of his or her eligibility.[22] Clients who may not have received these letters or who do not speak English can appeal their termination, but during the period of appeal they do not receive their benefits. Schram points out that the process of churning is furthered by the managerial decision "to count errors only in granting aid, not in denying it. This built-in bias, in effect, encouraged states to deny aid to many who are eligible."[23]

Challenging abuse of administrative power was in the late 1960s, and continues to be, a major target for welfare rights groups. By 1971, when the National Welfare Rights Organization had linked with 900 locals

19. Aid to Families with Dependent Children was renamed in 1962 from Aid to Dependent Children, which was established through the Social Security Act of 1935.
20. Federal Funding for legal services began in 1965 to provide the poor with access to legal counsel. Legal Services lawyers have filed class action suits to prevent welfare reductions and to protect welfare recipients from lack of due process in terminations from public assistance. Under regulations passed in 1997, legal services lawyers can no longer file class action suits or engage in lobbying on behalf of welfare recipients, prisoners, or migrant laborers, among other vulnerable groups. See Rael Jean Isaac, "Illegal Services," *National Review* 49, no. 5 (1997): 42–45, 60, for a conservative reaction to the restrictions on the Legal Services Corporation, as well as a discussion of the challenges made by legal services advocates to the new regulations.
21. Children's Defense Fund, "High Rates of Termination for Children with Disabilities: Children's Defense Fund Update," August 15, 1997.
22. Sanford F. Schram, *Words of Welfare: The Poverty of Social Science and the Social Science of Poverty* (Minneapolis: University of Minnesota, 1995), 94.
23. Ibid.

across the states, members lobbied local, state, and federal governments against arbitrary bureaucratic practices and mandatory work programs, as well as for increased benefits.[24] In today's policy environment, the state is divesting its administrative role to not-for-profit and for-profit agencies, and this divestiture withdraws important legal safeguards for poor people. Not only has the federal government ceded its role, but state governments have also privatized welfare. One major subcontractor that administers Wisconsin's workfare program, Wisconsin Works (W-2), is Goodwill Industries. It was featured in a story in the *New York Times Magazine* on Sunday, August 24, 1997.[25] As part of a campaign to "Stop the War on the Poor," Welfare Mothers, a Milwaukee-based welfare rights group, awarded Goodwill Industries a "Community Destruction Award" on April 1, 1997, for unfairly reducing or terminating welfare-reliant families.[26]

The PRA dismantles the social safety net by placing a life-long cap of five years on those who are eligible for assistance and by requiring recipients to work outside the home in exchange for the state's financial support. It narrowly defines what counts as "work" and eliminates support for four-year college education, which was included in the workfare provisions of the Family Support Act.[27] As a consequence, Michelle Billies and collaborators report, "over 9,000 students on welfare have been forced to leave the City University of New York to participate in workfare" since New York City began implementation of PRA.[28] The various provisions of the PRA limit who can make claims on the state,

24. See Mimi Abramovitz, *Under Attack, Fighting Back: Women and Welfare in the United States* (New York: Monthly Review Press, 1996).

25. Jason DeParle, "Getting Opal Caples to Work," *New York Times Magazine* (August 24, 1997): 32–37, 47, 54, 59–61.

26. "Stop the War on the Poor," *Welfare Mothers Voice*, Milwaukee, Wisconsin (Spring 1997): 1. The April Fool's award to Goodwill Industries and PIC (Private Industry Council) JOBS Administrators read:

> For their 1. Promotion of a new slave system and violation of the 19th Amendment (which forbids slavery) by using and exploiting "unpaid" labor of mothers in poverty. 2. For cruelty and abuse of their power, by reducing, terminating, and eliminating the meager welfare child support check and even food stamps (which is their unpaid workers entire family income) . . . 3. For scabbing by using unpaid labor to lower the wages of all. 4. For sexism by using the slave labor of mothers and not demanding equal responsibility from fathers. 5. Perpetuating poverty and violating human rights and dignity of workers by forcing mothers to do degrading and/or menial make-work—for no paycheck in the guise of "training." 6. For enlarging the gap between rich and poor by refusing to pay wages, not even minimum [wage].

27. Nancy A. Naples, "Bringing Everyday Life to Policy Analysis: The Case of White Rural Women Negotiating College and Welfare," *Journal of Poverty: Innovations on Social, Political, and Economic Inequalities* 2, no. 1 (1998): 23–53.

28. Michelle Billies, Heather Boushey, Heidi Dorow, Maureen Land, Andy Pollack, and Karen Jau, eds., *Welfare, Workfare, and Jobs: An Educator's Guidebook* (New York: The Urban Justice Center Organizing Project, 1997), 33–34.

impede education and training that would lead to above-poverty employment, and offer little protection for recipients who are denied state support as a result of arbitrary administrative practices. In some states, welfare-reliant residents and their advocates are also denied input in the design of welfare regulations, further limiting participatory democratic practices that have become an expected part of public policy implementation in most policy arenas. For example, Mike Lewis notes that California has gone so far as to exclude "itself from laws requiring public comment and notification when it begins the long and complicated task of writing regulations to decide specifically who will receive benefits and for how long." [29]

Within the contemporary antipoor and antistate policy environment, certain programs established through the War on Poverty nevertheless continue to receive state support. They include Head Start and Legal Aid, although, of course, their staffs' ability to engage in advocacy and other forms of political activism has been curtailed. CAPs continue to serve low-income residents across the country and have not been specifically targeted for extinction. Indeed, they accounted for the largest increase in domestic spending in the 1997 budget allocations. The same Congress that ended "welfare as we know it" in a bipartisan vote increased the allocations for CAPs—some of the most contested state-sponsored programs in recent policy history. What explains this seemingly incongruous legislative outcome?

Over time, certain features of Community Action—community-service employment, decentralization, empowerment, and "tripartite" community collaboration—have gained renewed popularity in legislative discourse. Privatization and depoliticization have displaced calls for community control and community action, but it is possible to trace popular contemporary policy strategies to features embedded in the Community Action title of the Economic Opportunity Act. The next two sections examine how community work, once viewed as a "new career" for low-income residents, has been class-differentiated in contemporary social policies. Welfare recipients are now expected to work in low-paid community service jobs to "earn" their welfare payments. However, these community service jobs do not provide the means to a career or above-poverty wages as they once did for those hired as community workers in Community Action Agencies. Simultaneously, college-bound young people are encouraged to perform community service as a way to finance their college educations at salaries much greater than their wel-

29. Mike Lewis, "New Law Is Freed of Procedure." *San Francisco Daily Journal* (Tuesday, August 12, 1997): 1.

fare-reliant counterparts. In the class-blind context of American policy discourse, the discrimination embedded in these contrasting approaches to community service remains uncontested.

FROM NEW CAREERS TO WORKFARE: CLASS REPRODUCTION THROUGH SOCIAL POLICY

The state depends on women's unpaid work as consumers of social welfare services and as mediators between the state and other targets of social welfare such as children, the elderly, or the disabled.[30] Women in their unpaid caretaking roles find themselves waiting with sick and disabled family members for increasing amounts of time for essential health care and social services. As child care programs and services for the disabled and elderly are eliminated, women must provide the unpaid labor to fill the gaps. With cutbacks in child care, health, and social services and increases in bureaucratic procedures that accompany shifts to managed care and other privatized services, women who work on the front lines of health and welfare bureaucracies also face increased demands with little to no increase in pay. Women in their socially constructed roles are expected to take up the slack left by the withdrawal of state resources from low-income communities. Policy designers, whether consciously or unconsciously, rely on such responses by women, yet rarely provide child care or other supports that would assist women in their triple day as family caretakers, paid workers, and unpaid community workers.

To a certain extent, through their hiring practices CAPs recognized the importance of the work women performed for their low-income communities. One of the most persuasive justifications for the movement to hire residents of low-income communities as community workers for paid employment was put forth by Arthur Pearl and Frank Riessman and termed "New Careers."[31] Pearl and Riessman argued that noncredentialed, resident workers would be able to relate more effectively to their neighbors than would strangers who did not share the same class and race background. Yet it would be inadequate to merely provide dead-end jobs to the poor. The job must give them an entree to an institutionalized career that is also socially useful or at least better than other options available to them. By distinguishing between the contri-

30. See, for example, Anne Showstack Sassoon, "Women's New Social Role: Contradictions of the Welfare State" in *Women and the State*, ed. Anne Showstack Sassoon (London: Hutchinson, 1987), 158–188.
31. Arthur Pearl and Frank Riessman, *New Careers for the Poor: The Nonprofessionals in Human Service* (New York: Free Press, 1965).

butions of resident community workers and outside professional experts, New Careers served to legitimate indigenous experience as a form of knowledge, which, in practice, surfaced women's social position as community caretakers while remunerating women's community caregiving work.

The New Careers concept was initially supported by the federal government through the 1966 Scheuer Amendments to the EOA, which established $3.3 million for New Careers.[32] In 1969, Congress designated the following programs to be included in New Careers:

> [Those] designed to improve the physical, social, economic, or cultural condition of the community or area served in fields of public service, including without limitation health, education, welfare, recreation, day care, neighborhood redevelopment, and public safety, which provide maximum prospects for on-the-job training, promotion, and advancement and continued employment without Federal assistance, which give promise of contributing to the broader adoption of new methods of structuring jobs and new methods of providing job ladder opportunities, and which provide opportunities for further occupational training to facilitate career advancement.[33]

This state-funded form of community work stands out for initially permitting workers the flexibility to respond to community needs as they defined them. However, EOA is not the only antipoverty measure that stressed the development of dignified work for unemployed and underemployed U.S. workers. As Nancy Rose details in her historical analysis of U.S. government-funded work programs, the federal government sponsored other approaches that respected individual dignity and choice; understood, to some extent, the need to provide child care for workers with children; and offered above-poverty wages for some workers.[34] These programs can also serve as models for supporting socially meaningful work and for countering assumptions that government-sponsored work programs create only "make-work" jobs.

Of course, the ongoing concern by labor organizers has been that the creation of such jobs, especially public service employment, is used to re-

32. Robert Cohen, "New Careers" Grows Older: A Perspective on the Paraprofessional Experience, 1965–1975 (Baltimore, Md.: Johns Hopkins University Press, 1976), 8.

33. Congressional Quarterly Service, Congress and the Nation: Volume II, 1965–1968 (Washington, D.C.: Congressional Quarterly Service, 1969), 834.

34. Nancy E. Rose, Workfare or Fair Work: Women. Welfare, and Government Work Programs (New Brunswick, NJ: Rutgers University Press, 1995).

place union-protected labor with low-waged, disenfranchised workers.[35] This process has been most evident in the implementation of the coercive welfare-to-work strategies begun in the 1980s. The dominant contemporary approach to "welfare reform" has assumed that women's poverty is a consequence of their reluctance to train for and accept paid employment and that women on public assistance need sanctions and other coercive behavioral measures to ensure their cooperation in moving from welfare to work. These coercive strategies were implemented through the 1967 Work Incentive Program (WIN), the first federal workfare legislation, and furthered through the WIN Demonstration programs funded under President Ronald Reagan's 1981 budget. Work requirements have never been concerned with the level of welfare mothers' earnings—only with making them work. Hence, union representatives and other advocacy groups have been particularly worried about the way workfare can be used to replace other workers.[36] Following passage of the PRA, labor unions and other antipoverty activists lobbied on behalf of welfare recipients who had been forced to work in state jobs to be paid at least minimum wage for their labor. The Labor Department finally ruled that workfare employees must earn the minimum wage of $5.15 per hour.[37]

Critics of government work programs are not mistaken when they worry about worker displacement through workfare. In his testimony before the Senate welfare reform hearings in 1987, Gerald W. McEntee, international president of the American Federation of State, County, and Municipal Employees, referred to an affidavit offered by Samuel Chini, a maintenance worker from Lackawanna, New York.[38] Chini attests that he lost his job to a person on workfare and after collecting unemployment for a number of months was rehired through workfare for a similar position. McEntee testified that 5,000 to 10,000 people in New York City in 1987 were working off their welfare grants alongside workers with higher pay and benefits.

35. See Nancy A. Naples "The 'New Consensus' on the Gendered Social Contract: The 1987–1988 Congressional Hearings on Welfare Reform," *Signs: Journal of Women in Culture and Society* 22, no. 4 (1997): 907–945.
36. See, for example, U.S. Congress, "Welfare Reform," Hearings Before the Subcommittee on Public Assistance and Unemployment Compensation, House Ways and Means Committee, January 28; February 19; March 4, 6, 10, 11, 13, 1987.
37. Peter T. Kilborn, "In Budget Deal, Clinton Keeps Welfare Pledge," *New York Times* (August 1, 1997): A1, A22.
38. U.S. Congress, "Welfare: Reform or Replacement? (Work and Welfare)," Hearings before the Subcommittee on Social Security and Family Policy, Senate Finance Committee, 100th Congress, First Session, February 23, 1987.

In a recent study of Wisconsin Works (W-2), one of the most aggressive workfare programs in the country, Gray Green and Greg Maney assessed the availability of jobs for welfare recipients in fifteen Wisconsin counties.[39] Their extensive survey of 6,000 households and 800 employer interviews revealed, not surprisingly, a wide variation in job availability across the fifteen counties. In one county, the ratio was "about four welfare recipients for every job opening," an estimate that was determined before one of the largest employers in the county closed its doors and that does not factor in the job needs of other unemployed residents.[40] Rachel Swarns reports that New York City has "sent nearly 8,000 women to pound the pavement with resumes and newly fired dreams, [but] the vast majority of these women fail to find work."[41] The majority of recipients have been in short-term (six-month) workfare placements where they work in exchange for their welfare benefits, most typically in what is termed "community-service jobs." The W-2 program also places a subset of recipients who are not "job ready" into community-service jobs that require thirty hours of work per week in exchange for their $555 monthly grant.[42] This version of community-service work as a marginalized form of employment for workers who are not job ready is a far cry from New Careers' emphasis on the benefits to low-income communities that derive from the commitment and skills possessed by resident community workers. It is also a far cry from New Careers' emphasis on the benefits to residents of poor communities that derive from social and economic recognition for community care giving. Furthermore, as welfare recipients enter the job market through workfare, they lose their autonomy to participate in work-based organizing and to join unions. Therefore, workfare strategies circumscribe the political empowerment of unions as well as of welfare recipients.

FROM NEW CAREERS TO AMERICORPS: CLASS SHIFTS IN COMMUNITY SERVICE

Most of the community workers I interviewed in the mid-1980s and mid-1990s emphasized the need for job training and job creation to counter some of the problems of low-income residents. However, many,

---

39. Gary P. Green and Greg Maney, *What Will It Take to Generate Enough Jobs for the W-2 Program?* (Madison: University of Wisconsin-Madison, 1997).
40. Ibid.
41. Rachel L. Swarns, "Welfare Mothers Prep for Jobs, and Wait," *New York Times* (August 31, 1997), 1.
42. DeParle, "Getting Opal Caples to Work," 35.

like African American community worker Vera Lane of Philadelphia, were critical of the government's efforts to address the employment issue. Vera was also skeptical of the job training programs, "unless there's a job at the end of the training." She believed that job training that offered "no place to go" at the end of the training "was worse than no training at all." Vera was more satisfied with the Comprehensive Employment Training Act (CETA), which created jobs for those trained in the programs. CETA was passed in 1973 to promote the establishment of employment and training programs designed and implemented in local community organizations. CETA merged training funds from the Manpower Development and Training Act of 1962 and the Economic Opportunity Act, thus removing substantial control over the content and direction of employment and training activities from CAPs. By the end of the 1970s, Howard Hallman reports that all but 30 of the 830 community action agencies operated some form of employment and training program funded by CETA.[43] Nancy Rose explains that CETA jobs included "a variety of socially useful jobs."[44] CETA workers found employment in battered women's shelters, neighborhood organizations, and child care programs among other community-based programs.

The AmeriCorps program established by the National and Community Service Trust Act of 1993 also allocates funds for service jobs in community-based programs, but shifts the focus from indigenous community workers of a wide range of ages residing in low-income communities to upwardly mobile youth who can use these job experiences to help cover future college expenses. The class differentiation between single mothers coerced into dead-end community-service jobs by workfare and those who "volunteer" for AmeriCorps as a step toward their bright futures is striking. Since President Bill Clinton's plan targets college-bound youth, community service is viewed both as a temporary service and one provided to others, rather than on behalf of one's own community— an approach that mirrors the Peace Corps rather than the New Careers model.[45] Indeed, the Peace Corps, rather than the War on Poverty, served as the stated model for this new program.

43. Howard W. Hallman, *Community-Based Employment Programs* (Baltimore: Johns Hopkins University Press, 1980), 47–48.
44. Rose, *Workfare or Fair Work: Women, Welfare, and Government Work Programs.*
45. This distinction has been blurred recently by AmeriCorps programs, which encourage welfare recipients who are college-ready to apply for AmeriCorps positions. For example, Delta Service Corps, a program of the Center for Community Development at Delta State University, Cleveland, Mississippi, includes welfare recipients in its AmeriCorps program. Delta Service Corps was established in 1989 before the passage of the AmeriCorps legislation. (Mary Tillis, presentation for session on "Welfare Reform and Rural Poverty: Community Voices," Rural Sociological Society, Portland, Oregon, August, 6, 1998.)

The AmeriCorps program was part of a general shift from state responsibility for maintaining community services to a reliance on volunteerism and private-sector initiatives. When he signed the bill, Clinton stated:

> This morning our Cabinet and the heads of our Federal Agencies were directed to redouble their efforts to use service—community grassroots service—to accomplish their fundamental missions. We want them to help reinvent our Government, to do more and cost less, by creating new ways for citizens to fulfill the mission of the public. We believe we can do that. Already departments have enlisted young people and not so young people to do everything from flood cleanup to housing rehabilitation, from being tour guides in our national parks to being teachers' aides in our schools.[46]

Echoing a major theme of the new welfare bill, Clinton added: "And I hope it [AmeriCorps] will remind every American that there can be no opportunity without responsibility."[47] However, unlike their college-bound counterparts, low-income women forced into community-service employment in exchange for welfare benefits derive no opportunity for social or economic advancement from fulfillment of their "responsibility."

Critics of the national service proposal raise concerns that are similar to those leveled against workfare, namely, that it contributes to worker displacement and union busting. However, since AmeriCorps targets college-bound youth, the carrot of higher education replaces the stick of workfare. Assessing the contradictions embedded in AmeriCorps, Lewis Solmon and Tamara Schiff argue that:

> A national service program can be viewed as an attempt to entice people to supply their labor at below-market rates to make available public services for which taxpayers or those who give private charity are unwilling to pay market prices. One way to achieve this is to convince participants that non-pecuniary benefits from volunteering compensate for these below-market wages. The proposed national service program confounds this goal by tying compensation in part to higher education. This linkage may be justified if college-bound volunteers

---

46. Bill Clinton, "Remarks by the President in Signing Ceremony of the National Service Bill," The South Lawn, September 21, 11:15 A.M. EDT, 1993 (Washington, D.C.: Office of the Press Secretary, The White House), 1824.
47. Ibid.

are preferable to others or if an argument can be made for additional subsidization for higher education. But if national service aims to favor higher education, why not do so explicitly [by locating it on college campuses] and avoid the need for a whole new bureaucracy? As a by-product, the quality of the program probably would be enhanced as well.[48]

From another political perspective, critics such as Republican Representative Todd Tiahrt from Kansas are concerned that the money would be better spent on veterans and other deficit reduction than to pay "people $31,000 to act as volunteers."[49] In fact, in the House debate on the 1997 appropriations bill, Tiahrt successfully sponsored an amendment to shift $40 million of the AmeriCorps allocations to veterans' health care and debt reduction.[50]

As was the case with arguments against the CAPs, critics of AmeriCorps debate from both right and left political positions. For example, Leslie Kaufman fears that the community service funds will be used for political organizing as was apparent during the Summer of Service (SoS) that preceded the passage of the legislation.[51] Kaufman was also concerned that SoS participants could "wander from their assigned tasks and design their own service projects."[52] From the left of the political spectrum, Claudia Horowitz offers a criticism that was also leveled at the War on Poverty, namely, co-optation of progressive leadership.[53]

Left critics of Community Action argued that the War on Poverty was partially motivated by the federal government's interest in diverting the energies of progressive leadership in low-income communities of color from radical political protest.[54] However, as Frances Fox Piven and Richard Cloward point out, "For a time these programs did not so much moderate unrest as provide the vehicles through which the Black ghettos mobilized to demand government services."[55] One major demand that erupted among low-income residents in New York City was the call for

48. Lewis Solmon and Tamara W. Schiff, "National Service: Is It Worth Government Support?" *Change* (September/October 1993): 41.
49. Siobhan Gorman, "House Acts to Strip National-Service Program of All Funds in 1997," *Chronicle of Higher Education* 42, no. 43 (July 5, 1996): A24.
50. Ibid.
51. Leslie Kaufman, "P.C. Corps: Clinton's National Service Prototype Was Largely a Poverty Program Disguised as a Sensitivity Seminar," *Washington Monthly* (October 9–11, 1993): 11.
52. Ibid.
53. Claudia Horowitz, "What Is Wrong with National Service," *Social Policy* 24, no. 1 (1993): 37.
54. Saul Alinsky, "The War on Poverty: Political Pornography" in *Poverty: Power and Politics*, ed. Chaim I. Waxman (New York: Grosset and Dunlap, 1968), 171–179.
55. Frances Fox Piven and Richard Cloward, *Poor People's Movements: Why They Succeed, How They Fail* (New York: Random House, 1977), 271.

community control of these services, especially education. Such challenges to the local state quickly eroded political support for Community Action and other policies of the Great Society and contributed to a narrowing of citizenship that reverberates in today's antipoor policy context. Decentralization, understood in the context of the late 1960s and early 1970s as a way to broaden participation, now forms the basis for shifting the fiscal burden of the welfare state and limiting the role of the poor in the decision-making process.

FROM COMMUNITY CONTROL TO DISINVESTMENT: DECENTRALIZATION AND BLOCK GRANTS

The Economic Opportunity Act incorporated a mechanism for assessing the multiplicity of community needs from the point of view of local residents and consequently led community workers to contest the provision of services in their communities through a variety of political strategies. Community Action Programs attempted to address the full range of needs, including political empowerment, which would help people living in poverty improve their lives. As the community workers labored to implement strategies to rectify the political, social, and economic problems of their neighborhoods, they confronted resistance from public officials as well as the social service establishment. However, they continued to envision new ways of solving the problems faced by their neighbors, friends, and family members, although bureaucratic pressures and funding cuts often interfered with their ability to implement many of their innovative approaches.

The community workers I interviewed frequently recounted their frustration as their concerns for problems in their communities were met by unresponsive public bureaucracies. This in turn led the women to organize protests against these organizations and, in many cases, to argue for community control of the key institutions serving their neighborhoods.[56] For example, New York City community worker Ann Robinson

56. Howard W. Hallman, *Community Control: A Study of Community Corporation and Neighborhood Boards* (Washington, D.C.: Washington Center for Metropolitan Studies, 1969) notes that the call for:

> community control emerged as a demand of black nationalists as a means of achieving "black power," a slogan that gained popularity during the Meredith Mississippi Freedom March of June 1966. As a reaction to the ineffectiveness of programs controlled by stagnant, big-city bureaucracies, neighborhood control became a major interest of Mayor John Lindsay's administration in New York City during the same period. (1).

described her involvement in protests against the city-run hospital in her Manhattan neighborhood and for improved housing, as well as for expanded child care services and community control of the public schools.[57] For a number of years parents were successful in gaining some control of the school system, hiring African American and bilingual teachers, and establishing local school boards that were, at one point, community led and community controlled. However, as with other community-based struggles to gain control of local institutions, changes within the wider political economy and backlash from powerful interest groups quickly compromised these efforts.

One strategy that was most effective in circumscribing the political activism of community workers was the reduction of funds through block grants to local governments, often justified by the appeal to community control of spending decisions. In fact, some federal legislators touted the Community Services Block Grant program through which the CAPs have been funded since 1981 as a model for the current block grant approach to welfare reform. The PRA of 1996 uses a modified block grant system to give states wide latitude in designing the program components of the new policy. Since the PRA drastically reduces the funds available for low-income residents, it will undoubtedly increase the rate of poverty more generally and place further demands on community workers remaining in poor neighborhoods.

Block grant approaches to funding are supported not only for the ways they help federal officials reduce spending while allowing them to avoid making the tough choices between different programmatic constituencies, but also because this approach dovetails with the rhetoric of states' rights and local autonomy. Ironically, as Jane Jenson points out, demands for decentralization in the name of democracy and community control opened spaces for "offloading" the fiscal problems of the other levels of government.[58] This offloading process also entails shifting the provision of services such as child care and health from state-run to private, for-profit institutions.

Other analysts argue that certain strategies of decentralization pit local groups against one another, thus undermining "the global challenge that race presented to the urban system and restor[ing] the territorial bound-

---

57. For further information on the community control of schools movement in New York City, see Mario Fantini and Marilyn Gittell, *Decentralization: Achieving Reform* (New York: Praeger, 1973).

58. Jane Jenson, Presentation for Conference on "Comparative Research on Gender and States," University of Wisconsin, Madison, January 31 to February 2, 1997.

aries of regular urban conflict."[59] Ira Katznelson found evidence for this process in his analysis of the Neighborhood Action Program and the District School Board in northern Manhattan during the 1970s. He explains:

These neighborhood institutions absorbed the energies of insurgents and transformed their protests and rendered them harmless. They did so by reconnecting the disaffected to political life and in this way making them part of the regular, legitimate, and predictable political process. And they did so by fragmenting issues into community-sized components, thus separating community from community, and one set of concerns, such as education, from each of the other policy areas. Once activists joined in this new version of the old game of city trenches, they lost their ability to challenge the urban system and, in time, their capacity to lead popular constituencies.[60]

Furthermore, though calls for decentralization and community control generate popular sentiment, they also channel social protest into less radical challenges to the status quo. Piven and Cloward stress this point in their assessment of the "decentralized apparatus of school administration."[61] They argue that this structure serves "to obscure the centralized and hierarchical imposition of school policy, while lending democratic legitimation to centralized and hierarchical imposition."[62] Decentralized structures, they argue, "generate politics . . . incapable of influencing crucial educational policies, which are decided elsewhere through other processes."[63] Yet, for the community workers I interviewed, decentralized institutional strategies did open up avenues of participation that increased their political efficacy, at least in the short run, as well as their politicization. Concern for their children's education and the activism they undertook on their behalf led them into other avenues of protest and enhanced their understanding of the ways in which relations of domination circumscribed the lives of the poor. In contrast, conceptions of empowerment embedded in 1990s policy approaches emphasize economic development and more limited forms of participation in local decision-making processes.

59. Ira Katznelson, *City Trenches: Urban Politics and the Patterning of Class in the United States* (New York: Pantheon Books, 1981), 179, paraphrasing Alan Altshuler, *Community Control: The Black Demand for Participation in Large American Cities* (New York: Pegasus, 1970), 203.
60. Katznelson, *City Trenches*, 179–180.
61. Frances Fox Piven and Richard Cloward, "Social Policy and the Formation of Political Consciousness," *Political Power and Social Theory* 1 (1980): 140.
62. Ibid.
63. Ibid.

FROM POLITICAL EMPOWERMENT TO EMPOWERMENT ZONES: DISENFRANCHISEMENT OF THE POOR

The history of CAPs under the auspices of OEO spans less then a decade. Over these years the autonomy of the CAPs was progressively curtailed. Before 1970, approximately 80 percent of the CAAs were private, nonprofit community organizations. In 1967, however, Congress passed the Green Amendments, which required that all CAAs be set up as political subdivisions of city governments with one-third of the community action board consisting of public officials.[64] Representative Edith Green (D-Oregon) introduced this "local-control feature" into the 1967 authorization for the antipoverty programs to gain support for these programs from Southern politicians as well as to mollify some representatives from Northern cities "where militant antipoverty groups had come in conflict with the city administration."[65] The "tripartite" approach to program management (one-third of the board representing city government, one-third representing private-sector interests, and one-third representing the local community) is one of the key features of CAP management that has gained renewed saliency in contemporary policy implementation strategies, most notably the Empowerment Zones and Enterprise Communities (EZEC) Program.

Variations in organizational structure and political history of the CAPs in Philadelphia and New York City contributed to differing contexts for the community workers' activism.[66] New York City's decentralized organizational approach to CAPs offered a more conducive environment for the politicization and grassroots mobilization of residents in poor neighborhoods. However, these political spaces were further and further constricted by withdrawal of state support for maximum feasible participation and community action. The community workers included advocacy and other political activities as basic components of their work in low-income neighborhoods. However, many supervisors, politicians, and funders did not share their view, as evidenced by the swiftness with which state officials limited CAP staffs' political activism. Josephine Card of East Harlem described the great limitations placed on the implementation of the maximum feasible participation component of the legislation

64. Dale Rogers Marshall, *The Politics of Participation in Poverty* (Berkeley: University of California Press, 1971), 45.
65. See Congressional Quarterly Service, *Congress and the Nation: Volume II, 1965–1968*, 766. The final version of the authorization bill (S. 2388) included a "bypass" provision that allowed "direct OEO administration of programs if public officials did not develop a satisfactory plan" (ibid).
66. Naples, *Grassroots Warriors*.

and exclaimed: "It all sounded great on paper, but . . . when they said maximum feasible participation and the poor decided that they meant on every level, including the policymaking level, no way!"

Philadelphia's citywide response to the EOA, the Philadelphia Anti-Poverty Action Committee (PAAC), was established as a centralized program with twelve area offices in poor communities around the city. The twenty-two-member central advisory board included a representative from Mayor James Tate's office, representatives from nine established social service agencies, and twelve elected representatives from the poverty communities—an illustration of the tripartite board structure. Matusow reports that despite the mandated involvement of the poor on Philadelphia's policy board, Samuel L. Evans ran the show. Evans was appointed vice chair of PAAC by Mayor Tate and from that position "set out to insulate the program from the influence of the poor and run it in Tate's political interest." [67] He helped diminish the poor's influence on the board by announcing that the elected poor representatives "were not bound in voting by their neighborhood councils and by personally courting them with lunches, dinners, and private caucuses." Evans also worked to isolate the different area offices from each other.

Programs were developed at the central office with input from the twelve local areas. Since the Philadelphia antipoverty agency operated as a quasi-city agency, all employees were prohibited from overt political action as a condition of their employment. The Philadelphia community workers I interviewed understood the administrative practices as efforts to control their activism and undermine collective protests in the low-income communities. Despite the major limitations involved in implementation of the participatory component of the Economic Opportunity Act, PAAC community workers claimed that their participation in the state-funded CAPs increased their sense of personal and political power.

Numerous critics of the War on Poverty from a range of political perspectives emphasized the limits of maximum feasible participation as a strategy to enhance democratic practice. Saul Alinsky, who described the War on Poverty as "political pornography," was especially critical when he attacked the number of consulting firms and high-paid administrators drawing inflated salaries from the antipoverty programs. [68] Senator Daniel Patrick Moynihan used the term "maximum feasible misunder-

---

67. Matusow, *Unraveling of America: American Liberalism During the 1960s,* 256.
68. Alinsky, "The War on Poverty: Political Pornography."

standing" in his assessment of the program.[69] However, from the community workers' vantage point, the War on Poverty, with its emphasis on maximum feasible participation, transformed their previously unpaid community work into paid work and, at the same time, empowered them as residents of low-income communities—resulting in a merging of social and political citizenship.[70]

Legislative efforts to constitute the poor as a political constituency were enacted in the period of the Civil Rights Movement, when African Americans were demanding political and economic justice from the dominant white society. As Jill Quadagno powerfully demonstrates, in some cities, Civil Rights Movement organizations drew on the CAPs to enhance their organizing efforts, which in turn fueled further concerns of the white political establishment that community action posed a basic threat to their power base.[71] However, not all cities provided a context for civil rights organizations to work effectively with CAPs. In some cities, civil rights organizations actively challenged the administration of the antipoverty programs as evidenced by a boycott against the 1966 poverty elections in Philadelphia sponsored by Freedom George of the Young Militants, Bill Mathias of CORE, Fred Mealy of SNCC, and Robert Brazzwell of the NAACP Youth Council.[72]

The centralized approach to CAP administration in Philadelphia laid the organizational framework for the shift away from the comprehensive antipoverty strategies of the Economic Opportunity Act to targeted economic development efforts in the 1990s—a citywide response to President Clinton's Empowerment Zones and Enterprise Communities (EZEC) Program, which was included in the Omnibus Budget Reconciliation Act of 1993. The enterprise zone program targets specific geographic communities with tax reductions and relief from certain government regulations to encourage business and industrial development. City CAP administrators I interviewed in Philadelphia in 1995 enthusiastically discussed the creation of three "Empowerment Zones" designed to feature different approaches to economic development. Former PAAC community workers, however, were less optimistic about the new approach than were their former supervisors. They explained that the management

---

69. Daniel P. Moynihan, *Maximum Feasible Misunderstanding: Community Action in the War on Poverty* (New York: Free Press, 1969).
70. Also see Sarvasy and Siim, "Gender, Transitions to Democracy, and Citizenship."
71. Jill Quadagno, *The Color of Welfare: How Racism Undermined the War on Poverty* (New York: Oxford, 1994).
72. Naples, *Grassroots Warriors*, 209.

structure created for the Empowerment Zones shifted the basis of power from the community residents to developers, city bureaucrats, and leaders of established social services agencies.

The EZEC program draws on themes that were evident in policy approaches that date back to the Model Cities community planning projects of the 1960s.[73] The Model Cities Program, another key component of President Johnson's Great Society, was created by the Demonstration Cities and Metropolitan Act of 1966.[74] Gerry Riposa analyzes the extent to which the Empowerment Zones and Enterprise Communities Program fosters "the community context necessary for greater local participation in economic development."[75] He quotes President Clinton's statement of the program's philosophy: "Our challenge is to provide opportunity to all Americans. We believe the best strategy for community empowerment is a community-driven comprehensive approach which coordinates economic, physical, environmental, community, and human needs."[76] However, with no mechanisms to ensure local community participation, it is unlikely that the EZEC programs will involve local residents to the extent that the CAPs initially did. As Riposa reports:

> Because community involvement is solicited, it does not necessarily follow that national and local governments will divide authority and decision-making powers with those whose input is sought. Community participation in the 1960s' Community Action Programs resulted in vehement mayoral complaints to Washington that neighborhood activists—particularly outspoken minorities—were usurping policy powers from city hall. This conflict contributed to a shift toward the model cities approach, which gave city officials greater policy discre-

73. See Marilyn Marks Rubin, "Can Reorchestration of Historical Themes Reinvent Government? A Case Study of the Empowerment Zones and Enterprise Communities Act of 1993," *Public Administration Review* 54, no. 2 (March-April 1994): 161–169.

74. Model Cities provided resources to encourage urban redevelopment and was funded until 1972 when President Nixon's administration failed to include a budget request for continued Model Cities funding (Rubin, "Can Reorchestration of Historical Themes Reinvent Government?"); see also Sarah F. Liebschutz, "Empowerment Zones and Enterprise Communities: Reinventing Federalism for Distressed Communities," *The Journal of Federalism* 25, no. 3 (1995): 117–32.

75. Gerry Riposa, "From Enterprise Zones to Empowerment Zones: The Community Context of Urban Economic Development," *American Behavioral Scientists* 39, no. 5 (March/April 1996): 536.

76. U.S. Department of Housing and Urban Development, Office of Community Planning; and U.S. Department of Agriculture, Office of Small Community and Rural Development, *Building Communities: Together: The President's Community Enterprise Board* (Washington, D.C.: U.S. Department of Housing and Urban Development and U.S. Department of Agriculture, 1993), 4, quoted in Riposa, "From Enterprise Zones to Empowerment Zones," 545.

tion. Presently, signs are emerging in empowerment zones that mayors are trying to avoid potential challenges to the existing distribution of power.[77]

Although EZEC draws on rhetoric that resonates with the Community Action title of the EOA, it offers little basis for the participation of poor residents. With the displacement of voices providing an alternative to the dominant business, professional, and government interests, it is unlikely that the economic empowerment strategies will benefit the poor in Philadelphia or elsewhere.

CONCLUSION

Certain occupational categories supported by the War on Poverty, such as health and education aide, are now established parts of the state (and private institutions), although they are gender-segregated, low paid, and the first to be eliminated during times of financial crisis. Because women, especially women of color, fill a large percentage of these positions, they were (and continue to be) disproportionately affected by the current downsizing of the welfare state. In the contemporary policy arena, community-based employment is bifurcated into low-waged marginal employment for stigmatized welfare recipients and temporary "volunteer" work at $31,000 per year for college-bound youth. Neither approach to community service retains the respect for indigenous experience as a form of knowledge or acknowledges women's contributions as community caretakers, most notably in low-income communities of color.

Policy designers of the War on Poverty hoped that participation in resident-led community institutions would increase poor residents' sense of connection to the wider social world and improve their access to resources outside their local neighborhoods. By gaining experience in decision making and acquiring leadership skills, these residents would develop the necessary framework for participating more fully as citizens. Norman Fainstein and Susan Fainstein[78] emphasize how "assertive community organizations"[79] "sometimes perform functions of political so-

77. Riposa, "From Enterprise Zones to Empowerment Zones," 549–550.
78. Norman I. Fainstein and Susan Fainstein, *Urban Political Movements: The Search for Power by Minority Groups in American Cities* (Englewood Cliffs, NJ: Prentice-Hall, 1974).
79. Kathleen McCourt, *Working Class Women and Grass Roots Politics* (Bloomington: Indiana University Press, 1977).

cialization and provide a ready-made communications network" in low-income neighborhoods that can be mobilized for urban social movements.[80] However, rather than a source of political empowerment, contemporary decentralization strategies are used to justify cuts in federal spending for the poor and to privatize the delivery of social services. With the shift from federally run to state-run to privately run services, poor residents lose their right to claim protection against misuse of power and mismanagement that was available to them under entitlement-based programs. Now that Legal Services lawyers are prohibited from filing class action suits on behalf of the poor, poor people have even fewer legal protections available to them.

The policy legacy of the War on Poverty includes both the political empowerment of the poor through their maximum feasible participation in defining local needs and designing community-based responses and, in the present context, the political restoration of the power of local officials, businesses, and traditional social services. Each has been justified in the name of decentralization and community control. Given the contradictory legacies of the War on Poverty, Community Action—once viewed as one of the most radical and controversial policy innovations in the fight against poverty—has provided some crucial building blocks for disenfranchising poor mothers and their children. The challenge for antipoverty and labor activists now is to create a coordinated response that harnesses the progressive possibilities of the War on Poverty to contest the disenfranchisement and further impoverishment of poor mothers and their communities.

80. Fainstein and Fainstein, *Urban Political Movements*, 53.

II

CLASS, RACE, AND GENDER IN THE NEW WELFARE REGIME

Welfare and Work

Frances Fox Piven

This chapter is about the bearing of the 1996 Personal Responsibility and Work Opportunity Act (PRA) on labor markets, and especially on the low-wage labor market. The nationwide debate that climaxed with the rollback of federal welfare responsibilities ignored this aspect of welfare policy. Instead, arguments fastened on questions of personal morality. A lax and too-generous welfare system was said to lead women to shun work in favor of habitual idleness and dependency. Welfare was also said to undermine sexual and family morality. Together these charges spurred something like a grand national revival movement to restore moral compulsion to the lives of the poor. Yet, throughout the long history of relief or welfare, charges that relief encouraged immorality always accompanied measures that worsened the terms of work for broad swaths of the population, as I have been at pains to argue elsewhere in work with Richard Cloward.[1] Here I show that this episode of reform is no different.

To make my points about labor markets, I first discuss the grounds for the charge that the availability of welfare distorts the individual's choice to work or not to work. Then I turn to the larger question of the systemic effects of welfare policy on labor markets, particularly in the context of the specific conditions that characterized the American labor market in the 1990s. And finally, albeit necessarily briefly, I try to unravel some of the tangled connections between labor markets and family stability, the other electrified pole in the campaign against welfare. I argue that,

---

1. See Frances Fox Piven and Richard A. Cloward, *Regulating the Poor: The Functions of Public Welfare*, rev. ed. (New York: Pantheon Books, 1993); see also by Piven and Cloward, "The Historical Sources of the Contemporary Relief Debate," and "The Contemporary Relief Debate" in Fred Block, Richard A. Cloward, Barbara Ehrenreich and Frances Fox Piven, *The Mean Season* (New York: Pantheon Books, 1987).

ironically, when labor market effects are taken into account, "welfare reform" is far more likely to weaken families than to restore them.

The public argument about welfare and work focuses on the impact of "the dole" on the choices of poor women and on the debilitating psychological and subcultural consequences of those choices. Welfare use or "dependency" is thus cast as a problem of personal morality. Liberals, for their part, defend a more generous policy by arguing in the same vein, claiming that welfare use is justified because most recipients rely on welfare only for relatively short periods and do not in fact become welfare dependent (a claim that rests, however, on just how the count is made).[2] The defenders also argue that there are not enough jobs for the relatively unskilled women on welfare, especially in the inner cities where these women, many of whom are minorities, are concentrated. And some defenders also point to circumstances beyond the control of poor women that prevent them from working, such as the violence of abusive men who are alarmed at the prospect that their female partners will become independent.[3] This in sum is an an effort to legitimate the decisions of the poor women who turn to welfare.

The arguments made by the defenders have a good deal of truth. Yet they also skirt the central charge, that there is a trade-off between welfare and work, and a more liberal welfare policy tilts individual choices toward welfare, while a restrictive policy tilts the other way. The skittishness is understandable, because acknowledging the trade-off raises the question of whether it is morally right for a mother to choose welfare over work, a question on which the American public seems to have made up its mind by large majorities, at least for the time being.

The underlying idea of the trade-off is clear, and it in fact makes sense. It is the logic of incentives and disincentives. The economic rewards of work have to be greater than the benefits available from unemployment insurance or social assistance or old-age pensions. This is the ancient principle of "less eligibility," a principle that asserts that even the lowest paid worker must fare better than the pauper. It is not the whole story, of course, since surviving on the dole can be demeaning, and people may want to work for reasons other than their wages. Nevertheless, if people

2. If we count as welfare users the total population that moves on and off welfare over a period of years, the argument is correct. Most people who turn to welfare do not remain on the rolls very long. However, some do, and if we use as the base the population on the rolls at any one time, about half are in fact long-term users of welfare.

3. See Jody Raphael, "Domestic Violence as a Barrier to Employment," *Poverty & Race* 6, no. 4, July/August 1997.

can survive without working, and survive in a manner judged reasonable by the standards of their community, a good many will, at least if the work available to them offers only dreary toil, low wages, and little reason for pride. It follows also that if there is no way of surviving except through low-wage drudgery, most people will work. The logic of the new welfare policies from this point of view is simply to eliminate the possibility of a welfare to work trade-off for many women and to worsen the terms of the welfare option for many others.

Thus the new lifetime limit of five years means that many women will have no recourse but to search for whatever work they can get. Moreover, unless a state opts out of this requirement, cash assistance is limited to two months, and in any case to no more than two years. This means that many women will be required to work in exchange for whatever benefits they get. In addition to the time limit on cash assistance, the federal law also establishes "quotas" backed up by fiscal penalties. Twenty-five percent of the recipients in a state must be working at least 20 hours a week by the end of 1997, rising to 50 percent and 30 hours by the year 2002. The states can meet these requirements either by cutting people off or by assigning them to some kind of "workfare" activity for enough hours to equal the amount of their welfare and food stamp benefits, sometimes but not always calculated at the minimum wage.

Finally, federal funding now takes the form of a block grant to the states, leaving them free to set even more restrictive policies. Many states are legislating tighter time limits, along with benefit cuts encouraged by the increasingly hostile climate toward welfare and new sanctions that mean reduced or terminated benefits for one or another kind of presumably undesirable behavior. The states are also freer to use administrative procedures that increase the rate of erroneous bureaucratic denials. A recent study by the Citizens Budget Commission of New York City, for example, found that the city's increasingly vigorous procedures to root out welfare fraud had resulted in the cutoff of aid to thousands of eligible people.[4] Indeed, even before the new legislation had passed, many states had initiated more restrictive policies under "waivers" approved by the Clinton administration. Wisconsin, for example, had embarked on a program to simply eliminate most cash assistance in favor of "the principle of immediate, universal work—no exemptions, exceptions or delays."[5]

---

4. See *New York Times*, August 12, 1997.
5. See Jason DeParle, ""Getting Opal Caples to Work," *New York Times Magazine*, August 24, 1997, 37. DeParle describes Jason Turner, the architect of the program, as someone so jolted at the

I think it obvious that these policies will succeed in pushing or cajoling or humiliating women who are now on welfare to search for work, and a good many of them will find it, especially if unemployment levels remain relatively low. I should note that many current welfare recipients already do work, although most do not report their earnings.[6] They rely on income from part-time or irregular work to supplement low and declining benefits. The new requirements will necessarily disrupt these informal arrangements and lead to lower family incomes.

A recently published study by Katherine Edin and Laura Lein makes clear how necessary these irregular sources of income are for these families.[7] It also illuminates the calculus underlying welfare or work choices among poor women raising children. Edin and Lein conducted a careful study of the household economies of two groups of poor mothers, one on welfare, another in low-wage jobs. Both groups lived precariously, managing to stay afloat only through elaborate stratagems, including some income from work and contributions from family and friends. But the women and their children endured periods of serious hardship nevertheless. For the most part, those on welfare did not match the caricature of people who have become "dependent" on welfare. Most of them had job experience—on average 4.2 years—and they expected to leave welfare for the labor force again. However, they had concluded that they could not afford to quit welfare for a low-wage job, and many were trying to acquire the education or skills that would make work a more practical alternative. As for the working mothers who do not use welfare, the Edin and Lein data show that they actually had a harder time than the women on welfare. Their income was a little higher, but their expenses were also higher, and they worried more about the supervision of their children. These women worked nevertheless because it made them feel better about themselves.

But when welfare is no longer an option, or when the terms worsen because benefits fall or harassment increases, or when the stigma intensifies, more women will inevitably choose work. The press has searched out the stories of such women, and reported delighted accounts of women

---

idea that women existed on government charity that, in junior high, while other students scribbled football plays, he designed plans to put women on welfare to work. DeParle appears to be approving of this odd childhood.

6. See Kathleen Mullan Harris, "Work and Welfare among Single Mothers in Poverty, *American Journal of Sociology*, 99, no. 2 (September 1993). See also Roberta Spalter-Roth, Berverly Burr, Lois Shaw, and Heidi Hartman, "Welfare that Works" (Washington, D.C.: Institute for Women's Policy Research, 1994).

7. See Kathryn Edin and Laura Lein, *Making Ends Meet: How Single Mothers Survive Welfare and Low-Wage Work* (New York: Russell Sage Foundation, 1997).

pushed into the workforce by the new policies or by the threat of the new policies. The stories are told as morality tales that exemplify individual moral rejuvenation through work. We read of an Opal or of a Shari prodded by the new policies to pull herself together and get a job and of how her life and those of her children improve.[8] Of course other stories tell of women who don't manage to find work or hold their families together, and as time goes on, there are likely to be more of these, especially if the economy weakens. Nevertheless, it is important to acknowledge that when the welfare-work trade-off worsens, or is eliminated altogether, more poor women will work. And there will even be a payoff. Edin and Lein show that welfare makes sense for poor women raising children, but it also exacts a toll in stigma and lost pride, and the din of publicity about the presumed moral deficits of recipients along with new sanctions necessarily raises that toll.

This helps explain the sharp decline in caseloads, by 44 percent from January 1993 to 1998, allowing the president and the press to proclaim that the new policies are a success.[9] To be sure, almost all of the drop began well before the implementation of the PRA, and the most important reasons are probably improvements in the job market and demographic shifts.[10] Nevertheless, welfare restrictiveness is a factor as well. Many states have been operating for several years under waiver plans which freed them to employ sanctions that could result in the termination of aid for one or another kind of disapproved behavior. We should not discount the impact of these increasingly restrictive welfare practices or the threat of more restrictions in the future. As the trade-off worsens and the level of insult rises, many poor mothers shrink from applying for welfare and exert themselves to find other ways of making do.

Although the impact of the trade-off on individual decisions has to be confronted, it is not my main point. Political talk notwithstanding, welfare is not mainly an institution to regulate individual morality. It is also, and more important, a labor market institution.[11] The impact of welfare

8. Shari Pharr was featured in John McCormick and Evan Thomas, "One Family's Journey From Welfare," *Newsweek*, May 26, 1997; Opal Caples was featured in the Jason DeParle article cited earlier.

9. See "CLASP Update" (Washington, D.C.: Center for Law and Social Policy, May 21, 1997). See also editorial, *New York Times*, August 20, 1997.

10. This conclusion was reached in a report by the Council of Economic Advisors, "Explaining the Decline in Welfare Receipt, 1993–96." The report is discussed in "CLASP Update" (Washington, D.C.: Center for Law and Social Policy, May 21, 1997).

11. On this point, see Richard Freeman, "How Labor Fares in Advanced Economies," in Richard Freeman, ed., *Working under Different Rules* (New York: Russell Sage Foundation, 1994).

cutbacks should be evaluated not only and maybe not mainly in terms of the morality of the individual choices it encourages poor women to make as they struggle to survive. Rather we have to consider the *systemic* consequences of the new policies. These are new institutional arrangements that will affect large aggregates of people, and these cumulative effects will alter the terms of the labor market, especially the lower tiers of the labor market where poor and unskilled women compete for work. There are moral issues here too, but they are issues that pertain to the social justice of our institutions, to the fairness of the choices that people face, rather than to the morality of the choices they make when confronted with narrowly limited alternatives.

In other words, the welfare-work trade-off needs to be writ large to appreciate its full significance. Public programs that provide people with income, at least if the income is not conditional on participation in the labor market, create a floor under wages; hence the persuasive comparative evidence that shows more generous social programs are correlated with higher wages, especially at the bottom end of the wage scale where social benefit levels can approach wage levels. Haveman points out that in countries with narrow and narrowing income protections (such as unemployment insurance or social assistance for poor families), including the United States, Canada, the United Kingdom, Australia, and Japan, the relative wages of low-skilled workers fell during the 1980s by 10 to 25 percent. But in continental European countries with more generous benefits, the relative wages of the unskilled remained stable, and despite rising unemployment, measures of income inequality remained substantially lower than in the United States.[12] In a word, the higher the benefits, the higher are the wages; and the lower the benefits are, the lower the wages.

More recently, Elaine McCrate has shown the close link between state-to-state variations in welfare benefit levels and variations in the earnings of young women with a high school diploma or less. McCrate combined the benefits available from AFDC, food stamps, and Medicaid and showed that wages fell by 3 percent with each state-to-state drop of one hundred dollars in the benefit package.[13] And Michael Hout develops McCrate's data to show that cuts in the real value of AFDC benefits dur-

12. Robert Haveman, "Equity with Employment," *Boston Review*, Summer 1997. See also *The OECD Jobs Study: Evidence and Explanations* (Paris: OECD, 1994).

13. See Elaine McCrate, "Welfare and Women's Earnings." Paper delivered at the Politics and Society conference "After AFDC: Reshaping the Anti-Poverty Agenda," November 16, 1996, New School of Social Research, New York City.

ing the 1980s combined with the erosion of the minimum wage to drag down the wages of less-educated women by 14 percent.[14]

In a nutshell, the new welfare policies will lower the floor that welfare has constructed under wages. As time limits go into effect, fewer women will be able to choose welfare, and the combination of benefit cuts, administrative obstacles, and rising public stigma will also make welfare a less and less tolerable alternative so that only the most desperate will turn to it. This means that a steady stream of hundreds of thousands of poor women will flow into the low-wage end of the labor market, competing with those who are already there. That segment of the labor market is still glutted, despite a tighter labor market overall. Jared Bernstein of the the Economic Policy Institute reports that the unemployment rate among women with a high school diploma or less is 13.6 percent, and the underemployment rate (which includes people who have given up the search for work) is 24.3 percent.[15] The rates for minorities are substantially higher. In other words, women barred from welfare aid will compete in a segment of the labor market that is already saturated with job seekers, with the result that low wages will be driven lower, particularly in states like California and New York with large welfare populations. Mishel and Schmitt estimate that wages for the bottom 30 percent of workers will fall by 11.9 percent; in California the drop will be 17.8 percent and in New York, 17.1 percent.[16]

Another way in which welfare affects the labor market is through policies that make benefits conditional on mandatory work. There is a long history of such programs, called "relief in aid of wages" in the nineteenth century English Speenhamland plan. Karl Polanyi's seminal work on Speenhamland castigated the plan, and nineteenth century English poor relief generally, for driving agricultural wages down and thus deepening rural poverty and demoralization. Polanyi's analysis confused relief with work relief, however. He looked at the effects of the Speenhamland system of work relief on wages and morale and attributed those effects to relief generally. But relief unconditioned by forced work would almost surely have raised wages, for then local farmers would have had to offer more to attract workers. Speenhamland, by contrast, gave the poor no

14. See Michael Hout, "Inequality at the Margins: The Effects of Welfare, the Minimum Wage, and Tax Credits on Low-Wage Labor Markets." Unpublished paper, University of California, Berkeley, March 1997.

15. Jared Bernstein, "The Challenge of Moving from Welfare to Work," Economic Policy Institute Issue Brief #116, Washington, D.C., 1997.

16. Lawrence Mishel and John Schmitt, "Cutting Wages by Cutting Welfare," Briefing Paper of the Economic Policy Institute, Washington, D.C., October 1995.

choice but to offer themselves to local farmers for whatever they could get, with the parish relief system supplementing that amount according to a formula that presumably guaranteed the "right to live." It was this arrangement that drove wages and morale down more generally for the rural population, for those not on relief had to compete with the minimal earnings of the parish poor.[17]

Consider the parallels. The new mandatory work requirements are leading states and localities to institute "workfare" programs that replicate key features of the Speenhamland plan. Recipients are assigned to some kind of work activity in exchange for their grants. We have had welfare work programs before, but the new requirements affect many more people, and the terms are now harsher. The education and training activities that once often counted for work no longer do; fewer exemptions are allowed; work rules have been stiffened; and recipients are being assigned not only to public and nonprofit agencies, but also to private employers (who receive substantial tax credits and often subsidies paid for by welfare "grant diversions"). Meanwhile, hotly contested disputes are being waged on both the state and federal levels over the question of whether these people are in fact "workers" and therefore entitled to the protections of current labor laws. A lot hinges on how these questions will be resolved, including, for example, whether welfare recipients assigned to work are entitled to the minimum wage,[18] or to unemployment insurance, or to OSHA protections, as well as the applicability of a host of state labor laws.

When the Department of Labor ruled that welfare workers were indeed covered by some federal labor laws, and particularly by the minimum wage provisions of the Fair Labor Standards Act, Republicans in the Congress tried to reverse the ruling during negotiations over the Balanced Budget Act of 1997.[19] They failed, but then-Speaker Newt Gingrich subsequently vowed to make the issue a central legislative effort.[20] Needless to say, in the absence of these protections, workfare means the

---

17. See Karl Polanyi, *The Great Transformation: The Political and Economic Origins of Our Time* (Boston: Beacon Press, 1957). See also the discussion in Piven and Cloward, "Historical Sources of the Contemporary Relief Debate," *op. cit.*

18. Observing the minimum wage typically means that work hours are adjusted so that welfare and food stamp benefits are equivalent to the minimum wage. The fairness of this is disputed, because other of the working poor are often eligible for food stamps. In any case, the principle of making a range of benefits subject to the calculation of a minimum wage cash equivalent could quickly make the minimum wage requirement meaningless.

19. See Mark Greenberg, "A Brief Summary of the Welfare-to-Work and Other Temporary Assistance for Needy Families Related Provisions in the Balanced Budget Act of 1997" (Washington, D.C.: Center for Law and Social Policy, August 1997).

20. See *New York Times*, August 23, 1997.

creation of a virtually indentured labor force of welfare recipients. This is, of course, hard on recipients. More to the point here, welfare recipients assigned to workfare no longer enjoy the privilege of calculating the welfare-work trade-off. If they refuse to work, they will not receive welfare. Thus they constitute a reservoir of exceedingly vulnerable labor for employers. And since the welfare budget pays all or part of such wages as they receive, and tax credits to employers may cancel out the rest, they are also exceedingly cheap. The threat of competition with vulnerable and cheap welfare workers may well have pervasive labor market effects.

The early reports are worrisome. New York City is a workfare pioneer, because it began its program before the federal welfare law was passed, with recipients who were on state- and city-administered general assistance. Only recently have former AFDC recipients also been channeled into workfare. In 1999, some 30 to 40,000 job slots were filled by people who wear the orange vests that are the workfare uniform, and the mayor boasted that all able-bodied recipients, even many of the handicapped, would soon have workfare assignments. Welfare recipients clean the parks, streets, and subways or do routine clerical work in exchange for welfare and food stamp benefits, often without the regulation equipment issued to other workers or the job related protections and sometimes even without elementary decencies like bathrooms and lockers. Some recipients who were in school are being forced to drop out to take workfare assignments. Eight thousand have already been pushed out of the City University where, like the women in the Edin and Lein sample, they were trying to equip themselves to get a step ahead of the dead-end jobs that characterize the low-wage end of the job market.[21] Such evidence as we have suggests that workfare does nothing to help people get ahead. Only minuscule numbers in New York City have moved into regular jobs in the agencies where they were assigned as workfare recipients.[22]

But although workfare doesn't lead to jobs for recipients, it is likely to worsen conditions for people who do have jobs, by depressing wages and displacing workers. Some 20,000 municipal jobs were lost in New York City during the last few years. To do the work that unionized workers once did, 6,300 workfare recipients were assigned to the Parks Department by early 1996, and 4,300 to Sanitation, for example. James Butler,

21. See John Mogulescu, "University Presses Case for Students on Welfare," *CUNY Matters*, Office of University Relations, City University of New York, 1997.
22. The city does not keep records of what happens to the recipients who move through workfare. However, even the claims of city officials amount to an absurdly low placement rate of less than 1 percent. See Liz Krueger, Liz Accles, and Laura Wernick, "Workfare: The Real Deal II" (New York: Community Food Resource Center, July 9, 1997).

President of the Municipal Hospital Workers Union Local 420, tells how workfare recipients were used in one municipal agency:

At the Health and Hospital Corporation, a total of 472 [workfare] workers . . . as of March 4, 1996, filled positions that had previously been occupied by 896 HHC employees who accepted the severance packages offered by the Giuliani Administration. . . . [T]hey were paid much more than the $4.25 per hour that the workfare workers replacing them are receiving. Not only is the city getting the same services for much less money, but because these workers are filling these jobs under the threat of the loss of their welfare benefits, they are, in effect, indentured servants.[23]

Other cities are now following in New York's footsteps, although in cities without New York's large public sector, the emphasis is likely to be on placements in private business. There appear to be two main methods. Sometimes recipients remain on the rolls, but are assigned to businesses as unpaid workers, an arrangement justified as "training." The other method is to divert the welfare grant to employers, who then pay recipients a wage. We so far have only scattered reports, but these suggest that thousands of companies are signing up for tens of thousands of welfare workers. In Salt Lake City, the manager of a temporary agency told the *New York Times* that "Without the welfare people . . . we would have had to raise the wage . . . maybe 5 percent."[24] In Baltimore, nine schools did not renew contracts with firms that supplied janitors at $6.00 an hour and instead brought in workfare workers who cost them $1.50 an hour because the welfare grant is diverted to the employer.[25] No wonder the unions are in a panic over the threat that existing workers will be displaced, especially relatively better-paid union workers.[26]

So far I have fastened on the labor market consequences of welfare considered mainly as a set of material incentives. But material practices are also cultural practices, in the simple sense that they help to shape the way people think about themselves and their world. Conversely, so are cultural or symbolic practices also material, in the sense that by helping to

23. Ibid., 10.
24. See Louis Uchitelle, "Push to Put Welfare Recipients to Work Pushes Others from Jobs," *New York Times*, April 1, 1997, A1.
25. See Mike Hall, "Corporate America's Welfare Windfall," *America@Work*, July 1997.
26. See Frances Fox Piven, "A New Reserve Army of Labor," in Steven Fraser and Joshua B. Freeman, eds., *Audacious Democracy* (New York: Houghton Mifflin, 1997).

shape the way people think about themselves and their world, they help to account for their responses to material conditions.

In key ways, poor relief has not changed very much since it emerged some five centuries ago in Europe during the waning days of feudalism. From the beginning, relief or welfare practices firmly and often brutally singled out and punished those of the poor who were not workers. This was accomplished in part simply by the pitiful sustenance they were allowed, and in that sense, material practices had cultural consequences. It was also accomplished through public rituals of degradation, by the brand and the stocks, by the surveillance to which paupers had to submit, and by the penal regimen of the workhouse. These practices were not intended simply to punish and chasten the pauper. They were also designed to teach a broader lesson to all who observed the rituals, a lesson about the moral imperative of work and the fate that would befall those who shirked.

Family and sexual morality has always figured largely in this process of ritual degradation. The magistrates who supervised the administration of relief in Lyon in the early sixteenth century monitored the intimate behavior of the paupers who turned to them as well as their work behavior. The English social critics who called for the elimination of relief to the poor in their own houses in the nineteenth century named licentious behavior prominently among their complaints. As the Poor Law Commission of 1834 said, outdoor relief had generated a "train of evils" including the loss of responsibility, prudence, and temperance. In a similar vein, the state and county officials of the American South made "unsuitable homes"—meaning those with the presence of a child born out of wedlock—grounds for cutting thousands of black women from the relief rolls.[27]

The contemporary campaign strikes similar notes by reiterating charges that welfare encourages sexual license and family irresponsibility among the poor. These public complaints are part of the larger ritual of degradation. So are the new procedures for monitoring and sanctioning recipient families for one or another kind of disapproved behavior.[28] And

27. See Frances Fox Piven and Richard A. Cloward, "Welfare Doesn't Shore Up Traditional Family Roles: A Reply to Linda Gordon," *Social Research* 85, no. 4 (1988).
28. The much talked about "learnfare" program, which sanctions families by cutting benefits if adolescent children are truant from school, is an example. The program was pioneered by the state of Wisconsin, which expanded the program even after research by the University of Wisconsin at Milwaukee demonstrated that it did not improve school attendance. See John Pawasarat et al., "Evaluation of the Impact of Wisconsin's Learnfare Experiment on the School Attendance of Teenagers Receiving AFDC," University of Wisconsin-Milwaukee Employment and Training Institute, February 5, 1992.

then there are the investigative procedures that are proliferating among the states, presumably to root out fraud, including multiple investigations to certify eligibility, "finger imaging" (or finger printing) applicants, and requiring recipients to submit to drug tests.

Workfare is not the workhouse. People are not incarcerated, family members separated, and then made to break stones on diets so meager that only the strong survive. Still, the New York City women in orange vests, carrying huge trash baskets to which their lunches in plastic bags are tied, are participants in a ritual oriented to a wide public. Mickey Kaus explains it well:

> [W]hat's most important is not whether sweeping streets or cleaning buildings helps Betsy Smith, single teenage parent and high school dropout, learn skills that will help her find a private sector job. It is whether the prospect of sweeping streets and cleaning buildings for a welfare grant will deter Betsy Smith from having the illegitimate child that drops her out of school and onto welfare in the first place—or, failing that, whether the *sight* of Betsy Smith sweeping streets after having her illegitimate child will discourage her younger sisters and neighbors from doing as she did.[29]

In other words, the public display of the humiliated recipient will terrify her sisters and neighbors with the threat of what awaits them and thus drive them to take any job at any wage.

These policies take on added significance when we consider them in relation to broader shifts in the labor market. One of the much-discussed anomalies of this period is that, while official unemployment is at a historic low, wages are not rising. A large part of the reason is the growing insecurity of much work. The key word is *restructuring*, and it means the increasing reliance of employers (or the threatened reliance) on outsourcing or on new forms of less-than-secure employment, such as the temporary or involuntary part-time employment that became the symbolic rallying point of the United Parcel Service strike, or on "independent contractors," who do the work that regular employees once did but without benefits or job security, or the right to unionize.[30]

Pervasive job insecurity has altered the power balance between work-

29. Mickey Kaus, "The Work Ethic State," *New Republic*, July 6, 1986.
30. See *New York Times*, July 20, 1997. And see Barry Bluestone and Stephen Rose, "Overworked and Underemployed," *The American Prospect*, no. 31, March/April 1997.

ers and employers. Workers who are worried about their jobs don't bid for higher wages, and they don't join unions that will fight for higher wages. As a consequence, the business share of the American economic pie is growing, and the worker share is shrinking. Corporate profit shares have risen to a 30-year high, largely as a result of the successful restraint of wages.[31] Meanwhile, executive salaries have spun upward to new heights of excess, while the real earnings of manufacturing workers declined throughout the 1980s, and the lowest-wage workers fell further and further behind.[32]

The striking redistribution of the American economic product from wages to profits argues a broad shift in class power. So does the fact that public policies have played an important role in the process, partly by increasing worker insecurity. Some of those policies, including the lagging level of the legislated minimum wage and eroding federal protections for labor unions, have been much discussed elsewhere. Here I want to make the point that welfare cutbacks are only the most publicized of a range of cutbacks in social policies, the consequence of which will be to systematically increase the insecurity of workers.

Take, for example, the Social Security program. When the program was initiated in the mid-1930s, it was with the goal of *removing* older people from a labor market where they competed with other workers for scarce jobs. Now, however, the direction of policy development has been reversed. The age at which people become eligible for pensions is already being gradually raised, from 65 to 67, with talk of eligibility at age 70 in the future. The rationale is that the old are healthier than they once were. But the consequence will be to ensure that millions of older people continue to work or search for work. Meanwhile, those already receiving social security are encouraged to remain in the workforce by new regulations that reduce the penalties on earnings. So far, these changes have not attracted much attention because they are being implemented gradually. There is the looming prospect, however, as talk of the so-called crisis in social security financing becomes more strident, of additional major rollbacks, including downward revisions in benefit levels and upward revisions in the age of eligibility.[33] Together these changes would result in a

31. See the Week in Review, *New York Times*, August 10, 1997. See also Lawrence Mishel, "Capital's Gain," *American Prospect*, no. 33, July-August 1997; and Paul Krugman, "The Spiral of Inequality," *Mother Jones*, November/December 1996.
32. See Robert Kuttner, "Workers on the Auction Block: Is Labor Just a Market?" *Working USA*, May-June 1997.
33. See for example Peter G. Peterson, *Will America Grow Up Before It Grows Old? How the Coming Social Security Crisis Threatens You, Your Family, and Your Country* (New York: Random House,

flood of many millions of pensioners and erstwhile pensioners bidding for jobs, especially low-wage jobs.

Then there are the new policies toward immigrants, some of which were also incorporated in the Personal Responsibility and Work Opportunity Reconciliation Act of 1996. Many legal immigrants will no longer be entitled to medicaid, food stamps, or cash assistance. Much of the public seems to go along with these exclusions, presumably because they don't think immigrants should enter the country unless they can support themselves. But no informed observer believes that denying these benefits will actually be a significant deterrent to immigration. Indeed, the conservative think tanks and business lobbyists that backed the benefit cutoffs, and the congressional bloc that pushed them through, also opposed new restrictions on immigration. The objective, apparently, is not to keep immigrants out, but to bring them in and keep them vulnerable to low-wage employers. Denying benefits ensures that once here, immigrants will be without any protections to tide them over periods of adversity or to supplement low wages.[34]

Or consider the cutbacks in food stamp benefits, by almost 20 percent, reducing the average benefit per meal from 80 cents to 66 cents.[35] These cuts affect not only welfare recipients and the elderly, but the working poor as well. Indeed, one of the especially harsh provisions limits unemployed adults without children to three months of food stamps during any three-year stint of unemployment. Again, the likely effects seem clear. Public benefits were intended in part to help the unemployed weather joblessness without being forced to accept sharply lower wages and working conditions. The withdrawal of those benefits inevitably will have the reverse effect.

These policy changes all work to squeeze wages, and raise business profits, contributing to the seismic shift of the last decades in the power

---

1996). Since social security recipients are numerous and well organized, benefit cuts run the risk of serious opposition. The stratagem being floated now is a statistical sleight-of-hand through which benefits would be lowered by reducing the official rate of inflation, which is the basis for calculating annual cost-of-living adjustments. One estimate is that, in high-cost areas of the country, a 1 percent reduction in the cost of living formula over 10 years would reduce real benefits by 10 percent. See Lars-Erik Nelson, "Gingrich's Stealth Tax Hike," *New York Newsday*, January 19, 1995.
34. American employers have in fact always lobbied for a policy of open borders for immigrants and closed borders for goods. On business opposition to restrictions on immigration in the current period, see Eric Schmitt, "Milestones and Missteps on Immigration," *New York Times*, October 26, 1996.
35. The estimate is from Douglas Henwood, "Demote the General Welfare," *Left Business Observer*, no. 74 (October 7, 1996).

balance between employers and employees. Not surprisingly, the business community mobilized to promote the policies that weakened workers, first by funding the think tanks and the policy intellectuals who developed the arguments against government social spending, and then orchestrating the media campaigns that made the arguments popular.[36]

This public campaign helps to explain an otherwise inexplicable aspect of the welfare debacle. Despite the effects of the new policies in increasing worker insecurity widely, popular unease has been channeled into an upsurge of indignation at the poor, especially poor women, and most especially minority poor women. The intensification of the rituals of degradation to which women on welfare are exposed also contributes to this indignation. I said these rituals increased the anxiety of insecure low-wage workers. But they also give them a perverse reason for pride, even for a sense of martyrdom, just because they have through their efforts, sometimes extraordinary efforts, managed to keep themselves and their families above the mudslinging of welfare.

Another part of the reason for popular indignation has to do with the intense emotions provoked by the charge that welfare encourages sexual and family immorality, which in fact became the dominant argument for welfare cutbacks as the congressional debate proceeded. Presumably, young women who knew they could turn to welfare engaged in irresponsible sex, and young men turned their backs on the babies they had fathered because they would be supported by welfare. In fact, the sex and family argument had little support in research data, if only because family forms do not change easily, and when they do, large-scale social changes are almost surely the cause, not welfare benefits.[37] Nevertheless,

---

36. Several studies have begun to document the role of business in the campaign against government programs. See for example Sally Covington, "Moving a Public Policy Agenda: The Strategic Philanthropy of Conservative Foundations," A Report from the National Committee for Responsive Philanthropy, Washington, D.C., July 1997. On the role of business in the campaign against welfare specifically, see Charles Post, "The Capitalist Policy Planning Network and the Welfare Reform Act of 1996," unpublished paper presented at the Annual Meeting of the American Sociological Association, New York City, August 1996. See also Lucy A. Williams, "The Right's Attack on Aid to Families with Dependent Children," *The Public Eye* X, nos. 3/4 (Fall / Winter 1996).

37. There is by now a large volume of research on this question. See for example Hilary Williamson Hoynes, "Does Welfare Play Any Role in Female Headship Decisions?" Institute for Research on Poverty Discussion Paper No. 1078–95, 1995; Daniel T. Lichter, Diane K. McLauglin and David C. Ribar, "Welfare and the Rise in Female-Headed Families," *American Journal of Sociology* 103, no. 1 (July 1997); Sarah McLanahan and Lynne Casper, "Growing Diversity and Inequality in the American Family," in R. Farley, ed., *State of the Union: America in the 1990s*, vol. 2 (New York: Russell Sage Foundation, 1995); Robert A. Moffitt, "The Effect of the Welfare System on Nonmarital Fertility," *Report to Congress on Out-of-Wedlock Childbearing* (Washington, D.C.: U.S. Department of Health and Human Services, National Center for Health Statistics, 1995).

repeated invocation of sexual and family transgressions also helps explain why a wider public, including many of the low-wage workers who were likely to be harmed by the effects of the new policies, nevertheless enthusiastically supported the need to "end welfare as we know it."[38]

But if welfare is an unlikely cause of changes in family structure, the labor market developments to which I have pointed, and to which welfare cutbacks are contributing, may indeed affect family forms. To compensate for declining or stagnant incomes, more people are working, and they are also working substantially longer hours.[39] Needing extra money, more workers hold two or more jobs. Indeed, Bluestone and Rose, after carefully reviewing the data, conclude that "in the span of just two decades, working husband-wife couples increased their annual market work input by a cycle-adjusted 684 hours or 4 months of full-time work."[40] And most of the new work time is the result of rising levels of market work by women.

Inevitably, this means time and effort taken away from family work, from caring for children and preparing family meals and keeping track of family members' needs and activities, or what Gwendolyn Mink calls motherwork.[41] Whether this is something to celebrate or not can be debated. Clearly, for some women it means expanded life alternatives, a chance for self-realization, for status, and for a good salary. For others, it means the intensification of work and stress. For many, it probably means some of both. But my point here is a different one. Family stability requires, if not motherwork, then someone to do family work, to track the children, organize the family occasions, maintain the domestic space, and create a sense of nurturing. When no one does that because no one is there, families as we knew them do indeed weaken.

---

38. An Associated Press poll in the summer of 1996 found large majorities favoring time limits, although they also thought government should provide training and jobs. See "CLASP Update" (Washington, D.C.: Center on Law and Social Policy, July 2, 1996).

39. According to the U.S. Bureau of Labor Statistics, between 1976 and 1993 the average employed man added 100 hours per year, while the average employed woman increased her workyear by 233 hours. Reported in the *Left Business Observer* no. 77 (May 14, 1997), 8. Freeman reports that labor force participation in the United States has risen from 65 percent to 71 percent of the population since 1974, while comparable figures for OECD countries show a decline from 65 to 60 percent. See Richard B. Freeman, "Solving the New Inequality," *Boston Review*, December 1996–January 1997. This trend is usually reported as an American success, but its meaning is ambiguous as when women who are already unpaid domestic workers, or students, are forced into the labor market solely by the stagnant or declining earnings of primary earners.

40. Barry Bluestone and Stephen Rose, op. cit., 66.

41. See Gwendolyn Mink, *The Wages of Motherhood: Inequality in the Welfare State, 1917–1942* (Ithaca: Cornell University Press, 1995).

Which brings me to the final irony of the campaign against welfare. Cutbacks that were justified by invoking traditional family norms will almost surely contribute to the continued erosion of family life in the United States, not only among the families headed by poor women, but also among the many Americans already faltering under the burdens of family and work.

CHAPTER FIVE

Asian Immigrant Communities and the Racial Politics of Welfare Reform

Lynn H. Fujiwara

The politics surrounding welfare reform remain inseparably tied to the racial politics in the movement for immigration reform. As we begin the twenty-first century we are reminded of an anti-immigrant movement that 100 years ago was central to the definition of citizenship and the national identity. Coined the "New Nativism," the past decade of anti-immigrant sentiment and discourse resonates racialized hostility and insists on saving America for "Americans." To the proponents of immigration reform, immigration in general is a threat to the "nation" that is conceived of as a singular, predominantly Euro-American, English-speaking culture.[1] New nativist discourse is in response to the fear of an emerging majority of people of color that challenges assumed understandings of American culture and questions assimilationism and asserts racial diversity. Presidential candidate Patrick Buchanan voiced this threat in 1994 by stating "A nonwhite majority is envisioned if today's immigration continues."[2] The Personal Responsibility and Work Opportunity Reconciliation Act signed by President Clinton on August 22, 1996, codified the popular racial politics that scapegoats immigrants and demands their exclusion and disenfranchisement from our increasingly multicultural society.

---

1. Leo R. Chavez, "Immigration Reform and Nativism: The Nationalist Response to the Transnationalist Challenge," in *Immigrants Out: The New Nativism and the Anti-Immigrant Impulse in the United States*, ed. Juan F. Perea (New York: New York University Press, 1997), 63. According to Chavez, new nativism is characterized by the perceived threat brought by contemporary *transnational* migrants (immigrants no longer bound by national borders and who maintain linkages to their home countries), whose presence and communities challenge cultural assumptions of what "American" is and by doing so push multiculturalism and dismiss cultural assimilation.

2. Patrick J. Buchanan, "What Will America Be in 2050?" *Los Angeles Times*, October 28, 1994. Also cited and discussed by Chavez (1997).

The assault on immigrants' rights to public benefits became most striking in 1994, with California's Proposition 187, popularly known as the "Save Our State" initiative.[3] Passed with a strong majority by Californians, Proposition 187 reflected fears that undocumented immigrants were overutilizing public resources, such as health care, education, and economic assistance, at the expense of poor working-class "Americans." Racial-gendered images of migrant women crossing the border to have their children and receive medical care through state-funded health care services played on working- and middle-class voters' resentments against "non-Americans" who allegedly received benefits from their tax dollars. Shortly after the passage of Proposition 187, U.S. Representative Newt Gingrich promised, as Speaker of the House, that he would preside over a freewheeling congressional debate about the "cultural meanings of being American."[4]

Federal programs have never been available to undocumented immigrants, with the exception of emergency health care, immunizations, WIC (nutritional assistance for poor women, infants, and children), and education (in *Plyler v. Doe*, the Supreme Court ruled that the United States Constitution guarantees undocumented children an equal education). Yet, "illegal aliens" have been charged repeatedly with draining the public welfare system. Despite counterevidence that undocumented immigrants contribute more to national, state, and local economies than they take out in assistance (one study concluded that immigrants contribute $90 billion in taxes while taking only $5 billion in social services),[5] a 59 percent majority of California voters believed them to be a drain on the public treasury.

By the mid-1990s the sharp economic downturn seen in the earlier years of the decade had been reversed. However the mood and hostility

3. Proposition 187 consisted of five major sections: (1) illegal aliens are barred from the state's public education system, and educational institutions are required to verify the legal status of students and their parents; (2) providers of publicly paid, nonemergency health services are required to verify the legal status of persons seeking their services; (3) persons seeking cash assistance and other benefits are required to verify their legal status before receiving services; (4) service providers are required to report suspected illegal aliens to the state attorney general and the Immigration and Naturalization Service (INS); and (5) it is a state felony to make, distribute, and use false documents that conceal one's legal status to obtain public benefits or employment. See Adalberto Aguirre Jr., "Nativism, Mexican Immigrant Workers, and Proposition 187 in California," in *California's Social Problems*, ed. Charles F. Hohm (New York: Addison Wesley Longman, 1997).
4. Melissa Healy, "Gingrich Lays out Rigid GOP Agenda," *Los Angeles Times*, November 12, 1994, AI. This statement by Gingrich is also discussed by Leo Chavez (1997) in the context of new nativism and transnational migrants.
5. Berta Esperanza Hernandes-Truyol, "Reconciling Rights in Collision: An International Human Rights Strategy," in *Immigrants Out*, 254.

toward immigrants had escalated to a national "immigration problem." The movement for tougher restrictions on legal immigrants focused on limiting immigration altogether and restricting access to public services to noncitizens. In June 1995 the U.S. Commission on Immigration Reform, headed by Barbara Jordan of Texas, recommended that legal immigration into the United States be sharply reduced.[6] Florida representative E. Clay Shaw Jr. proposed that only citizens be provided benefits such as AFDC, food stamps, and medicaid, arguing that such measures would take away the attraction of people to come to this country.[7] By 1996 Pat Buchanan promised voters that if he were elected, all immigration would be halted for five years. Thus, the perceived "immigration problem" soon encompassed all immigrants entering this country, and the availability of public assistance and social services to noncitizens would be a primary venue for policy reform.

THE RACIAL POLITICS OF ANTI-IMMIGRATION AND WELFARE REFORM

The social and political context in which Proposition 187 ripened included shifting racial demographics and an increasingly depressed California economy. According to the 1995 *California Policy Seminar Brief,* "By 1992, California was experiencing the worst economic downturn since the Great Depression: 4.9 million Californians (15.9 percent) lived in poverty, including one out of every four children."[8] The restructuring of industry, the migration of manufacturing to third world countries, and the military base closures made California one of the few states in which median household incomes fell, by 2.1 percent between 1992 and 1994.[9] Health care, secondary education, and housing became less affordable for a wider segment of the population as poverty in general became more widespread and intense.[10] At the same time, Latino and Asian immi-

---

6. Janet Hook, "Immigration Cutback Urged by U.S. Panel," *Los Angeles Times,* June 8, 1995, A1. Also cited by Chavez (1997).
7. Elizabeth Shogren, "Plans to Cut Safety Net Leave Legal Immigrants Dangling," *Los Angeles Times,* November 21, 1994, A1. Also cited by Chavez (1997).
8. Patricia Zavella, "The Tables Are Turned: Immigration, Poverty, and Social Conflict in California Communities," in *Immigrants Out,* 141. For poverty statistics Zavella cites Linda Neuhauser, Doris Disbrow, and Sheldon Margen, "Hunger and Food Insecurity in California," *California Policy Seminar Brief* 7, no. 4 (April 1995): 3.
9. See Zavella, "The Tables Are Turned."
10. Ibid.

grants became more visible as a proportion of the California population. The coincidence of changing racial demographics and economic anxiety catalyzed the demonology of "illegal aliens."

Although most of the anti-immigrant hysteria has centered around a perceived invasion of foreigners from Mexico, the Asian population actually grew at nearly twice the rate of the Mexican population between 1980 and 1990.[11] According to Immigration and Naturalization Service (INS) statistics for 1990, 38 percent of California immigrants came from Mexico, and 62 percent were listed as arriving from other countries. Moreover, despite that the majority (64 percent) of all Latinos in the United States are born in the United States, Latinos are generally perceived by the public as immigrants.[12] Between 1980 and 1990, the overall Asian Pacific American population increased 95.2 percent. In comparison, the non-Hispanic white population grew 4.2 percent, while the Latino population increased 53 percent from 1980 to 1990. Since 1990, the Asian Pacific American population has grown by an average of 4.5 percent annually. Eighty-six percent of this growth is attributable to immigration and the remainder to natural increase.[13] Furthermore, between 1980 and 1990, 70 percent of those who arrived as refugee/ asylees in the United States came from Asia, and 52 percent settled in California.[14]

The "Save Our State" campaign wrongly assumed that "illegal aliens" come to this county to take advantage of social services rather than to work. First ruled unconstitutional in November 1995, U.S. District Judge Mariana R. Pfaelzer struck down Proposition 187 based on the 1982 Supreme Court decision in *Plyler v. Doe*, which ruled that the equal protection clause of the Fourteenth Amendment prohibits states from denying undocumented children a free public education.[15] In November 1997 Judge Pfaelzer ruled again that Proposition 187 is unconstitutional based on the grounds that the enactment of the Personal Responsibility and Work Opportunity Reconciliation Act of 1996 effectively "ousts state

11. Paul Ong and Suzanne J. Hee, "The Growth of the Asian Pacific American Population: Twenty Million in 2020," in *The State of Asian Pacific America: Policy Issues to the Year 2020* (Los Angeles: LEAP, 1993), 11.

12. Adalberto Aguirre Jr., "Nativism, Mexican Immigrant Workers, and Proposition 187 in California," in *California's Social Problems*, ed. Charles F. Hohm (New York: Longman, 1997).

13. Larry Hajime Shinagawa, "The Impact of Immigration on the Demography of Asian Pacific Americans," in *Reframing the Immigration Debate*, ed. Bill Ong Hing (Los Angeles: LEAP, 1996), 61.

14. Ibid.

15. Lynn Schnailberg. "Judge Rejects Prop 187 Bans on Calif. Services." *Education Week*, November 29, 1995.

power to legislate in the area of public benefits for aliens."[16] Although the Court ruled that California does not have the power to enact its own legislation scheme to regulate immigration, then-Governor Pete Wilson and State Attorney Dan Lundgren intended to appeal Judge Pfaelzer's ruling and take the case to the U.S. Supreme Court.

The stereotype of the welfare-abusing "illegal alien" has assumed saliency at the national level, as well. Peter Brimelow's national bestseller, *Alien Nation: Common Sense about America's Immigration Disaster*, presents immigrants as a drain on society. Articulating what has become common alarmist rhetoric, Brimelow's fear of an alien nation moves far beyond the "invasion" of "illegal aliens" and argues that all immigration, including legal immigration, is the crux of the nation's problems. As a simply written polemic on our nation's immigration/race problem, Brimelow's narrative expresses a popular sentiment that blames immigrants from the "third world" for increased crime, loss of jobs, failing public schools, welfare dependency, and a weak national identity.

Concerned with the complexion of the United States, Brimelow demands a complete overhaul of U.S. immigration laws to restore to 90 percent the white majority population. An immigrant himself from Great Britain, Brimelow argues that white homogeneity be reestablished, as "the American nation has always had a specific ethnic core. And that core has been white."[17] The recommitment to Western European immigration should coincide with the dismantling of all "third world" funding, "all diversion of public funds to promote 'diversity,' 'multiculturalism' and foreign-language retention must be struck down as subversive of this American ideal."[18] Most threatening in his proposals is the abolition of birthright citizenship to children born to undocumented parents, who would then be ineligible for all publicly funded programs.

Unfortunately, Brimelow's sentiments have taken hold in larger political struggles over welfare, education, health care, language, crime, "the border," and citizenship. Hostility toward all immigration established the context for national welfare and immigration reform that attacks poor immigrants legally residing in the United States, particularly those who need social supports. Consequently, although courts refused to implement Proposition 187, Congress resurrected its spirit in the Personal Responsibility and Work Opportunity Reconciliation Act (PRA) of 1996

16. ACLU Press Release. "Federal Judge Says States May Not Set Immigration Policy," November 14, 1997.
17. Peter Brimelow, *Alien Nation: Common Sense About America's Immigration Disaster* (New York: Harper Perennial, 1995).
18. Ibid., 264–265.

(Public Law 104–193) and the Illegal Immigration and Immigrant Responsibility Act of 1996 (Public Law 104–208).

IMMIGRANT RESTRICTIONS THROUGH WELFARE AND IMMIGRATION REFORM

When President Clinton signed the PRA on August 22, 1996, the immigrant provisions (which have undergone considerable reform since the act's initial passage) clearly tied eligibility for basic public benefits to citizenship. The immigrant provisions set forth in the PRA excluded documented noncitizen immigrants, except under certain circumstances. Under the new provisions, noncitizen immigrants are no longer eligible for Supplemental Security Income (SSI) and food stamps unless they meet one of the exemption criteria. The welfare law exempted only noncitizen veterans, military personnel and their dependents, along with those who could show proof of working forty qualifying quarters; it allows refugees and asylees to receive benefits during their first five years here.[19] All legal immigrants who entered the country after the enactment of the PRA on August 22, 1996, were not eligible for any federal means-tested public benefits for a period of five years beginning on the date of the immigrant's entry into the country. All other noncitizens, categorized as "nonqualified" for government benefits, are barred from nearly all federal public benefits except emergency medical assistance.

Under the PRA, the two programs that would have most immediately imposed a heavy cost on immigrant populations were SSI and food stamps. As enacted in 1996, noncitizens (other than refugees and asylees) would no longer be eligible for either program, regardless of the nature of their need. However, following a yearlong grassroots struggle by immigrant communities and advocacy groups, and the stunning visibility of poor elderly immigrants and refugees soon to lose their primary means of subsistence, Congress restored SSI benefits through the Balanced Budget Act of 1997 to immigrants already receiving them as of August 22, 1996, and expanded eligibility to legal immigrants who were in the country on that date and who become disabled in the future. Unlike SSI pro-

19. The term *refugee* is complex when discussing Asian immigrants and refugees. Although those who entered as Asian refugees or asylees at any time are referred to as refugees, they may not still qualify for refugee or asylee status exemptions for public benefits. Under the welfare law, only those refugees who have entered the country within the past five years will qualify for public benefits; this excludes most refugees from Asia who entered the country under refugee status between 1975 and 1990.

visions for citizens, poor noncitizen immigrants over the age of sixty-five are not automatically eligible for SSI based on their age, but must become disabled. Likewise, immigrants arriving after August 22, 1996, remain unqualified for SSI regardless of whether they become disabled. The Balanced Budget Act did not restore food stamps to immigrants, and states still have the option to prohibit immigrants from receiving Temporary Assistance to Needy Families (TANF) and medicaid.

One month after signing the Personal Responsibility Act, on September 30, 1996, President Clinton signed the Illegal Immigration Reform and Immigrant Responsibility Act of 1996 (IIRIRA, Public Law 104–208). Aiming to crack down on illegal immigration, the immigration reform law addressed the popular concerns expressed in the campaign for Proposition 187 and the increased hostility toward third world immigrants expressed by Brimelow as well as Republican politicians such as Patrick Buchanan. The dramatic intensification of patrol and facilities focused on the U.S./Mexico border and stiffer penalties for undocumented immigrants who overstay visas or enter the country without inspection are primary elements of immigration reform. Furthermore, the Immigration Reform Act established broader and more comprehensive restrictions in both immigration and welfare provisions directed at immigrants already residing in the country, as well as those desiring or planning to emigrate to the United States.

Provisions in the Immigration Reform Act limit welfare benefits for immigrants by increasing the earnings requirement for U.S. residents wanting to sponsor immigrant family members from 100 to 125 percent of the poverty level. In addition, legally binding Affidavits of Support are enforceable by the sponsored immigrant, the federal government, and any state or local government that provides any means-tested public benefits. After the immigrant meets his or her five-year bar from any federal means-tested benefits, the public benefits agency must incorporate the income of the sponsor and the sponsor's spouse as part of the immigrant's income in determining whether the immigrant is eligible to receive public benefits. The "public charge" provision also inhibits access to public benefits for immigrants wanting to immigrate, reenter the United States, or become legal permanent residents. Factors such as age, health, income, family size, education, and skills influence the INS evaluation of the possibilities for becoming a "public charge."[20] Thus, immigrants who are here lawfully, yet still need to obtain legal permanent

20. P.L. 104–208, section 531(a)(B).

resident status, are at great risk if they receive any public benefits involv-ing cash assistance, which indicates the inability to support oneself and one's family.

Another policy attack against immigrants was instituted through the Anti-Terrorism and Effective Death Penalty Act, which was signed into law on April 24, 1996, four months before the PRA. The immigrant pro-visions of this law require that any immigrant who has committed a seri-ous crime could face deportation regardless of the age at which he or she entered the country or the duration since the crime was committed and regardless of time served of their sentence. The antiterrorism law elimi-nates an immigrant's right to apply for a waiver of deportation or to ap-peal the case in federal court. Once they come to the attention of immi-gration authorities, immigrants are subject to mandatory detention, no matter how many years have passed since they were convicted or how se-rious their offense.[21]

By the time these bills were signed into law during election year 1996, the anti-immigrant movement had accelerated far beyond California's movement for immigration reform expressed through Proposition 187. Anti-immigrant legislation passed through both the House and Senate under nativist pressures that successfully equated "immigrants" with "crime," "welfare," and "illegality." Anti-immigrant sentiment pivoted on fear of "foreign invasion" by Latinos, given the proximity of the U.S.-Mexico border. The imagery that drove anti-Latino sentiments traded on stereotypes of Latina fertility. These sentiments gained momentum from claims that Latinos overuse public health services and education, and take jobs from "American citizens."

Often lost within debates over immigration and welfare reform is the importance Asian immigration plays in the making of social policy, as well as the devastating impact these provisions have on Asian immigrant communities. Although Asian immigrants comprise the fastest grow-ing immigrant group in the United States, their struggles with language barriers, economic constraints, racism and discrimination, or domestic violence rarely receive public consideration.[22] The pervasiveness of the "model minority" myth conceals the increasing utilization of public as-sistance by Asian immigrants and refugees; thus there remains a dearth of sociological research that comprehensively examines the racial politics

21. Louis Freedberg, "Immigrants' Peril—'One Strike and You're Out.'" *San Francisco Chronicle*, September 3, 1996, 1.
22. *Civil Rights Issues Facing Asian Americans in the 1990s.* A Report of the United States Com-mission on Civil Rights, February 1992, chap. 1.

and economic structures that Asian immigrants and their families must negotiate as they operate in a system that defines them as outsiders and undeserving of public support.

Asian immigrants have been precariously situated within a racial discourse that confuses their role and impact. On the one hand, prevailing cultural narratives of the Asian "model minority" have been politically employed to legitimize existing systems and impose "group" or cultural blame on other people of color to justify dismantling federally mandated social programs. At the same time, contrary to popular narratives of "Asian success" is the reality that between 1990 and 1994, poverty among Asian Pacific American families rose from 11.9 in 1990 to 13.5 percent in 1994.[23] With the resulting increase in their use of public assistance, Asian immigrant and refugee groups have become nativist targets, denounced for their welfare "dependency" and failure to assimilate to the "American" way of life and work.

Academic discussions concerning immigration reform and welfare reform neglect the critical role and traumatic impact both policies have on Asian immigrant communities. A more comprehensive understanding of the patterns, circumstances, and continuing challenges for each group remains a critical and urgent necessity because of the drastic shifts in public support. To fully assess the impact on Asian immigrant communities, analysts need to understand the complex and heterogeneous nature of Asian immigrant experience and different communities' relationships with the public welfare system. Different immigration patterns based on immigrant or refugee/asylee status have significant consequences in how a particular community may experience welfare reform. The historical, social, and economic circumstances within immigrant ethnic groups directly affect age, gender, and education characteristics, which influence the types of public assistance most used and needed by particular Asian immigrant groups. Given the historical trajectory of Asian immigration, the relationship between Asian immigrants and public assistance is a relatively recent phenomenon. To understand the unique circumstances around the utilization of public assistance by Asian immigrants it is important to contextualize Asian immigration patterns within a framework of shifting welfare and immigration politics. Thus, before examining the immediate policy implications on the Asian immigrant community, I

23. Shinagawa, "The Impact of Immigration." Among individuals, the figure rose from 14.1 percent in 1990 to 15.3 percent in 1994. Of the Asian Pacific American population 66.8 percent were foreign born.

first provide a brief schematic examination of the relationship between Asian immigrants and the public welfare system since 1965.

ASIAN IMMIGRANTS AND PUBLIC ASSISTANCE SINCE 1965

Driven by the international political contradictions of the United States' long-standing race-based exclusionary immigration policy, the Immigration Act of 1965 intended to end a long history of discrimination aimed particularly against Asian countries. The elimination of the "national origins quota" was meant to eliminate offensive racial provisions that persisted even after the McCarran-Walter Act of 1952 softened the absolute exclusions of the Asiatic Barred Zone Act of 1917. Under the 1965 law, families could reunify, and persons from Asian countries could emigrate to seek new opportunities as workers in occupations where labor was in short supply in the United States.[24]

Although the 1965 Immigration Act removed all traces of directly discriminatory provisions against Asians in immigration law, policymakers, nativist organizations, and other bill supporters believed that the new law would have little practical effect on immigration flows from Asia.[25] Given that four family reunification preferences added up to 74 percent of the total number of quota immigrants (170,000 visas per year to applicants from all the countries outside the Western Hemisphere), it appeared that the very minuscule Asian population at the time would not be able to make wide use of the "family reunification" provisions of the new law. Because the prior exclusion of Asians kept the number of Asian American citizens and legal resident aliens low, few Asian Americans were available to sponsor relatives compared to citizens and legal residents with European backgrounds.[26]

However, regardless of what proponents of the 1965 act predicted, the

---

24. The Preference System established by the immigration act of 1965, in descending order of preference: (1) unmarried sons and daughters of U.S. citizens, (2) spouse and unmarried sons and daughters of an alien lawfully admitted for permanent residence, (3) members of the professions and scientists and artists of exceptional ability, (4) married sons and daughters of U.S. citizens, (5) brothers and sisters of U.S. citizens, (6) skilled and unskilled workers in occupations for which labor is in short supply in the United States, (7) refugees to whom conditional entry or adjustment of status may be granted, and (8) nonpreference: Any applicant not entitled to one of the above preferences.

25. Charles B. Keely, "The Immigration Act of 1965," in *Asian Americans and Congress: A Documentary History*, ed. Hyung-Chan Kim (Westport Conn: Greenwood, 1995).

26. Ibid., 531. See also Sucheng Chan (1991).

demographic shifts in the Asian Pacific American population were dramatic. Between 1953 and 1965, under the McCarran-Walter Act, about 19,000 Asians became immigrants annually (about 7 percent of immigration flows). In 1966, the number of Asian immigrants increased to about 40,000, or 12.3 percent. In 1967, the total jumped once again to 59,000 immigrants, or 16.4 percent. In the last year of the transition, 1968, the Asian total was 57,000, or 12.6 percent.[27] After the transition period, the flow of Asian immigration continued to increase with the exception of immigrants from Japan. In 1978, modifications to the policy unified Western and non-Western immigrants into a global system of 290,000 preference visas. Parents, spouses, and children of citizens continued to be exempt from the overall preference limit, set at 20,000 preference visas per country.

According to Bill Ong Hing (1993), the reason for the unexpected surge in Asian immigration patterns was that policymakers did not understand how the political, economic, and social dynamics in Asian countries would influence immigration. They knew little about Asian American communities, Asian countries, and their relationship to one another; their analyses by and large were cursory and highly inaccurate.[28] The family reunification provisions would prove to be highly utilized, and as immigrants naturalized, the numbers of sponsored immigrants rose. Thus, from 1961 to 1970, 12.88 percent of immigrants came from Asia, while from 1971 to 1980 immigrants from Asia increased to 35.35 percent of all immigrants. From 1981 to 1990 Asian immigration hovered at 38.39 percent, and from 1991 to 1994, 30.50 percent of all immigrants to the United States came from Asia.[29]

Simultaneous with the "opening" of immigration policy was passage of the 1964 Civil Rights Act, the 1965 Voting Rights Act, the 1968 Fair Housing Act, and the implementation of the Great Society and War on Poverty programs. Provisions established in the 1972 reform of the Social Security Act would have a lasting impact on Asian immigrant communities, especially on the elderly. Public assistance programs most closely associated with the Asian immigrant population have been Supplemental Security Income (SSI), along with medical coverage for the poor (medicaid), food stamps, AFDC, and job training programs.

Initially, Asian immigrants were known for underutilizing publicly

27. Ibid., 538.
28. Hing, *Reframing the Immigration Debate*, 79.
29. Shinagawa, "The Impact of Immigration." Data source for figures is the U.S. Immigration and Naturalization Service.

funded programs due to feelings of mistrust and fear of government agencies. However, with the Civil Rights Movement, community mobilization, grassroots organizing, and an increased political consciousness for equal rights within the APA community, by the mid-1970s Asian immigrants increased their use of public benefits. Community-based services more sensitive to language and cultural needs also helped make programs more accessible.

However, more recent immigrants had to be sponsored by an employer or by a financially solvent relative willing to guarantee that the new immigrant would not become a "public charge."[30] The immigrant's "sponsor" was (and still is) required to complete an *affidavit of support* in order for their immigrating relative to obtain lawful permanent resident status. The process of "deeming" requires that "for a period of time, the income and resources of an alien's 'sponsor' (and usually also the sponsor's spouse) will be considered, or 'deemed,' to be available to the sponsored alien when he or she applies for certain public benefits."[31] Deeming did not automatically mean that a permanent resident was ineligible for public benefits: if the sponsor's current income was very low, the immigrant might still qualify for a particular program. However, if the sponsor's income proved to be relatively high, the income was applied toward the immigrant's available income, even if the sponsor failed to actually provide financial support.[32] The deeming period for food stamps and AFDC was established as three years from the date the immigrant became a lawful permanent resident and five years (unless the permanent resident became blind or disabled after entry) for SSI.

Although the Asian immigrant population increased dramatically under the 1965 Immigration Act, public attention toward the increasing utilization of public assistance programs by Asian Pacific Americans did not win serious notice until the 1980s. Public concern over elevated levels of welfare use by Asian immigrant communities tracked the impact of refugee/asylee policies following the war in Vietnam. Because of the unique influence of the Vietnam War on refugee policies since 1975, a separate examination of the social and historical events surrounding policy implementation and Southeast Asian refugees is in order.

In the immediate aftermath of the Vietnam War, policymakers stressed

30. Mary Elizabeth Kelsey, "Negotiating Poverty: Welfare Regimes and Economic Mobility." Ph.D Dissertation, University of California at Berkeley, 1994.
31. See *Guide to Alien Eligibility for Federal Programs*, 3d ed. (Los Angeles: National Immigration Law Center).
32. Hing, *Reframing the Immigration Debate*, 88.

that public assistance was a necessary entitlement in the resettlement process. With the enactment of the Refugee Act of 1980 the seventh preference for refugees was removed from the Immigration Act of 1965, and the 1980 law mandated that refugee admissions be handled separately from immigration.[33] Congress enacted sweeping changes in domestic policies aiding refugees once they had been admitted to the United States.[34] To coordinate the federal resettlement programs, Congress established the Office of Refugee Resettlement (ORR) within the Department of Health and Human Services. The ORR has its own budget to "administer assistance programs designed to help refugees achieve economic self-sufficiency as quickly as possible."[35] Under the 1980 act, refugees were given thirty-six months of stipends including special refugee cash assistance, medical assistance, and other support services.[36] However, with the entry of the poorer, less-educated, and more devastated second wave of refugees (popularly referred to as the "boat people") in 1982, the 1980 Refugee Act was amended to reduce refugee cash assistance to eighteen months to pressure refugees to become economically independent more quickly.[37]

According to the 1980 Census the percentage of Laotian and Hmong families with incomes below the poverty level was over 65 percent, over 46 percent for Cambodian families, and over 33 percent for Vietnamese families.[38] Bill Ong Hing provides a general assessment of the economic patterns of Southeast Asians in his examination of Asian Americans and immigration policy. According to Hing, "Nationwide, 64 percent of all Southeast Asian households headed by refugees arriving after 1980 are on public assistance, three times the rate of African Americans and four times that of Latinos."[39] Data as recent as 1991 reveal that the proportion of Southeast Asians using public assistance has remained significantly high. Of those whose first year in the United States was fiscal year 1991, about 45 percent of Vietnamese, 44 percent of Laotians, and almost 100 percent of Cambodians depended on welfare.[40] Economic differences between the first wave and second wave of refugees lay behind mounting

33. Keely, "The Immigration Act of 1965," 537.
34. Kelsey, "Negotiating Poverty," 84.
35. Ibid., 84–85.
36. Hing, *Reframing the Immigration Debate*, 137.
37. Ibid.
38. *Civil Rights Issues Facing Asian Americans in the 1990s.* A Report of the United States Commission on Civil Rights, February 1992, 17.
39. Hing, *Reframing the Immigration Debate*, 137.
40. Ngoan Le, "The Case of the Southeast Asian Refugees: Policy for a Community 'At-Risk.'" in *The State of Asian Pacific America: Policy Issues to the Year 2020* (Los Angeles: LEAP Asian Pacific American Public Policy Institute and UCLA Asian American Studies Center, 1993), 171.

pressures for reducing public assistance and eliminating some support services altogether.

The first wave of refugees consisted of the more educated and professional upper classes and was predominantly Vietnamese. They resettled under the Refugee Assistance Act of 1975, which provided reimbursements to state governments for the cash assistance and medical and social services that the refugees received.[41] The Department of Health, Education, and Welfare (now the Department of Health and Human Services) also gave grants to public or nonprofit private agencies to provide the refugees with English instruction, employment counseling, and mental health services.[42] However, as the more war-traumatized second exodus, a much more ethnically heterogeneous people consisting of ethnic Chinese from Vietnam, Kampucheans (usually still referred to as Cambodians), lowland Lao, and highland Hmong, began settling in the United States, their presence and visibility stirred public concerns of "cultural conflict" and resentment against public assistance to outsiders.

The view that refugees were "victims of war" for whom the United States bore responsibility was short-lived among policymakers and never quite gained currency among the "American" public. Instead, as Hing argues, Southeast Asians have been accused of having developed a welfare mentality, as their relatively low rate of labor force participation (primarily due to language, skills, education, racism, and discrimination) has in fact led many refugees to depend on government assistance. According to Hing, "Many attribute this dependency to a welfare system that purportedly creates disincentives to work."[43] Thus after the 1982 amendments, when refugee aid was reduced to eighteen months,

> most programs stressed employment-enhancing services such as vocational, English-language, and job-development training. Most refugees are unable to acquire the skills that would qualify them for anything other than minimum wage jobs in eighteen months. They were nonetheless constrained to take these positions in the absence of continued public assistance.[44]

Hing concludes that as a result of these more stringent and inefficient assistance programs, many refugees have been relegated to entry-level

41. Sucheng Chan, *Asian Americans: An Interpretive History* (Boston: Twayne Publishers, 1991), 156–157.
42. Ibid., 156.
43. Hing, *Reframing the Immigration Debate*, 137.
44. Ibid.

jobs with minimal earnings (even more so for refugee women), thus explaining the over 50 percent poverty rate of all Southeast Asian refugees by 1985. Consequently, many refugees have had to turn to AFDC, SSI, and other income programs that were not subject to the same eighteen-month limit for refugee aid.

Although resettlement aims were to disperse refugees widely across the nation to minimize the financial burden to any single locality, California, with its sizable Asian American population and possibilities for greater community support systems, became the state with the largest population (45 percent, or 453,363) of Southeast Asian refugees (based on 1990 census data).[45] In California, the Department of Social Services (DSS) serves as the state's refugee services coordinator. Sucheng Chan describes the role of DSS in terms of the services and programs the government agency has been established to provide:

> DSS administers the Food Stamp and Aid to Families with Dependent Children programs, monitors the federal Supplementary Security Income/State Supplementary program, and oversees the provisions of Title 20 social services—all of which eligible refugees may partake of. The Office of Refugee Services within DSS coordinates the various programs. Title 20 services available to refugees include instruction in English as a second language, vocational training, employment services, services to facilitate social adjustment, mental health services, and health assessment.[46]

Given the gravity of the situation faced by poor Southeast Asians, relatively few studies have been conducted that comprehensively examine the overall implementation and impact DSS services and programs have had and how well the programs work today given the state's fiscal crises, budget cuts, and political attacks on these very programs. In a 1987 survey of 2,773 Southeast Asians between 18 and 64 years of age in California, Gong-Guy found that the economic problems and need for public assistance remained severely high. Examining family income and employment, Gong-Guy found that the percentage of families completely dependent on public assistance was 79.3 percent for Cambodians, 76.3 percent for Chinese-Vietnamese, 81.1 percent for Hmong, 81.1 percent for Lao, and 49.7 percent for Vietnamese.[47] Clearly, such high rates of

45. Le, "The Case of the Southeast Asian Refugees," 171.
46. Chan, Asian Americans: An Interpretive History, 161.
47. Elizabeth Gong-Guy, California Southeast Asian Mental Health Needs Assessment (Oakland, Calif.: Asian Community Mental Health Services, 1991).

public assistance remain interconnected with high levels of unemployment among these refugees. According to Laura Uba's examination of
refugees and stress from a mental health perspective, "Unemployment
among Southeast Asians for the first few months after settling in the
United States has been almost 90 percent, and after more than three
years in the United States, about one-third are still unemployed."[48] Research by Anson Moon and Nathaniel Tashima found unemployment to
be a problem for 68 percent of the Cambodians and 85 percent of the
Chinese-Vietnamese in their 1982 study.[49] In a similar study by Woodrow Jones Jr. and Paul Strand in 1986, Hmong and Laotians discussed
their greatest difficulties: language barriers, insufficient funds, and lack of
job skills that are of use in the American economy.[50]

The interconnections between immigration policy and public assistance have greatly influenced the demographic configuration of the Asian
Pacific American (APA) community. As of 1990, the total APA population was 7,273,662, and 2.9 percent of the total U.S. population. In California, the total APA population was 2,845,659, or 9.6 percent of the
total state population, and 39.1 percent of the total APA population. Co-
inciding with a devastating domestic economic recession, increasing
deindustrialization in the United States, and more than ten years of harsh
social and economic policies under Reagan and Bush, poor and low-
skilled Asian immigrants have faced a difficult challenge to find above
minimum wage employment in our postindustrial economy. Overall,
poverty levels among Asian Pacific American families rose from 11.9 percent in 1990 to 13.5 percent in 1994. Among individuals, poverty increased from 14.1 percent in 1990 to 15.3 percent in 1994. The utilization
rate of public benefits by Asian immigrants has increased with their poverty, underemployment, and unskilled labor pools.

Backlash against Asian refugees' use of public assistance escalated during the 1980s as many "Americans" felt that public assistance should not
be spent on "foreigners." Despite mass trauma and dislocation caused
by the U.S. involvement in the Vietnam War and the participation of
Hmong men and boys on the U.S. side of that war, Asian refugees and
immigrants were demonized as culturally unassimilable and overdepen-
dent on welfare. Jeremy Hein's (1995) analysis of racial conflict and resentment expressed through anti-Indochinese incidents reveals hostility

48. Laura Uba, *Asian Americans: Personality Patterns, Identity, and Mental Health* (New York: Guil-
ford Press, 1994), 146.
49. Anson Moon and Nathaniel Tashima, *Help Seeking Behavior and Attitudes of Southeast Asian
Refugees* (San Francisco: Pacific Asian Mental Research Project, 1982).
50. Woodrow Jones and Paul Strand, "Adaptation and Adjustment Problems Among Indochinese
Refugees," *Sociology and Social Research* 71: 42–46.

toward the increased presence of Asian immigrants and refugees, not to mention toward their enrollment in public benefits. The fall of the pro-American governments in Vietnam, Laos, and Cambodia led to the arrival of 147,000 refugees between 1975 and 1978. Then political turmoil and persecution resulted in 453,000 refugee arrivals between 1979 and 1982. Finally, migration primarily based on family reunification brought another 350,000 refugees between 1983 and 1990. According to Hein,

> Each wave is associated with a different pattern of aggression toward the refugees. The earliest period was marked by protest over the refugees' arrival. The next period produced conflict over jobs and social services—as large numbers of refugees arrived during a severe recession—and a rise in violence. The final period, when Vietnamese, Laotian, and Cambodian communities took root in the United States, is characterized by destruction of property, harassment, assaults, and murders.[51]

Between 1981 and 1990, 38.39 percent percent of immigrants to the United States came from Asia, and 37.20 percent came from countries of "Hispanic" origin.[52] The demographics of immigration spurred broad mobilization of an anti-immigrant movement by the early 1990s. The short-lived "open" period of immigration and welfare assistance soon succumbed to nativist resentments and pressures against immigrants' access to public services, as well as against immigration itself. Passage of the Personal Responsibility and Work Opportunity Act and the Illegal Immigration Reform and Immigrant Responsibility Act codified this nativism.

IMMEDIATE IMPACT ON ASIAN IMMIGRANT COMMUNITIES

Immediately following the enactment of the welfare and immigration reform laws, Asian immigrant communities were faced with the fear, panic, and despair of poor immigrants who were confused and fearful of losing their primary means of support. Immigrant rights coalitions and community-based organizations worked quickly to assess the impending impact of the new laws on poor immigrants and directly galvanized a

---

51. See Jeremy Hein, *From Vietnam, Laos, and Cambodia: A Refugee Experience in the United States* (New York: Twayne Publishers, 1995, 72–73.
52. See Shinagawa, "The Impact of Immigration," 86.

broad base of community and political support by making visible the level of hardship and tragedy that would unfold if all enacted provisions were to be implemented. The most immediate effects would follow from the new prohibitions on Supplemental Security Income and food stamps for immigrants. Title IX of Public Law 104–193 (Personal Responsibility Act) defines the provisions for "Restricting Welfare and Public Benefits for Aliens." The act grants limited eligibility to qualified aliens for certain federal programs, but states that a person who is a qualified alien[53] is not eligible for other specified federal programs (SSI and food stamps).[54]

Although refugees and asylees remain eligible for designated federal programs such as Temporary Assistance to Needy Families during their first five years here, Asian refugees who have been in the United States for five years and have since adjusted their status to legal permanent residents do not. Certain lawfully admitted permanent residents also are eligible for certain federal benefits if they can show proof of having worked forty qualifying quarters (approximately ten years); are veterans with an honorable discharge; are on active duty in the Armed Forces of the United States; or are the spouse or unmarried dependent child of a veteran or person on active duty.

Even with the exceptions, the majority of permanent residents would no longer be eligible for SSI and food stamp benefits. Immediate estimates predicted that under the new provisions of the Personal Responsibility Act, 500,000 elderly and disabled immigrants would lose their Supplemental Security Income and almost one million immigrants would lose their food stamps.[55] While the rhetorical purpose of welfare reform was to encourage people to enter the workforce, the SSI population is, by definition, unable to work. For the Asian immigrant community the loss of SSI benefits and food stamps would have been devastating, especially given the utilization rates of public assistance among persons over the age of 65.

According to the 1990 Census, 29.9 percent of Asian immigrants over 65 use public assistance. Among the different Asian immigrant groups, public assistance rates for persons over the age of 65 were: Hmong Americans, 66.6 percent; Laotian Americans, 57.8 percent; Cambodian Americans, 53.2 percent; Vietnamese Americans, 51.1 percent; Korean Ameri-

53. According to the Immigration and Nationality Act: e.g., lawfully admitted permanent resident; alien granted asylum; a refugee.
54. See Public Law 104–193, Title IV, Section 402(b)(1).
55. See "Immigrants and Public Benefits, Facts and Figures," The Northern California Coalition for Immigrant and Refugee Rights.

cans, 42.1 percent; and Thai Americans, 37.5 percent.[56] Other Asian immigrant ethnic groups maintain fairly high utilization rates, although proportionately less than most Southeast Asian groups: Filipino Americans, 29.3 percent; Asian Indian Americans, 28.4 percent; and Chinese Americans, 25.9 percent.[57] These figures predict an urgent crisis if SSI were cut off from all legal permanent residents who did not qualify for an exemption. In 1995, in California, of the 309,383 noncitizen SSI/SSP (SSP are state supplementary payments) recipients, 58.1 percent were aged, 40.6 percent were disabled, and 1.3 percent were blind. Fifty-six percent of these SSI immigrants came from Asia.[58]

The exceptions for continued eligibility must be critically examined in terms of their gendered impact. There are more foreign-born Asian Pacific American women than men (71.8 percent of women compared to 69.7 percent of men are over 65), and among the foreign born, 26 percent of the women rely on public assistance, while 18.5 percent of the male Asian immigrants do. Approximately 72 percent of the immigrants scheduled to lose their SSI benefits were women. Hence women would be disproportionately harmed. Moreover, the eligibility requirement of forty qualifying quarters of "work" is biased against women immigrants, who are systematically relegated to domestic forms of labor in an "invisible sector" where work typically is not documented by payment of withholding taxes into the social security system. Further, the exemption based on military service and veteran status is biased against women immigrants who are very unlikely to have served in the U.S. armed forces. With the exception of wives and children of U.S. veterans, the majority of Asian immigrant and refugee women do not meet eligibility exemptions for public benefits.

As the Social Security Administration began the first wave of sending notices informing elderly, disabled, blind, and all other immigrants on SSI that they must show proof of citizenship to keep their monthly public aid, the reaction was frantic and fearful. Immigrant advocacy groups, community-based organizations, and immigrant legal services were overwhelmed with the surge of confused, frightened, and desperate immigrants and their families who saw their primary source of income being taken away. Receiving from $640 to $695 per month, they used this amount to support a large extended family or to provide con-

56. See Shinagawa, "The Impact of Immigration," 121.
57. Ibid.
58. See the *San Francisco Profile of Immigrants and Refugees: A Research Tool for Welfare Reform, Job Readiness and Self-Sufficiency*. International Institute of the East Bay, March 1997.

valescent or skilled nursing care for disabled or elderly parents needing institutional care. The only real recourse for immigrant SSI recipients was to naturalize.

Until August 22, 1996, elderly immigrants had no pressing need to learn English. When they came to the United States, legal immigrants were not required to become citizens within a set number of years. Federal laws made no mention of denying government aid to the disabled or elderly who had not been naturalized. The cover story in the *SF Weekly* exposed the difficulty for many of these elderly and disabled immigrants to successfully achieve naturalization.

At 9:30 on this gray Thursday morning in January, Tuan Van Dang is setting out to accomplish what some have called an impossible task. He is trying to teach women old enough to be his grandmothers — women who can't read, write, or speak English — the civics fundamentals the INS requires for citizenship. Van Dang's deadline is tight — and, like the law that spawned it, unforgiving.[59]

Suicides by elderly immigrants who had just received "cut-off" letters were reported to have occurred in Fresno and Sacramento, California; New York; and Dane County, Wisconsin. The suicide of Chia Yang, a Hmong refugee, mother of seven children, whose husband and two brothers were enlisted by the CIA from 1961 to 1974, gained particular public attention with in-depth cover stories and interviews with family and friends printed in the *Sacramento Bee* and the nationally distributed *Asian Week*. At 54, and illiterate, Mrs. Yang received her notice stating that her SSI of $640 that she received because of her disability status would be discontinued because she was not a U.S. citizen. The loss of her SSI benefits would leave only her husband's $400 welfare check and $180 in food stamps for the couple and their two youngest children to live on each month.

According to an interview with the family in *Asian Week*, Mrs. Yang panicked, then slid into depression.[60] She already suffered from major health ailments, but fell deeper into despair as she tried twice to become a U.S. citizen, but failed because of her poor English. She suffered a stroke in April, around the time she received a letter stating that her SSI

59. *San Francisco Weekly*, February 12–18, 1997.
60. For a more extensive discussion concerning Mrs. Chia Yang's situation and suicide see Deborah Hastings, "Reform Hits Hard Among Refugees," *Asian Week*, 19, no. 26 (February 19–25, 1998).

would not be cut off after all. But four months later, when her family received another letter stating that their food stamps were to be cut in half because noncitizens between 18 and 64 were no longer eligible for food stamp benefits, Mrs. Yang was "inconsolable." After waiting for her family to fall asleep, she changed her clothes, looped a cord around her throat, tied it to an overhead beam of the garage, and jumped off the back of her husband's truck. She left behind audio cassettes blaming the government.

Coalitions for immigrant rights, Catholic Charities, immigrant legal centers, and other nonprofit organizations came together in large-scale "naturalization" drives. Naturalization assistance involves helping fill out the necessary and daunting N-400 form to begin the naturalization process, checking for "red flag issues" that may require an immigration lawyer, conducting the required fingerprinting, providing two photographs, and photocopying the front and back of the INS card. Thousands of immigrants sought help during the first quarter of 1997. With the SSI cutoff scheduled for August 22, 1997, and with a naturalization interview taking 6–8 months to obtain, the panic for many immigrants was unmeasurable. County citizenship programs were established, and advocacy groups continued to pressure congressmen, legislators, and President Clinton to revise the welfare law. The impending SSI cutoff would disqualify severely disabled immigrants for nursing home care, and many disabled and elderly immigrants did not have sponsors or family able to pay for their care. The end of SSI eligibility would burden counties to provide aid through General Assistance (which pays only $345 a month in San Francisco) and other local programs.

Nationwide advocacy groups and lobbyists actively petitioned, demonstrated, and protested the inhumane and discriminatory cuts to legal permanent residents. Stories of disabled and elderly immigrants who were so cognitively impaired or mentally disabled that it would have been impossible for them to learn enough English to pass the fifteen-minute conversation with an INS officer, pass the 100-question[61] citizenship exam, and then be able to "meaningfully" take the loyalty oath, flooded Congressional offices. The first major federal adjustment was the establishment of a new disability waiver affecting the English language and citizenship exam requirements. Under new regulations, naturalization applicants with physical/developmental disabilities or mental impair-

61. They developed a twenty-five-question abridged version based on a person's age and length of residency in the United States. Applicants can opt to take the civics and history test in writing before their appointed interview with INS but must still be able to pass the fifteen-minute conversation in English.

ments can now file for a disability waiver with form N-648, to be filled out by medical doctors. While doctors need to be explicit enough to show the direct connection between the claimed disability and the applicant's inability to perform the test or to do so in English, they cannot imply that the applicant is so impaired that they cannot "meaningfully" take the loyalty oath. The loyalty oath has not been waived, and that still remains a great obstacle for many impaired elderly and disabled applicants.

Under tremendous pressure to restore some of the $24 billion in benefits that legal immigrants stood to lose under welfare reform, Congress restored $11 billion in SSI benefits for all current recipients who were in the United States as of August 22, 1996.[62] The 1997 Balanced Budget Act restored SSI benefits, establishing that the 500,000 elderly and disabled immigrants are assured of continuing to receive financial support of up to $474 a month.[63] Now immigrant provisions provide that,

> All immigrants currently on SSI will continue to receive their benefits; all legal immigrants who were here as of August 22, 1996, and later apply for SSI based on disability will continue to qualify, but those legal immigrants who were here as of that date and later apply for SSI based on age will not qualify for SSI; Refugees and asylees are now eligible to receive SSI for the first seven years after they receive that status. But refugees can only receive Food Stamps for five years. In addition, the term "refugee" now includes Amerasians — children fathered by U.S. citizens in certain Southeast Asian countries while there was U.S. conflict there. Other immigrant provisions of the Act expand the category of "veteran" to include Filipino veterans who fought under U.S. command during World War II, allowing them to avoid the SSI and Food Stamp cutoffs. The act also includes a "Congressional Statement" that Hmong and other Highland Lao veterans who fought on behalf of the U.S. armed forces during the Vietnam War should be considered veterans.[64]

Although SSI benefits were restored in the 1997 Balanced Budget Act for legal permanent residents who were in the United States before August 22, 1996, the struggle to restore food stamps has been a prolonged

---

62. *San Francisco Chronicle*, June 26, 1997.
63. Ibid.
64. See "Federal Balanced Budget Act Averts SSI Cutoffs, Partially Restores Benefits for Legal Immigrants" (San Francisco: The Northern California Coalition for Immigrant and Refugee Rights, August 8, 1997).

one. After the implementation of the food stamp restrictions, an estimated 940,000 immigrants receiving food stamps in 1997 lost eligibility to receive them.[65] On September 1, 1997, all immigrant adults aged 18 to 64 were terminated from the food stamp program. Some states such as California established a state-funded food assistance program, restoring benefits to about one-fourth (primarily children) of those who lost federal food stamps.[66] Legal and immigrant rights coalitions, nutritional rights organizations, and immigrants themselves directed immense pressure on Congress through a national "paper plate campaign" that pushed for enactment of the Agriculture Research, Extension, and Education Reform Act which would restore federal food stamps for the disabled, children under 18, adults 65 and older, and Hmong, Laotian, and Mien veterans who were enlisted by the Central Intelligence Agency but who were not directly included in veteran exemptions established in the Balanced Budget Act of 1997.

On June 23, 1998, the Agriculture Research, Extension, and Education Reform Act of 1998 (P.L. 105–185) was signed into law, restoring food stamps only to immigrants who were in the United States before August 22, 1996, and are disabled, younger than 18, or aged 65 and older, as well as to Southeast Asian veterans. The Agriculture Research Act also extended food stamp benefits to refugees from five years to seven years. Legal residents arriving after August 22, 1996 are ineligible for food stamps and other assistance, unless they become naturalized citizens or work forty qualifying quarters. According to the California Food Security Monitoring Project, even though immigrant children who were here before August 22, 1996 retain eligibility for food stamp benefits, many of these children live in "mixed" households where the adult heads of household lost benefits. The average food stamp recipient in California receives $71.00 per month in coupons used to supplement the family's food budget, which works out to 78 cents per meal. The food purchasing power lost when food stamps are cut is therefore substantial and potentially places these households—both those of single adults and those with children—at risk for increased food insecurity and hunger.[67] Furthermore, the Agriculture Research bill reinstated food stamp eligibility to only an estimated 250,000 immigrants, primarily those from the same

65. See the Report to the Ranking Minority Member, Subcommittee on Children and Families, Committee on Labor and Human Resources, U.S. Senate, "Welfare Reform: Many States Continue Some Federal or State Benefits for Immigrants." (Washington, D.C.: General Accounting Office. GAO/HEHS-98–132, July 1998).
66. See the "Impact of Legal Immigrant Food Stamp Cuts in Los Angeles and San Francisco" California Food Security Monitoring Project (Sacramento: California Food Policy Advocates, May 1998).
67. Ibid.

groups targeted by state-funded food stamp programs.[68] Thus, to continue to deny federal or state-funded food stamps to immigrants between the ages of 18 and 64 will put immigrant families at risk for greater levels of hunger and poor nutrition.

The yearlong battle to reinstate SSI and medicaid benefits to elderly and disabled immigrants, and the two-year movement for the restoration of food stamps to elderly, disabled, and minor immigrants involved political advocacy by immigrant rights groups. More important, success required the public testimony and visibility of those immigrants who were soon to face the most dire of situations with the loss of their benefits. Executive director of the Asian Law Caucus, Angelo Ancheta, explained, "Saving SSI eligibility for most current noncitizens was a great accomplishment for immigrant communities and their advocates. For many representatives in Congress it took the suicides of scores of elderly and disabled immigrants (and the resulting media coverage) to raise doubts about the original welfare reform bill."[69] As the impending deadline neared, the Caucus staff had been preparing and practicing procedures for responding to calls from suicidal elderly clients who were being cut off from assistance. Although there was much to celebrate with the yearlong efforts of many organizations and individuals to restore SSI benefits to the most vulnerable communities, the full extent of the welfare law was just beginning to affect the lives of thousands more immigrant families.

Undocumented Immigrants: Ineligible for Federal Benefits

For undocumented immigrants, the federal provision basically states that "an alien who is not a qualified alien is not eligible for any federal public benefits."[70] According to the federal immigrant provisions the only exceptions are for emergency medical treatment; short-term noncash disaster relief; immunizations; programs, services, or assistance specified by the Attorney General (such as soup kitchens, crisis counseling and intervention, short-term shelter); and programs for housing. Moreover, under the new law, a state to which a federal grant is made is required on request of the Immigration and Naturalization Service to

---

68. Report to the Ranking Minority Member, Subcommittee on Children and Families, Committee on Labor and Human Resources, U.S. Senate.
69. Angelo Ancheta, "A Costly Victory But More Battles to Come," *The Reporter, Asian Law Caucus* 19, no. 2.
70. See Public Law 104–193, Title IV, section 402(b)(1).

furnish the INS with the name and address of, and other identifying information about, any individual who the state knows is unlawfully in the United States. Thus, the Housing Department and some social service agencies must report undocumented immigrants to the INS if they know them to be undocumented. With the tightening of penalties for undocumented immigrants caught in acts of fraud or false claims to citizenship under the Illegal Immigration and Immigrant Responsibility Act, undocumented immigrants are left with very little recourse or few avenues to pursue economic assistance or legal justice.

With little ambiguity over the disqualification of undocumented immigrants from public benefits, and the implementation of more stringent reporting and verification procedures, the one issue that remained controversial in the years to follow was centered around undocumented women's access to prenatal care. Particularly in California, Governor Pete Wilson aggressively pushed to further deny undocumented women access to prenatal care. Since 1988, California's Medi-Cal program has provided state funds for checkups and other prenatal aid for pregnant women with family incomes up to 200 percent of the federal poverty level without regard to immigration status. Governor Wilson planned to impose the ban by January 1, 1998, for new undocumented pregnant applicants and by February 1 for current recipients, directly affecting tens of thousands of undocumented immigrant women in California.

At least three court rulings blocked Wilson's planned implementation of the ban. In December 1997, a superior court judge in Oakland ruled that California must wait for federal guidelines before denying subsidized pregnancy care to undocumented immigrants.[71] Similarly, in March 1998, a superior court judge in Los Angeles blocked Wilson's plans based on the federal welfare law's public health exception allowing undocumented immigrants continued access to subsidized care for screening and treatment of communicable diseases, as well as for immunizations. The judge argued that prenatal care is an important diagnostic tool for discovering communicable diseases and that Wilson's plan would result in the state failing to ensure that women would still have access to screening and treatment for infectious ailments regardless of immigration status.[72] Unfortunately, the rules established by the immigration law stating that hospitals and health care services need to report the immigration status of clients in order to receive federal reimbursements

71. Patrick J. McDonnell. "State Court Delays Ban on Illegal Immigrants' Prenatal Care," *Los Angeles Times*, December 22, 1997.
72. Patrick J. McDonnell, "Ban on Prenatal Care for Undocumented Immigrants Halted," *Los Angeles Times*, March 6, 1998.

have left many undocumented immigrants fearful of deportation if they use public health facilities. Community organizations report that undocumented immigrants are avoiding public health care services even in emergencies.

Sponsorship Deeming and the Affidavits of Support

Immigrants who arrive after August 22, 1997 will have to negotiate the "Attribute of Income and Affidavits of Support" provision established under the "Sponsorship Deeming" requirements of the Illegal Immigration and Immigrant Responsibility Act. According to the immigration reform law, the affidavit of support executed by a sponsor of the alien is a contract: "the sponsor agrees to provide support to maintain the sponsored alien" and must show that they earn at least 125 percent of the federal poverty level for themselves, their family, and the immigrant or immigrants they intend to support.[73] The affidavit is legally enforceable against the sponsor by the sponsored alien, the federal government, the state, or any other entity that provides any means-tested public benefit. Before the Personal Responsibility Act became law, affidavits of support were not always required to demonstrate self-sufficiency, nor were they always legally enforceable. However, the new provisions have established the affidavit as enforceable until the sponsored immigrant naturalizes, is credited with forty qualifying work quarters, permanently leaves the country, or dies.

With the new law, an immigrant's sponsor must prove an income of about $19,500 for a family of four. That income is assumed to be available to the immigrant even after the first five years, during which he or she is ineligible for federal means-tested benefits. Before the recent reform, the sponsor's income was generally included for only the first three or five years of an immigrant's residency. The law now requires states to deem a sponsor's income in federal means-tested programs until the immigrant becomes a citizen or can be credited with forty work quarters.[74] All of the income and resources of the immigrant's sponsor and the immigrant's sponsor's spouse are added to those of the immigrant to determine whether the immigrant qualifies for public assistance. Family-based immigrants who are exempt from deeming are those who satisfy the forty quarters exemption from the SSI and food stamp bar, some battered

---

73. See Public Law 104–208, section 551(a)(1).
74. Report to the Ranking Minority Member, Subcommittee on Children and Families, Committee on Labor and Human Resources, U.S. Senate.

spouses and children who are exempt for up to a year if the need for assistance has a substantial connection to the battery (and if an official certifies that the battery occurred), and persons who need assistance to avoid hunger or homelessness and who may obtain help for up to a year.

The affidavit of support raises more complicated problems for women who are experiencing abuse or battery from their sponsors. The 1990 immigration act was the first legislation by Congress to address the specific problems faced by battered immigrant women. The problem is especially acute for those immigrant women who have been petitioned here through marriage and are still in the process of gaining legal permanent residency. The Violence Against Women Act (VAWA) of 1994 allowed women immigrants who were victims of abuse to complete the process for gaining permanent status without requiring the participation of their abusers. Under previous conditions women were forced to rely on the relative who petitioned her to the United States regardless of the conditions she faced, and if the petitioner threatened to discontinue his or her sponsorship before she became a legal permanent resident, she could then face deportation. VAWA allows women who are victims of abuse by husbands to file their own petitions or suspend deportation if the INS has instituted removal action. However, if a VAWA applicant receives federal means-tested aid, it can be used against her in regard to public charge provisions established in the immigration reform law of 1996.

As for immigrant women who are already legal permanent residents, the Illegal Immigration and immigrant Responsibility Act makes some exceptions for battered women regarding the stricter rules for the affidavit of support. Under the new affidavit of support if a woman or her child has been battered or subjected to extreme cruelty in the United States by a spouse, parent, or a member of the spouse or parent's family residing in the same household, she can be exempt from the sponsor deeming requirements.[75] The woman must demonstrate a connection between the battery or extreme cruelty and the need for public assistance.

ELIGIBILITY FOR STATE AND LOCAL PUBLIC BENEFITS PROGRAMS IN CALIFORNIA

Also established through the federal provisions of the federally mandated welfare law are block grants to states for Temporary Assistance for Needy Families (TANF). Under the welfare law, the family assistance

75. P.L. 104–208, section 552(f)(1).

program known as Aid to Families with Dependent Children (AFDC) was replaced with TANF, which imposes strict time limits and requires parents to "work" in order to receive aid.

The federally mandated provisions for immigrants concerning state and local public benefit programs give states authority to limit TANF eligibility for qualified legal immigrants. According to the welfare law, "A State is authorized to determine the eligibility for any state public benefits of an alien who is a qualified alien, a nonimmigrant under the Immigration and Nationality Act, or an alien who is paroled into the United States for less than one year."[76] Thus, for legal permanent residents, states have the option to ban TANF and social service block grants until naturalization. Under federal provisions, undocumented immigrants do not qualify for federally funded state and local public benefits, except emergency medical treatment; short-term noncash disaster relief; immunizations; and programs, services, or assistance specified by the attorney general. However, the federal provisions also mandate that a state "may provide that an alien who is not lawfully present in the United States is eligible for any State or local public benefit for which such alien would otherwise be ineligible under subsection (a) only through the enactment of a State law after the date of the enactment of this Act which affirmatively provides for such eligibility."[77]

Although the federal provisions provide states authority to determine immigrants' eligibility for some public benefits, the state's "flexibility" will be particularly threatening for immigrants who reside in states hostile to noncitizens receiving public assistance. In California, for example, where Governor Pete Wilson was very vocal about denying public benefits to immigrants, the 1997 state budget left "immigrants with almost nothing." According to the California Immigrant Welfare Collaborative, "Speaker Cruz Bustamante (D-Fresno) accepted a paltry offer on immigrant benefits from Governor Wilson rather than hold up the state budget and push for more meaningful benefit programs. Despite the fact that 33 of the 43 Democratic Assembly members were willing to hold up the budget for immigrant benefits, the Speaker asked them not to for fear of going home with nothing."[78]

The immigrant welfare provisions in California's 1997 budget provided for a state food stamp program for immigrant children under the age of 18 and for adults over the age of 65, but only if they were in the

76. See Public Law 104–193, Title IV, Section 412(a).
77. See Public Law 104–193, Title IV, section 411(d).
78. See "State Legislative Update: Budget Deal Closes, Leaves Immigrants with Almost Nothing" (Sacramento: California Immigrant Welfare Collaborative, August 13, 1997).

United States before August 22, 1996. In Santa Clara County alone, it is estimated that 8,000 legal permanent residents between the ages of 18 and 65 were cut off from any nutritional support by the state and federal government. One year later, the 1998 California budget reinstated state-funded food stamps—with work requirements—for immigrant adults who were in the United States before August 22, 1996. Immigrants who arrive in the United States after August 22, 1996 can receive state-funded food stamps only if they have a sponsor who is abusive, disabled, or deceased.

The 1997 California budget did not create state-level SSI provision for immigrants who lose federal SSI eligibility. However, the 1998 California budget reestablished some portions of state-funded SSI benefits. Immigrants in the United States before August 22, 1996, or who are currently receiving federal SSI benefits, will also be eligible for state-funded benefits. Immigrants who arrive in the United States after August 22, 1996 can receive state-funded SSI only if they have a sponsor who is abusive, disabled, or deceased.

As for health services, at this point all legal permanent residents remain eligible for Medi-Cal benefits regardless of their date of entry. However, because so many fewer immigrant families will be getting assistance under CalWORKs than under AFDC (primarily due to new income requirements), many recipients will have to find other pathways to receive Medi-Cal benefits. California has also instituted a program called Healthy Families,[79] a health care program for children under 19 with family incomes up to 200 percent of the poverty level and who are not eligible for Medi-Cal. Under Healthy Families, parents pay premiums and copayments, with strict federally imposed limits on the amount. Although immigrants are eligible for the Healthy Families program, immigrants who entered the United States after August 22, 1996 are still barred for five years.

Although California has decided to provide TANF to immigrants regardless of their date of entry into the country, the new work requirements and time limits prevent Asian immigrant families from receiving the assistance they need. After California passed its state program (Cal-WORKs—California Work Opportunity and Responsibility to Kids) implementing TANF, the counties then needed to develop local plans by January 10, 1998. Faced with a complete overhaul from AFDC to Cal-

79. Under the Balanced Budget Act of 1997, Congress allocated $24 billion to states (over five years) to provide health care to low-income uninsured children whose families do not qualify for medicaid. States can elect to expand their medicaid programs, create new programs, or both. With these funds, California created the Healthy Families program.

WORKs, county-level departments of social services have been scrambling with local governments to develop plans to address the needs of their constituencies.

The newly established CalWORKs program consists of time-limited employment and job training services, work requirements, and time-limited cash assistance. Under the welfare-to-work approach, time limits for employment and training services for new applicants is eighteen cumulative months (counties may extend the time limit by six months if the county determines that added time would lead to employment or local conditions are such that employment is not available); current recipients are limited to twenty-four months of cumulative employment training from time of agreement to welfare-to-work plan. According to the 1998 California state budget, immigrants receiving CalWORKs will have to complete twenty-six or thirty-two hours of work per month in unsubsidized or subsidized work. Cash assistance is set at a sixty-month lifetime limit for adults, beginning from initial receipt of aid, after which a safety net aid is provided for recipient children only. Currently, immigrants who arrived by August 22, 1996, are eligible for CalWORKs benefits after their first five years here.

In May 1997, the immigrant caseload of 199,381 accounted for almost 22.5 percent of California's total TANF caseload.[80] In San Francisco, approximately 41 percent of immigrant families receiving AFDC were headed by single mothers. The consequences of the sixty-month lifetime limit are that poor immigrant mothers will quickly run out of options for long-term support of their families. Meeting the work requirement for benefits will undoubtedly create great hardship for immigrant families as well, especially those who came here as refugees from Southeast Asia more than five years ago. Inadequate skill and job training, English-language limitations, and racial discrimination in the labor market will confine poor immigrant parents in menial and low-wage service-sector jobs, which many of them already have. For immigrants arriving after August 22, 1996, eligibility for CalWORKs will be limited by federal deeming rules regarding their sponsor's income and resources.

By January 10, 1998, counties were required to submit their plans for CalWORKs implementation to the State Department of Social Services. As clocks began to tick for noncitizen recipients enrolled in CalWORKs, counties confronted the complicated needs of a very heterogeneous clientele that Congress did not consider when it mandated welfare-to-work

80. Report to the Ranking Minority Member, Subcommittee on Children and Families, Committee on Labor and Human Resources, U.S. Senate.

as a way to move women from "dependency" to "self-sufficiency." Transitioning recipients into work requires counties to provide support for child care, transportation, English instruction, job training, and services to assist poor women who are dealing with domestic abuse, mental disabilities, or drug- and alcohol-related issues. However, such supports are not guaranteed.

As cash assistance, food stamps, and health care for needy families have become exponentially more difficult to receive, Asian immigrant and refugee women, who have always had to piece together a multitude of ways to support their families, will find that the new system requires a lot of work to get a small amount of money. These punitive measures directed at poor women and noncitizens have already affected the stability and security of poor Asian immigrant and refugee families, as the means for security and self-sufficiency are stripped away.

THE COST OF WELFARE

The profound impact of welfare reform on Asian immigrant communities continues to unfold as policy implementation continues. Although politicians have recognized the severe cruelty of denying SSI benefits to economically vulnerable disabled and elderly immigrants by restoring SSI to those here on or before August 22, 1996, the cost of continued restrictions to the Asian immigrant community is staggering. The traumatic loss of food stamps, even though partially restored, means that immigrant families have to get by with less food and worse nutrition and that they must rely on free food distribution centers to keep their families from starving.

For immigrants who are eligible for the other cash assistance program, TANF, the implementation of welfare-to-work has proved so confusing that the drop-off rates in California counties have been astounding. With immigrants unable to read and understand the Notices of Action explaining the transition from AFDC to CalWORKs, as well as informing them of their required interview appointment, they are confused by or unaware of the new work requirements and time limits. In Bay Area Counties, 60 percent of adult CalWORKs recipients are not showing up for their contract interview. It is likely that many immigrant clients are falling through the cracks, most likely because the notices are so unclear.

Welfare-to-work time limits and work requirements will have a devastating impact on poor Asian immigrant women and their families because of their limited English and low-level marketable skills. Already in a highly vulnerable position because they are viewed by employers in the service and manufacturing sectors as a "globally exploitable" labor pool, being forced into labor agreements as welfare workers will further jeopardize their ability to expect fair and safe working conditions. Given the compounding barriers of language, low education levels, lack of jobs at living wages, and appropriate child care services—not to mention sexual inequality and harassment in the workplace—Asian immigrant and refugee CalWORKs recipients live precariously, with no other options but to take menial exploitive work, place their children in the care of others, and hope to survive on very little. The end of welfare and immigration reform thus have made survival a struggle for poor immigrants in this country. Although President Clinton placed race at the top of the national agenda, immigrants of color have lost security, basic rights, and social guarantees.

CHAPTER SIX

Women, Welfare, and Domestic Violence

Demie Kurz

Male violence is a problem for women of all income, race, and ethnic groups and affects an estimated 3–4 million women in the United States every year.[1] This problem creates serious hardship for women because most abused women experience fear and emotional pain, as well as physical injury. Children can also suffer from witnessing the physical abuse of their mothers.[2] As well as depriving women of their basic right to safety, male violence is very costly to society. The public pays billions of dollars for the direct and indirect costs of this problem, including health and criminal justice services.[3]

This chapter focuses on poor women, their experience of male violence, and the impact of violence on their lives. Although research and policy must address the violence that affects women in all social groups, the situation of poor women needs particular attention because poor women have so few resources. Those who wish to leave violent relationships, particularly those with children, face serious problems gaining the financial stability they need. Government assistance can be critical for

The author wishes to thank Gwendolyn Mink, and Martha Davis and Pat Reuss of the NOW Legal Defense and Education Fund, for helpful comments on this paper. They are not responsible, however, for any errors or omissions.

1. Joan Zorza, "Woman Battering: High Costs and the State of the Law," *Clearinghouse Review* (Special Issue) 1994: 386.

2. Peter Jaffe, David Wolfe, and Susan K. Wilson, "Children of Battered Women," *Developmental Clinical Psychology and Psychiatry* 21 (Newbury Park, Calif.: Sage, 1990); Janet Johnston, "High Conflict Divorce," *The Future of Children: Children and Divorce*, 4, no. 1 (Spring 1994): 165–182.

3. Jane Maslow Cohen, "Private Violence and Public Obligation: The Fulcrum of Reason," in Martha A. Fineman and Roxanne Mykitiuk, eds., *The Public Nature of Private Violence* (New York: Routledge, 1994), 369; and Louise Laurence and Roberta Spalter-Roth, "Measuring the Costs of Domestic Violence against Women and the Cost-Effectiveness of Interventions: An Initial Assessment and Proposals for Further Research" (Washington, D.C.: Institute for Women's Policy Research, 1996).

poor women. The previous welfare system, Aid to Families with Dependent Children (AFDC), although in many ways inadequate, provided a guaranteed safety net for all poor women. Unfortunately, the termination of poor women's entitlement to benefits in the Personal Responsibility and Work Reconciliation Act (PRA), along with other severe cuts to welfare programs, have deprived poor women who are trying to escape abusive partners of a very important resource.

The purpose of this chapter is to examine the impact of the PRA on the lives of poor, abused women who are enrolled in or qualify for welfare programs. I examine what this legislation does and does not provide for battered women and demonstrate how, although the new law does make some provisions to take the situation of abused women into account, it fails such women in critical respects. I argue that federal and state policymakers must make greater commitments both to protecting abused women and to helping them rebuild their lives.

The policies for battered women contained in the PRA reveal a lot about the state's views of violence against women, including what kinds of commitments the state is willing to make to reduce male violence and whether it will honor them. One of the main justifications for government is the protection of citizens from harm. Until recently, women abused by male partners fell outside the purview of the law's protection because the home was defined as part of the "private" sphere, insulated from the law, in contrast to the "public" sphere which is protected by legal codes. Beginning in the 1980s, however, due to pressure from a movement of activists in grassroots and institutional settings, important changes took place. The federal government and states passed stricter laws outlawing and punishing violence against women, and local law enforcement began to make major changes, such as granting women temporary restraining orders against their abusers, creating tougher arrest policies, and training criminal justice personnel in how to intervene in cases of woman abuse.[4]

The efforts of this movement culminated in the Violence Against Women Act (VAWA) of 1994, landmark federal legislation that provides for improved prevention and prosecution of violent crimes against women and children and for the care of victims. The law authorizes funds for increased efforts to reduce violent crimes against women, including improving arrest procedures, tracking domestic violence cases, and prosecuting stalkers. VAWA also provides funding for prevention

---

4. Cohen, "Private Violence and Public Obligation."

and victim services, including money to expand shelter services, educate judges about violence against women, develop legal advocacy service programs for victims of domestic violence, create more school- and community-based education programs, and improve research databases on violence against women.[5] VAWA is an indication of a positive change in the way the state views violence, compared with earlier times when violence against women was considered a private affair. Despite the increased public recognition of this issue, however, violence is still overlooked in many areas of social life,[6] and it continues to cause great harm to women.

Fortunately, the new welfare law does recognize that abused women have particular needs and seeks to provide certain protections for them. However, it does not provide abused women with badly needed resources. Temporary Assistance to Needy Families (TANF), the new public assistance program, assumes that many opportunities exist for poor women to escape poverty, an assumption that must be challenged. In the first section of this chapter, I examine the situation of poor, abused women and discuss their needs. In the second section, I examine the PRA to determine what assistance it does and does not provide for poor, abused women. I conclude with a consideration of what a law would need to include if it were truly to serve the interests of poor and abused women.

WOMEN, POVERTY, AND VIOLENCE

In this section, using data from my own and other studies, I examine the extent of the problem of violence toward poor women and its impact on their lives. My own study is based on a random sample of divorced women with children, some of whom were recipients of welfare under the previous system, AFDC,[7] and many of whom had experienced vio-

5. National Resource Center on Domestic Violence, "The Violence against Women Act Analysis Series." Prepared by and for the National Resource Center on Domestic Violence and the Battered Women's Justice Project (Harrisburg, Pa.: National Resource Center on Domestic Violence, 1997).
6. Demie Kurz, "Old Problems and New Directions in the Study of Violence Against Women," in Racquel Kennedy Bergen, ed., *Issues in Intimate Violence* (Newbury Park, Calif.: Sage, 1998), 197–208.
7. Demie Kurz, *For Richer, For Poorer: Mothers Confront Divorce* (New York: Routledge, 1995). My divorce study was based on interviews with a random sample of 129 divorced women with children, who were living in the city of Philadelphia, also a county of Pennsylvania. The racial distribution of the sample approximates that of the county, with 61 percent white women, 35 percent Black women, and 3 percent Hispanic women. Nineteen percent of the women in the sample were on AFDC. This is similar to the percentage of divorced women nationwide who receive welfare in-

lence during their marriages and during the period of separation.[8] The continuing threat of violence had an impact on these women's lives throughout the divorce process, as they attempted to secure the resources to which they were entitled, particularly child support, and begin their new lives.[9]

The High Levels of Violence Experienced by Poor Women

Recent studies from a variety of jurisdictions, including Chicago, Massachusetts, and New Jersey, have reported that women on welfare experience high rates of male violence.[10] In the Massachusetts study, which was based on a random sample of welfare recipients, researchers found that 20 percent of current welfare recipients had been abused by a former or current boyfriend or husband within the preceding twelve months, and 65 percent had been victims of abuse at the hands of a husband or boyfriend or former husband or boyfriend at some point in their lives.[11] Other studies report similar findings of 15–20 percent of women using welfare services reporting that they are currently experiencing abuse by a male partner and 57–65 percent that they have experienced abuse at some time in their lives.[12] In my study as well, the poorest divorced women, those on welfare, experienced higher rates of violence than any

---

come, which is 10 to 20 percent (Peterson [1989], 49–51). The AFDC women were the poorest women in the sample.

8. Overall, 50 percent of the women in the sample experienced violence at least 2 to 3 times in their marriages. An additional 16 percent experienced violence once. For this analysis I did not count this latter group, however. Although one act of violence could certainly have had serious repercussions for their outlook and behavior, the 16 percent of women who experienced only one act of violence stated that the violence, usually a slap, was an isolated event that did not affect other aspects of their lives. The amount of violence experienced by women who reported several or more incidents during their marriages is similar to rates of violence reported elsewhere.

9. An additional 4 percent of the women experienced violence during the separation only. According to women's reports, the actual percentage of women who experienced violence during the separation is higher than 4 percent, but due to the wording of one question in the interview about violence during both the marriage and the separation, it was not possible to determine the extent of separation abuse.

10. Ellen L. Bassuk, Angela Browne, and John C. Buckner, "Single Mothers and Welfare," *Scientific American* (October 1996): 60–67; Martha F. Davis and Susan J. Kraham, "Protecting Women's Welfare in the Face of Violence," *Fordham Urban Law Journal* 22, no. 4 (1995): 1145; Washington State Institute for Public Policy, "Over Half of Women on Public Assistance in Washington State Reported Physical or Sexual Abuse as Adults" (October 1993).

11. McCormack Institute and Center for Survey Research, *In Harm's Way? Domestic Violence, AFDC Receipt, and Welfare Reform in Massachusetts. A Report from the University of Massachusetts Boston* (Boston, Mass., 1997).

12. Jody Raphael and Richard Tolman, *Trapped by Poverty, Trapped by Abuse: New Evidence Documenting the Relationship between Domestic Violence and Welfare* (Chicago, Ill.: Taylor Institute, April 1997).

other group of women.[13] Not only did poor women experience the most violence, but also the poorer the women, the more serious was the violence they experienced; women on welfare experienced the most serious violence. I defined *serious violence* as more than three incidents of violence, or one very serious incident of violence.[14]

Whatever the exact rates of abuse currently experienced by welfare recipients, we do know that the poorer women are, the more likely they are to experience violence at the hands of their intimate partners. According to the U.S. Department of Justice's National Crime Victimization Survey, "women with an annual family income under $10,000 were more likely to report having experienced violence by an intimate than those with an income of $10,000 or more."[15] Further, rates of violence at the hands of intimates decrease with each increase in income category. Thus, the rates of "violent victimizations" per 1,000 females age 12 or older for those with an annual family income of $9,999 or less was 19.9 percent; for those with annual family incomes of $10,000 – $14,999, 13.3 percent; $15,000 – $19,999, 10.9 percent; $20,000 – $29,999, 9.5 percent; $30,000 – $49,999, 5.4 percent; and $50,000 or more, 4.5 percent. In their nationwide survey of the use of violence by married couples, Murray Straus and Richard Gelles found that the lower a woman's education, income, and occupational level, the more likely she was to be battered.[16]

What is the reason for the higher levels of violence reported by low-income women? Are poorer women more forthcoming about the amount of violence they experience, or do more of them report the violence to the police because they have less access to other kinds of legal assistance? These are possibilities, but at this point no data answer this question. It is also possible that something about the circumstances of those living in poverty contributes to the higher rate of violence among poorer men. For example, men from lower income groups may have a

13. Seventy-one percent reported experiencing violence at least two to three times during their marriage or the separation, in contrast with the 50 percent average for the sample.

14. Fifty-eight percent of welfare women experienced serious violence, while 37 percent of the sample as a whole experienced serious violence.

15. U.S. Department of Justice's National Crime Victimization Survey 15 (1995: 4); U.S. Department of Justice, Bureau of Justice Statistics, Special Report, National Crime Victimization Survey, "Violence Against Women: Estimates from the Redesigned Survey" (Washington, D.C., August 1995), 4.

16. Murray A. Straus and Richard J. Gelles, "Societal Change and Change in Family Violence from 1975–1985 as Revealed by Two National Surveys," *Journal of Marriage and the Family* 48 (1986): 465–479.

stronger belief in the legitimacy of violence than other men, since they typically hold more traditional gender ideologies than other men.[17] It is not clear, however, that lower-income men actually behave in more gendered ways than do other men.[18] Another explanation for the higher rates of violence reported by poorer women could be that lower-income men have fewer ways of controlling their partners than other men. The higher men's social class, the more ability they have to control their female partners through their greater economic resources. In my study, many divorced women in all social classes volunteered that their husbands tried to control their social life, their friendships, and major family decisions. Interviewers did not specifically ask about this kind of behavior, but many women volunteered that they felt their husbands were controlling and that they did not like this. So while according to women's volunteered statements, men of all different backgrounds were controlling, perhaps higher-income men, who control greater amounts of family income and property than poorer men do, felt as though they did not need to resort to violence to control their female partners or family decision making more generally.

The Economic and Social Impact of Violence on the Lives of Poor Women

All abused women, but particularly those who are poor, need access to resources. According to some researchers, a major factor in whether or not battered women will permanently leave their abusers is whether they have enough economic resources to live outside the abusive relationship.[19] Sometimes women leave a violent relationship but return when they realize they cannot survive financially. One of the most serious disadvantages that poor, abused women face is that they frequently have little job experience and thus have difficulty gaining access to stable employment, the most important means to secure economic well-being. Some abused women in my study, for example, had not been able to gain employment experience during their marriages because their hus-

17. Randall Collins, *Sociology of Marriage and the Family: Gender, Love, and Property* (Chicago: Nelson-Hall, 1988).

18. Arlie Hochschild, *The Second Shift* (New York: Avon Books, 1989).

19. B. E. Aguirre, "Why Do They Return? Abused Wives in Shelters," *Social Work* 30 (1985): 350 – 54; Edward W. Gondolf and Ellen R. Fisher, *Battered Women as Survivors: An Alternative to Treating Learned Helplessness* (Lexington, Mass.: Lexington Books, 1988); Lewis Okun, *Woman Abuse: Facts Replacing Myths* (Albany: State University of New York Press, 1986).

bands had prevented them from working. In answer to the question, "Why did you go on welfare?" women gave a variety of answers—that they couldn't get child care or jobs with health care benefits or they had married young and had no job experiences. In addition, some women who had suffered physical abuse said they had to go on welfare because they hadn't been allowed to work while they were married, and thus they had no job skills and no prospect of a job. The following quotes are from several different women on AFDC who had this problem.

> I was not allowed to go out. I wasn't really allowed to talk on the phone. . . . I wasn't allowed to have a job. I wasn't allowed to have friends.
>
> I wanted to work but my ex-husband wouldn't let me. He said I might meet a man. He was very jealous. But then I did work for a while in a firm that a relative owned. He said that was OK because he knew the men there.
>
> He was very insecure. He wanted me at home. He didn't mind if I worked when he was working, but if he got laid off, which he sometimes did, then he wouldn't let me work. One time he said that the worst thing that ever happened was that I went to school. . . . He also wanted to control everything about my life. He wanted to control my friends, my time. He wouldn't let my son see my brother, who is a successful businessman.

One woman reported that her confidence in her work abilities was destroyed by her ex-husband.

> I went for a job interview recently. I did great until I came to the part where you have to type something on the computer. I did bad. They must have thought I was lying. I froze up. They didn't have machines like that at [local business school], not at all. Also, one thing that happened during my marriage was that my confidence in my ability to work got a bit destroyed. He tore me down all the time. Fortunately my new husband has given some of that back to me.

Other data confirm that some batterers prohibit their partners from working.[20]

---

20. Melanie Shepard and Ellen Pence, "The Effect of Battering on the Employment Status of Women," *Affilia* 3 (1988): 55; Raphael and Tolman, *Trapped by Poverty, Trapped by Abuse*, ii.

Child Support

One very important resource that abused mothers need is child support. Research shows that the regular receipt of child support payments helps women escape poverty.[21] Most of the mothers in my sample were very anxious to receive child support. The new welfare system is premised on the idea that women can escape poverty through their wages from jobs and through the receipt of child support from the fathers of their children. To ensure that women receive child support, the law requires that women applying for welfare cooperate in locating the father, so that he can be issued a child support order.

Unfortunately, for many mothers, particularly those who are poor, obtaining child support has not been easy. Fewer than one-third of single mothers receive child support. Divorced mothers receive slightly more, but less than half of them receive the child support to which they are entitled. Further, the lower a woman's income, the less likely she is to receive child support, and Black women receive child support at much lower rates than white women. In my sample, women on welfare received less child support than any other group of women. Eighty-three percent of women on welfare received no child support and many of these women had no child support order.[22]

Poor women receive so little child support for several reasons. One is that a number of poor fathers are not able to pay much child support, although the average income of fathers whose partners or former partners are on welfare is $13,000 to $21,000,[23] which is higher than the average woman receives in welfare payments.[24] These figures indicate that income is not the only barrier to payment of child support. Another reason so few women on welfare receive child support is that the child support system for women on welfare, which has been different from the one for nonwelfare women, has discouraged women from seeking, and men from paying, child support. Previously, AFDC regulations stipulated that recipients receive only $50 of the child support paid by the father; AFDC appropriated the rest of the award to offset the cost of welfare to the fam-

21. Ann Nichols-Caseboldt, "The Economic Impact of Child Support Reform on the Poverty Status of Custodial and Noncustodial Families," in Irwin Garfinkel, Sara McLanahan, and Philip Robins, eds., *Child Support Assurance* (Washington, D.C.: Urban Institute Press, 1992), 189–202.
22. All data cited in this paragraph are from the U.S. Bureau of the Census, *Child Support and Alimony: 1989*, Current Population Reports, Series P-60, No. 173 (Washington, D.C.: U.S. Government Printing Office, 1991).
23. Paula G. Roberts, *Ending Poverty as We Know It: The Case for Child Support Enforcement and Assurance* (Washington, D.C.: The Center for Law and Social Policy, 1994), 36–38.
24. Kurz, *For Richer, For Poorer*, 30.

ily. Under TANF, the new welfare program, the states can decide how much of the father's child support payment a mother will receive. Some states have increased the amount of child support a mother may receive, some have decreased it, and some have decided that women should continue to receive $50 of the father's payment.[25]

An additional, very important factor that prevents many women from securing child support, and one that has unfortunately not been sufficiently recognized, is fear of violence. Some mothers, particularly those who experienced violence at the hands of their husbands during their marriage, will not apply for child support because they fear their ex-husbands will be violent toward them if they do. In my sample, 30 percent of all women stated that they were fearful during their negotiations for child support, with few race or class differences among them. In addition, 38 percent of the women reported being fearful during negotiations for custody. (There is overlap between these two groups: 74 percent of those who were fearful during negotiations for child support also reported being fearful during negotiations for custody.)

These women's fears were strongly related to their experience of violence during marriage. A statistically significant relationship exists between women's fear during the negotiations for child support and their experience of violence during marriage and separation. The more serious or frequent the violence these women experienced, the more fearful they were during negotiations for child support. Some women were also fearful because of their experience of violence during the separation. Increasingly, researchers believe that women are at risk of violence during separation. Mahoney calls the violence that women experience at this time "separation assault."[26]

There are strong indications that their fears caused some of the women in my sample to reduce their requests for child support. There is a statistically significant relationship between feeling fearful during negotiations for child support and receipt of child support. Only 34 percent of the women who reported being fearful received regular child support, in contrast to 60 percent of those who did not report fear during negotiations for child support. There was also a statistically significant relationship between women's fear of losing custody and the lower rates at which

25. Telephone conversation with Sue Frietsche, Child Support Initiative, Women's Law Project, Philadelphia, Pa., September 28, 1998.
26. Martha Mahoney, "Legal Images of Battered Women: Redefining the Issue of Separation," *Michigan Law Review* 90 (1991): 1–94. See also Demie Kurz, "Separation, Divorce, and Woman Abuse," *Violence Against Women* 2 (1), 1996: 63–81, for a discussion of separation assault.

they received child support. Fear of losing custody, like fear of negotiating for child support, was also significantly related to a woman's experience of violence.

Women's accounts of their experiences illustrate their fears. One woman, a 24-year-old mother of two on AFDC, initially spoke of just wanting to "get away from her husband," who had been using drugs. But on further questioning, she says that she was fearful of him.

> I really wish now that I had gotten money for child support. I feel like I just threw it away. Then I was trying to get away from him. I just wanted to get away and to get divorced.
> Int.: What do you mean?
> I was afraid. I felt that if I had pushed him for things, he would have beat me up. I also figured he never would pay.

Another woman, who spoke of her fear that her ex-husband might take her children, said, "I was fearful the whole time [I was negotiating for child support]. He was always threatening. By this time I had been to abuse court. He was under orders not to come near the house, the kids, or me. The teachers were notified. I was terrified he would take the kids."

Because of their difficulty finding jobs and obtaining child support, women who leave marriages and other relationships with men face hardship, and poorer women face the most difficult circumstances. An astonishing 47 percent of never-married women heads of households in the United States live below the official poverty level,[27] as do 39 percent of divorced women with children.[28] Battered women who leave their partners face particular difficulties getting out of poverty, as they often leave with no financial resources. Davis and Kraham point out that batterers commonly isolate their partners from financial resources.[29] For example, many battered women do not have access to cash, checking accounts, or charge accounts.[30] Women of color endure particular hardship. Higher percentages of Black than white women are poor, despite the fact that Black women have a similar level of education to the white women.[31]

27. Elyce Rotella, "Women and the American Economy," in Sheila Ruth, ed., *Issues in Feminism* (Mountain View, Calif.: Mayfield Publishing, 1995), 320–333.
28. U.S. Bureau of the Census, *Poverty in the United States: 1992.* Current Population Reports, Series P-60, No. 185. (Washington, D.C.: U.S. Government Printing Office, 1993).
29. Davis and Kraham, "Protecting Women's Welfare in the Face of Violence."
30. Lisa G. Lerman, "Model State Act: Remedies for Domestic Abuse," *Harvard Journal On Legislation* 21 (1984): 90.
31. Ruth Sidel, *Women and Children Last* (New York: Penguin, 1986), 23.

Discriminatory policies in education and employment continue to disadvantage Black women, whose experience reflects not only the "feminization of poverty," but also the "racialization of poverty."[32]

Homelessness is also a problem for battered women, as evidenced by the fact that a significant portion of the homeless population is battered women.[33] Women in shelters describe housing as one of their greatest needs.[34] In my sample, several mothers on welfare, who were both poor and abused, experienced periods of homelessness along with their children. In their study of women on welfare, many of whom had been abused, Bassuk and colleagues found not only that many of the women had high rates of homelessness but also that the abuse these women suffered, combined with the experience of being homeless, caused them to experience high rates of both physical and emotional problems.[35]

These data indicate that large numbers of women who are entitled to welfare services have been abused. These women not only need jobs, but many also need job training and the things that support job training—day care, transportation, and health insurance for themselves and their children. They also need child support. The data presented here indicate that we must give much more serious attention to how the experience of violence prevents women from obtaining child support and further contributes to their poverty. Still, although battered women need and frequently want child support, policymakers must not force women to interact with abusive fathers to get that child support.

THE PERSONAL RESPONSIBILITY ACT
AND PROVISIONS ABOUT VIOLENCE

The Personal Responsibility and Work Opportunity Act, which became law on August 22, 1996, marked a radical break from recent social welfare policy by ending six decades of guaranteed federal assistance to poor parents and their children under the Aid to Families with Dependent Children program. In place of AFDC, the law offers Temporary As-

32. Margaret B. Wilkerson and Jewell H. Gresham, "The Racialization of Poverty," in Alison Jaggar and Paula S. Rothenberg, eds., *Feminist Frameworks* 3d ed. (New York: McGraw Hill, 1993), 297–303.
33. Zorza, "Woman Battering: High Costs and the State of the Law."
34. Chris M. Sullivan, Joanna Basta, Cheribeth Tan, and William S. Davidson II, "After the Crisis: A Needs Assessment of Women Leaving a Domestic Violence Shelter," *Violence and Victims* 7 (1992): 267–272.
35. Bassuk et al., "Single Mothers and Welfare."

sistance for Needy Families (TANF). The law's most significant features are that it ties cash assistance to work requirements and that it strictly limits the total amount of time during which women can receive support (P.L. 104–193). The legislation also severely restricts eligibility for food stamps, medicaid, and other benefits, cutting $56 billion from antipoverty programs.[36] In addition, unlike the previous welfare system over which the federal government had authority, TANF transfers most of the power over welfare programs to states.

These changes have, and will continue to have, many negative consequences for the 12.8 million people on welfare, 8 million of whom are children.[37] The five-year time limit on welfare benefits has especially serious implications for poor women, particularly those who have been abused. There are serious questions as to whether jobs will be available for poor women who must go off assistance when they have reached the time limit mandated by welfare law, and whether these jobs will pay a living wage or provide health and other benefits. As demonstrated earlier, it can take an abused woman with children some time to get out of a battering relationship and to establish her own household. In this and many other ways, the PRA is a punitive measure, based on faulty assumptions about poor women's unwillingness to work, assumptions that are fed by racist stereotypes of women having babies to get on welfare.

Fortunately, the PRA does recognize the problem of abuse through the Wellstone/Murray Amendment, added to the welfare bill as a result of lobbying by activists.[38] The Family Violence Option (FVO) [Sec. 402(a)(7)] permits states (1) to screen for domestic violence both for candidates applying for assistance and for those being dropped from assistance programs; (2) to refer victims of domestic violence to counseling; and (3) to make a determination whether certain welfare requirements should be waived for abused women, such as time limits or other restrictions that would unfairly penalize them for things they cannot do while in an abusive relationship or while recovering from the relationship. This last provision, the waiver on time limits, can be extremely important to battered women. Although not all abused women need such waivers, some do, in order to leave or escape violent relationships or to obtain job training that they were unable to secure while in a violent relationship. Another welfare requirement that can be waived is the mandatory coop-

---

36. Ibid.
37. Ibid., 60.
38. The NOW Legal Defense and Education Fund has spearheaded efforts to gain recognition for victims of domestic violence in the new welfare law and worked closely with Senators Murray and Wellstone to develop the Family Violence Option.

eration in the child support enforcement process. The Personal Responsibility Act puts a priority on collecting child support and requires that mothers cooperate in identifying fathers; however, the FVO does recognize that cooperation with the child support enforcement process may carry risks for abused women.

Congress decided to recommend, rather than require, that states adopt the FVO. All fifty states plus Puerto Rico and the District of Columbia were permitted to implement the amendment, to implement parts of it, or to reject it altogether. Thirty-one states have implemented the provision in its entirety (most of them only very recently), and nine states claim that they are planning to adopt it. Ten states have not adopted the amendment but have some domestic violence language or provisions in their state plans. The remaining two states have not adopted the Family Violence Option, and their state welfare plans do not include any domestic violence provisions.[39]

Limitations of the Family Violence Option

The FVO is an extremely important resource for battered women, but there are some serious limitations to the current provision. First, Congress failed to take certain measures that would have greatly improved the effectiveness of the FVO. As it is currently written, a "hardship exemption" allows states to exempt 20 percent of welfare recipients from work requirements and time requirements.[40] Hardship is something that would prevent a person from fulfilling the requirements of PRA, through no fault of their own. The definition of *hardship* includes battering and extreme cruelty. Since the passage of the welfare law, however, there has been confusion about whether battered women who receive FVO waivers could be counted separately from the 20 percent of women who may be granted a hardship exemption. The welfare law also requires states to move half the people from their welfare caseloads into jobs by 2002. There has been a similar confusion about whether states can count battered women above and beyond this 50 percent. It is very important that states be allowed to count battered women above and beyond the level of exemptions allowed in the welfare law. Otherwise, abused women will be forced into competition with other groups for protection and help, and many will not receive the waivers that they need because states

39. Jody Raphael and Sheila Haennicke, "The Family Violence Option: An Early Assessment, A Taylor Institute Report Submitted to the Federal Department of Health and Human Services" (Chicago: Taylor Institute, September 1, 1998).
40. Institute for Women's Policy Research, *Welfare Reform Network News*, issue no. 4 (April 11, 1997).

risk losing their funding if they do not follow the guidelines of the welfare law.

The U.S. Senate did produce a clarification that its intent was that battered women could be granted exemptions in numbers above and beyond the 20 percent of women granted hardship exemptions.[41] This clarification of the Family Violence Option had strong support in both houses of Congress. In the fall of 1997, however, a House-Senate conference committee failed to pass this clarification. In the wake of Congress's failure to pass the clarification, the Department of Health and Human Services (HHS) has proposed regulations that would waive the penalties for states that fail to meet work or time-limit requirements because of waivers granted to victims of domestic violence. HHS proposes to grant "good cause" exceptions to the penalties for states "as long as those waivers are temporary and include services to help the individual prepare for work and self-sufficiency."[42] HHS has also stipulated in its proposals that to qualify for these waivers, states must have adopted the Family Violence Option. Unfortunately, this means that deserving women in states that have not adopted the FVO will not be eligible for these waivers.

Another group that will not be able to benefit from these reforms is noncitizen immigrant women, who cannot count on welfare funds to help them escape an abusive situation. The law permits states to deny all noncitizens welfare (TANF) benefits and requires states to subject immigrant welfare applicants to tough sponsor deeming requirements. There is no specific provision in the PRA to waive the denial of TANF benefits to immigrant women in cases of abuse, although the Illegal Immigration and Immigrant Responsibility Act did loosen deeming requirements for battered immigrant women. The 1994 Violence Against Women Act also made it easier for battered immigrant women and their children to become permanent residents; as such, the new immigration law permits them to receive welfare without meeting deeming requirements if they can show a connection between their abuse and their need for welfare—and if their state permits noncitizen immigrants to receive welfare.[43]

Implementation of the Family Violence Option

Another issue that is critical for the success of the FVO is how it will be implemented. For example, the privatization of welfare casework

---

41. *Congressional Record*, the United States Senate, S4872, May 21, 1997.
42. U.S. Department of Health and Human Services, "HHS Fact Sheet." November 17, 1997, 3.
43. Data reported in this paragraph are from Institute for Women's Policy Research, *Welfare Reform Network News*, issue no. 4 (Washington, D.C., 1997).

raises the questions of whether caseworkers will have any knowledge of the FVO and of how to question eligible women about the violence they have experienced, or whether these workers will have any commitment to implementing the FVO. In fact, caseworkers are rewarded first and foremost for seeing that as many women as possible are dropped from welfare programs.

Further, welfare caseworkers may not receive any training in violence against women and the options that are available to such women. Some very important issues must be considered when welfare personnel interact with women: What screening procedures will be used to determine whether abuse has occurred? How should women be screened given that some women may be fearful for their safety? Will there be adequate numbers of personnel to do the screening? Will the confidentiality of women be protected? How much assistance should welfare office staff provide for abused women? Many battered women want to work and to secure child support and other benefits, as long as they can do so safely. What consideration will caseworkers give to abused women in comparison to other needy clients? States must also be prevented from introducing punitive measures. For example, states could require that to qualify for the FVO, women have to secure protection orders or undergo mandatory counseling, decisions that should be left in the hands of women. States must be prevented from exacting a price from battered women in exchange for protecting them.

Another important part of the FVO that must be implemented with great care is the enforcement of child support obligations. Although the FVO permits states to exempt battered women from child support enforcement rules, it leaves it up to states to decide which women to exempt and when. Thus states decide when women have been battered and when there is "good cause" for not cooperating with paternity establishment and child support enforcement rules. States also determine such things as what penalties to give women for not cooperating with paternity establishment and whether women with "good cause" exemptions should still receive medicaid (currently they can). It is not clear how generous or understanding states will be of the situations of abused women. As indicated earlier, states are now under heavy pressure to reduce their welfare caseloads. This means they must help women to gain access to the only other potential sources of income: jobs and child support from their children's fathers.

Paternity establishment and child support enforcement raise serious concerns about the screening process to determine "good cause" exemptions. Under TANF, state child support departments and bureaucracies have exclusive responsibility for determining whether or not a woman is "cooperating" with the child support process. If the agency determines she is not, then a woman may lose her rights to receive TANF, medicaid, and possibly food stamp benefits.[44] Because of the serious consequences of a determination of noncooperation, personnel in these child support agencies will need training about violence against women. Determining whether women are abused can be a delicate matter, as well as one involving knowledge of technical issues. Where will the money come from for such training? Further, what incentive will these workers have to carefully screen for domestic violence, given that they are burdened with large caseloads of clients?[45]

Research on the treatment of battered women by front-line workers in the health care and criminal justice systems shows that they do not always take the issue of woman abuse seriously.[46] Even when hospital personnel and criminal justice officials are told to identify battered women, some fail to recognize woman battering, while others give low priority to abused women. For example, emergency department personnel may view battered women as less deserving of attention than other patients whose conditions they perceive as "truly serious,"[47] and criminal justice personnel may view abused women as people with social problems brought on by their own behavior, not as "real" victims of crimes.[48] Research shows that the best way to get battered women the services they need is for organizations to have advocates who are trained to look out for their interests.[49]

In conclusion, the FVO is very important to abused women. However, it will take serious pressure by advocates for battered women at the state level to ensure that its provisions are enforced. Fortunately, one very positive development is that battered women's groups at the state level have become involved in monitoring the implementation of the FVO.[50] This is the best hope for ensuring fair and effective policies. Advocates for battered women must also pressure the government to add benefits for

---

44. Telephone conversation with Cristina Firvida, National Women's Law Center, Washington, D.C., September 4, 1998.
45. Ibid.
46. Kathleen Ferraro, "Policing Woman Battering," *Social Problems* 36 (1989): 61–74; Demie Kurz, "Responses to Battered Women: Resistance to Medicalization," *Social Problems* 34 (1987): 501–13.
47. Kurz, "Responses to Battered Women: Resistance to Medicalization."
48. Ferraro, "Policing Woman Battering."
49. Demie Kurz, "Battering and the Criminal Justice System: A Feminist View," in Eve S. Buzawa and Carl G. Buzawa, eds., *Domestic Violence: The Changing Criminal Justice Response* (Westport, Conn.: Auburn House, 1992).
50. National Resource Center on Domestic Violence, "The Violence against Women Act Analysis Series."

those immigrant women who are currently excluded from protection by the FVO.

Even if the FVO is fully implemented and battered women are given certain protections, however, the welfare law fails to address what poor, battered women, and all poor women, really need to build safe and secure lives. For example, the welfare law severely limits the kind of job training women are able to get, compared to what was provided under its predecessor, the Family Support Act. Education now counts as a "work activity" for only one year, and funding for job training has been cut. Without training and jobs, the poorest women will face extreme hardship, including homelessness. In the following section, I explore the kinds of resources and benefits that battered women, and all poor women, need to provide them with security.

POLICY MEASURES IN SUPPORT OF ABUSED WOMEN ON WELFARE

Although the Personal Responsibility Act does provide protections for battered women through the FVO, in many respects it is a step backward for abused women because in its current form, it does not provide women with the basic social and economic resources they need to rebuild their lives. At the same time that the PRA has stipulated strict work requirements, it provides even fewer resources than the previous welfare system, AFDC, to help poor women get jobs—resources such as education, job training, and child care. Although all women need access to jobs, this welfare law overlooks the fact that many women also need effective job training and education and that the jobs for which poor women are qualified pay little and offer no health care benefits. The new welfare law does provide some money for child care, but it is not adequate; moreover it eliminates the child care entitlement for welfare mothers trying to enter the labor market.

Another important goal of TANF is to get more child support paid to mothers. It is assumed that mothers will be able to support themselves on a combination of income from jobs and from child support paid by the fathers. To increase the rate of receipt of child support, the new welfare system strengthens the child support enforcement system. While tougher child support enforcement is in women's interests, the existing system for providing child support has many limitations. Because of their fear of their former partner's violence, his ability to evade the child support system, or his inability to pay child support, a quarter to a third of mothers who are eligible for child support will still not receive it.[51]

How are poor, single mothers, particularly those who are formerly battered women, going to get the economic security they desperately need so that they can permanently leave violent relationships without falling into poverty? First, we need to change our thinking about citizenship. States should give highest priority not only to the physical safety of all citizens, but also to their economic security. The failure of our policies to support poor, abused women shows how women lack adequate civil and human rights.[52] We must challenge the state to change this situation. First, we need a host of social benefits to increase women's economic independence and enable them to build lives independent of their abusers. Government social policies need to provide women with job training and with child care and health care benefits so they can take advantage of this training. Family allowances and income subsidies are also critical for abused women because, as described above, poor women may have difficulty obtaining adequately paying jobs and child support. Women workers also need higher wages. Further, since some women must work part-time to adequately care for their children, we need a strategy of "income packaging" for single mothers, which would help them combine income from work, from assistance programs, and from fathers.[53]

Similarly, the government should adopt a child support assurance system, such as is found in some European countries.[54] Such a system guarantees that if a woman does not receive all the child support she is owed by her child's father, the government will make up the difference to her. Thus, unlike in our system, under a child support assurance system, all children receive child support due to them. This takes a great burden off mothers, who usually find the child support system very difficult to negotiate. Such a system may also help some mothers to keep their distance from abusive fathers.

Finally, the state must be much more aggressive in enforcing laws against violent offenders. The state should also engage in a vigorous ed-

51. Kurz, *For Richer, For Poorer*.
52. Isabel Marcus, "Reframing 'Domestic Violence': Terrorism in the Home," in Martha A. Fineman and Roxanne Mykitiuk eds., *The Public Nature of Private Violence* (New York: Routledge, 1994), 11–35.
53. Roberta Spalter-Roth and Heidi Hartmann, "AFDC Recipients as Care-Givers and Workers: A Feminist Approach to Income Security Policy for American Women," *Social Politics*, 1 no. 2 (Summer 1994): 190–210.
54. Irwin Garfinkel, *Assuring Child Support: An Extension of Social Security* (New York: Russell Sage, 1992).

ucational campaign about violence against women and should encourage major social institutions to do likewise. Employers must initiate campaigns against violence in their businesses and professional organizations and should make it clear that they will not tolerate violence by any employees. Medical insurers, for example, could increase the fees of those who perpetrate violence, a measure that would also make people aware of the wider social costs of violence.[55]

Although rates of male violence are unacceptably high for all women, this is particularly true for poor women, whose poverty can affect their ability to leave relationships. Poor women who do leave violent relationships face the possibility of continuing threats of violence, as they struggle to make new lives and to escape poverty. Government policies provide meager support for women living independently of men. By refusing to make it easier for women to escape male violence, the state in effect condones violence against women. The current direction of social policies should be reversed. Social welfare policies must provide guaranteed assistance to poor women, particularly those who have been abused, and work with them until such time as they are able to support themselves and their children through gainful employment.

This brief examination of male violence toward poor women has shown not only how the violence can have a dramatic and sometimes life-threatening effect on their lives, but also how neglected this topic has been in social policy. It is also neglected in the scholarly literature. Based on a review of articles in key scholarly journals of the family over the last ten years, Thompson and Walker conclude that there is still little recognition of male violence toward female partners in the literature on the family.[56] Similarly, until very recently, the welfare literature has ignored this subject. We must stop compartmentalizing the study of violence and instead look for evidence of domestic violence whenever we study women's lives. Increased recognition of the high rates of male violence experienced by poor women and its consequences for their lives is vital for developing policies that will support poor women, but it is also very important to make sure this fact isn't used against poor women and men. Many conservative thinkers, and probably many mainstream ones as well, would happily use the fact that poor women experience high rates

55. Cohen, "Private Violence and Public Obligation."
56. Linda Thompson and Alexis J. Walker, "The Place of Feminism in Family Studies," *Journal of Marriage and the Family* 57 (November 1995): 847–865.

of domestic violence as yet another way to demonize poor men as villainous and poor women as hopeless victims. Men from all races and classes can commit violence against women, and women from all races and classes can experience violence. Not all women who are abused need special attention because of the abuse. What poor women need is a means to break free from abusers. What all women need is the ability to live independently of male support.

CHAPTER SEVEN

Welfare's Ban on Poor Motherhood

Dorothy Roberts

The Personal Responsibility and Work Opportunity Reconciliation Act of 1996 (PRA) executed welfare's new social role: government aid to the poor is no longer seen as charity but as a means of modifying their behavior. The chief behavior to be reformed by the new policies is poor women's mothering. Welfare reform is an assault on the right of poor women to be mothers. Programs adopted by a majority of states seek to curtail the birthrate of women on welfare and make it difficult, if not impossible, for many of them to care for the children they have. Work requirements enforce the disparate values placed on the domestic labor of poor and middle-class women. They proclaim the message that poor women are fit only for performing menial care of other people's children and are not entitled to care properly for their own. This devaluation will have tragic material consequences for many poor families: as poor women are forced to mother under increasingly harsh conditions, some will lose custody of their children to foster care and state institutions.

The ferocity of this assault on mothers can only be explained by the long-standing degradation of Black motherhood in the dominant American culture.[1] Beginning with the brutal denial of slave women's maternal rights, many white Americans have viewed Black mothers as less fit, less caring, and less hurt by separation from their children. Because welfare reform measures disproportionately disrupt Black families, who are perceived to be the majority of welfare recipients, they have become the principal tool for perpetuating this oppressive legacy.

I would like to thank Dominique Day for her excellent research assistance.
1. See generally Dorothy Roberts, *Killing the Black Body: Race, Reproduction, and the Meaning of Liberty* (New York: Pantheon, 1997).

Discouraging Procreation

One of the goals of welfare reformers is to reduce the number of children born to women receiving public assistance. During the 1990s, state legislators proposed a number of avenues to pressure women on welfare to have fewer children. The most benign measure has been to make Norplant and other long-acting contraceptives available to poor women in every state through medicaid. At a time when legislatures nationwide were slashing programs for the poor, states spent millions of dollars providing expensive birth control methods to medicaid recipients. Some lawmakers proposed adding extra incentives to prevent welfare mothers from conceiving. Several introduced bills that would offer women on welfare a financial bonus to use Norplant. Yet others proposed the more coercive measure of mandating Norplant insertion as a condition for receiving future benefits.

Finally, many states passed laws denying any increase in payments for children born to women who are already receiving public assistance. States typically determine a standard of family need according to the number of family members, sources of income, and other factors. The birth of a new baby to a family on welfare used to increase the total payment the family received by a prescribed increment. Child exclusion laws, however, deny this new birth benefit increase for children born or conceived while the mother is receiving aid. Although the most draconian birth-deterring provisions failed to become law, child exclusion policies, popularly known as "family caps," are permitted by the PRA and are widely accepted. In the four years before the PRA was passed, twenty states enacted family caps. The Clinton administration routinely approved state requests for federal waivers of AFDC eligibility requirements to put family caps in place and vigorously defended these measures in the press and federal court.

Child exclusion laws are explicitly designed to keep mothers on welfare from having more children. They are based on the erroneous assumption that the promise of a meager increase in benefits encourages women on welfare to have additional children. These laws reflect a national consensus that the government has no obligation to support poor women's decision to have children or to sustain the children that poor women have. More troubling, they enforce the view that childbearing by poor women is pathological and should be deterred through social policy. Poor mothers violate the middle-class norm of childbearing that holds that it is irresponsible to have children when one cannot afford to support them. Politicians typically couch their defense of family caps in terms of taxpayers' rights to withhold payment for other people's reproductive choices. Florida Republican Rick Dantzler, for example, asked rhetorically, "Does a man have the right to impregnate a woman and does that woman have the right to bear a child knowing Uncle Sam will pick up all the responsibility? Do they have a constitutional right to do that and make us pay for it?" This way of framing the issue avoids the question of why taxpayers have the right to use welfare policy to regulate poor women's procreative lives.

The new child exclusion laws are reminiscent of attempts by Southern legislators in earlier decades to limit the fertility of poor Black women in their states. These proposals focused on out-of-wedlock births and were advocated in explicitly racial terms. As their economies became increasingly mechanized, southern states found that Blacks were no longer as useful as a source of cheap, unskilled labor. Schemes to lower the Black birthrate were seen as a way to reduce Blacks' welfare burden and to force Blacks to migrate to the North. In 1958, for example, Mississippi state representative David H. Glass introduced a bill mandating sterilization for any unmarried mother who gave birth to another illegitimate child. Glass explained that his objective was to reduce the number of Black children on welfare: "During the calendar year 1957, there were born out-of-wedlock in Mississippi more than 7,000 negro children, and about 200 white children. The negro woman, because of child welfare assistance, [is] making it a business in some cases of giving birth to illegitimate children. . . . The purpose of my bill was to try to stop, or slow down, such traffic at its source." [2]

Bills denying additional welfare benefits to women who had more than two children or conditioning future payments on their sterilization were introduced in several states during the 1970s.

The claim that welfare creates a financial incentive for recipients to have more children is refuted by empirical studies and common sense. It would be completely irrational for a mother on welfare to assume the tremendous costs and burdens of caring for an additional child given the meager increase in benefits that results. The vast majority of women on welfare have only one or two children. This does not mean, however, that government funding schemes have no effect on poor women's reproductive decisions. Welfare may not induce childbearing by indigent women, but refusing to provide welfare might discourage it. The availability of

---

2. Julius Paul, "The Return of Punitive Sterilization Proposals: Current Attacks on Illegitimacy and the AFDC Program," 3 *Law and Society Review* (1968): 77, 89.

public assistance lessens the burden that poor mothers would otherwise have to bear and therefore reduces the incentive to take every possible precaution against pregnancy. We can predict that family caps will achieve, to some extent, their desired end—deterring some welfare recipients from having children. For some women this will mean using failsafe and risky forms of birth control such as Norplant, Depo Provera, and sterilization. For some of those who become pregnant, it will mean getting an abortion.

Although it is too early to determine conclusively the impact of child exclusion laws, there is some evidence that they affect reproductive practices. A Rutgers University study of the New Jersey family cap law found a significant effect on the rate of abortions and births among women on welfare.[3] It found a decline in the number of births, with welfare recipients having 14,000 fewer children in the four years after the family cap was enacted compared with what would be expected due to trend and population composition changes. It also concluded that the law contributed to an increase of 1,400 abortions among women on welfare over expected rates. The law constrained Black women's reproductive decisions more than those of any other group. Abortions among Black women on welfare exceeded births from March 1993, five months after the family cap went into effect, until September 1996.[4]

Current constitutional jurisprudence provides poor mothers little protection against government attempts to manipulate their procreative decisions. In *C.K. v. Shalala*, a federal class action lawsuit filed against the Secretary of Health and Human Services in 1994, several New Jersey welfare recipients challenged the government's authorization of the country's first family cap law. Judge Nicholas H. Politan rejected the plaintiffs' contention that the law violated their constitutional right to reproductive liberty. He reasoned that the law furthered New Jersey's legitimate interest in promoting individual responsibility and stabilizing family structure. Judge Politan did not see the family cap as a penalty for childbearing. Rather, he believed that the law "puts the welfare household in the same situation as that of a working family, which does not automatically receive a wage increase every time it produces another child."

Judge Politan's decision simply extended the U.S. Supreme Court's jurisprudence on the constitutional liberties of welfare recipients. Privacy doctrine, which is supposed to protect citizens' intimate decisions about

---

3. Jennifer Preston, "With New Jersey Family Cap, Births Fall and Abortions Rise," *New York Times*, November 3, 1998, A29.
4. Associated Press, "Jersey Welfare Law Tied to Fewer Babies," *San Francisco Chronicle*, June 9, 1998, A7.

their families, does not shield people on welfare from government interference or give them any affirmative claim to government assistance. Shortly after the *Roe v. Wade* decision ensured women's constitutional right to an abortion, the Court held that the Constitution did not require the government to pay for abortions for poor women. Because poor women are not entitled to government support, the Court has reasoned, the government may force them to comply with standards of sexual and reproductive morality to qualify for benefits. On numerous occasions the Court has upheld welfare regulations that determine eligibility for benefits based on household composition, despite their negative effects on families' chosen living arrangements.

Child exclusion policies, however, do penalize reproductive decisions the government disapproves. The state denies benefits only to children who are born or conceived while their mothers are on welfare. "Family cap," then, is a misnomer because the laws do not put an absolute ceiling on the number of children in a family who may receive benefits. Rather, they exclude only children born to mothers who are already on welfare. What is discouraged is not having too many children, but having any children at all while on welfare. These laws achieve the same end as a government fine assessed against welfare mothers for each additional child that they have. But because they work indirectly, they are not seen to pose a constitutional problem.

Judge Politan's reasoning also displayed incredible blindness to the difficulty poor mothers have in caring for their children. Welfare, unlike working people's salaries, is geared toward a family's minimal needs. Families receiving government aid are already living in poverty. The new birth increment does not bring the family out of poverty; it merely adjusts the benefits to minimally accommodate the additional child. Moreover, working families also receive government benefits, in the form of earned income tax credits, tax exemptions, and child care credits, that subsidize the cost of an additional child. It is ludicrous to think that a middle-class family with a new baby is in the same situation as a mother receiving public assistance. Far from "equalizing" the circumstances of poor and middle-class mothers, family caps send their worlds spiraling even farther apart.

THE VALUE OF WELFARE MOTHERS' WORK

In addition to discouraging childbirth, the second central tenet of welfare reform is requiring mothers to leave home for paid employment.

This aspect of the new law also devalues the mothering performed by women on welfare. While family caps interfere with the right to bear children, work requirements interfere with the right of women to maintain a relationship with the children they have. Even women with babies may be required to work part-time to keep their benefits. Work requirements for welfare mothers with young children reflect an inability to see the value in their care for their children.[5] The devaluation of welfare mothers' work is reflected as well in behavior modification programs designed to reform poor women's lifestyles—programs that assume that poor mothers need moral supervision.[6]

Why do reformers focus on welfare mothers' dependence on public assistance rather than on their children's dependence on them for care? This focus certainly reflects a radical departure from the original welfare policy toward mothers and the contemporary view of middle-class mothers' role. The logic that propelled "widows' pensions," championed by women activists in the late nineteenth century, was precisely the opposite of that backing contemporary work requirements: widowed mothers needed government aid so that they would not have to relinquish their maternal duties in the home to join the wage labor force.

The depreciation of welfare mothers' care giving work also contradicts attitudes toward middle-class mothers. While it is widely assumed that single welfare mothers should take paid jobs outside the home, more affluent mothers are expected to stay home full-time to care for their children and to depend on their husband's income to meet their financial needs. Katherine Teghtsoonian's textual analysis of child care policy debates in the late 1980s reveals this stark disparity in the value placed on different mothers' care giving.[7] Teghtsoonian found that conservative opponents of the Act for Better Child Care Services (the ABC bill), which extended public support for out-of-home child care, "articulated a strongly held belief that full-time care by mothers is the best arrangement for children and that government policy ought to be facilitating it."[8] They expressed their preference for full-time motherhood by criticizing child care centers as well as women with children who worked outside the home. Even some Democratic supporters of the ABC bill conceded that full-time maternal care was best for children, but that out-

5. Gwendolyn Mink, *Welfare's End* (Ithaca: Cornell University Press, 1998).
6. See generally Lucy A. Williams, "The Ideology of Division: Behavior Modification Welfare Reform Proposals," 102 *Yale Law Journal* (1992): 719.
7. Katherine Teghtsoonian, "The Work of Caring for Children: Contradictory Themes in American Child Care Policy Debates," *Women & Politics* 17, no. 2 (1997): 77.
8. Ibid., 83–84.

of-home child care services were critical for women forced into paid employment by economic necessity.

This support for full-time motherhood was reserved for middle-class women alone, however. The conservative congressmen excluded mothers receiving AFDC benefits from their support of full-time care giving. According to Teghtsoonian, "[t]he prescription for these women who are poor, without husbands, and racially coded black in American public discourse was *not* full-time motherhood, but mandatory labor force participation, with their children placed in out-of-home child care contexts while they are at work."[9] Advocates of the ABC bill took advantage of this devaluation of welfare recipients' mothering to garner support for child care funding. Because child care was viewed as a service for needy mothers rather than a universal social program, however, it failed to receive adequate federal support.

Part of the reason that maternalist rhetoric applies only to middle-class women and can no longer justify public financial support is that the public views this support as benefiting primarily Black mothers. The dominant society devalues Black mothers' work in particular because it sees these mothers as inherently unfit and even affirmatively harmful to their children. There is little reason, then, to support their care giving work at home. To the contrary, contemporary poverty rhetoric blames single mothers, and especially Black single mothers, for perpetuating poverty by transmitting a deviant lifestyle to their children. Far from helping children, this view holds, payments to Black single mothers merely encourage this transgenerational pathology.

Spiritual and Menial Housework

The devaluation of welfare mothers' work reflects what I have called the dichotomy between spiritual and menial housework.[10] This dichotomy exists within the nineteenth-century ideology that distinguishes between work in the public sphere, associated with men, and work in the private sphere to which women were consigned. Just as persistent as the *gendered* division of labor into market and domestic work is the *racialized* division of domestic labor into spiritual and menial work.

9. Ibid., 89.
10. Dorothy E. Roberts, "Spiritual and Menial Housework," 9 *Yale Journal of Law and Feminism* (1997): 51. I define housework to include household chores and care for children and other family members.

The "cult of domesticity" legitimized the confinement of women to the private sphere by defining women as suited for motherhood (and unsuited for public life) because of their moral or spiritual nature. Household labor, however, is not all spiritual. It involves nasty, tedious physical tasks—standing over a hot stove, cleaning toilets, scrubbing stains off floors and out of shirts, changing diapers and bed pans. The notion of a purely spiritual domesticity could be maintained only by cleansing housework of its menial parts. The ideological separation of home from market, then, dictated the separation of spiritual and menial housework. Spiritual housework is valued highly because it is thought to be essential to the proper functioning of the household and the moral upbringing of children. Menial housework is devalued because it is strenuous and unpleasant and is thought to require little moral or intellectual skill.

While the ideological opposition of home and work distinguishes men from women, the ideological distinction between spiritual and menial housework fosters inequality among women. This is because spiritual housework is associated with privileged white women, and menial housework is associated with minority, immigrant, and white, working-class women. Housework has always been women's work, but polishing floors, scrubbing clothes, and tending to children for pay has been seen as Black and other minority women's work. Even as aspects of housework have shifted from the home to the market—to day care centers, fast-food restaurants, maid services, nursing homes, and recreation facilities—women of color continue to fill a disproportionate share of the menial jobs.[11] Not only has the assignment of household work to women persisted in the face of monumental changes in the workplace, but so has the racialized distinction between spiritual and menial housework.

An early example of the spiritual/menial dichotomy is embodied in the relationship between Mammy and her mistress. The image of Mammy was that of a rotund, hankerchiefed house servant who humbly nursed her master's children. Mammy was both the perfect mother and the perfect slave; whites saw her as a "passive nurturer, a mother figure who gave all without expectation of return, who not only acknowledged her inferiority to whites but who loved them."[12] It is important to recognize, however, that Mammy did not reflect any virtue in *Black* motherhood. The ideology of Mammy placed no value on Black women as

---

11. Evelyn Nakano Glenn, "Cleaning Up/Kept Down: A Historical Perspective on Racial Inequality in 'Women's Work,'" 43 *Stanford Law Review* (1991): 1333, 1347–53.
12. bell hooks, *Ain't I A Woman: Black Women and Feminism* (Boston: South End Press, 1991): 84–85.

mothers of their *own* children. Rather, whites claimed Mammy's total de-
votion to the master's children, without regard to the fate of Mammy's
own offspring. Moreover, Mammy, while caring for the master's children, remained under the constant supervision of her white mistress.[13]
She had no real authority over either the white children she raised or the
Black children she bore. Mammy's domestic labor is the perfect illustration of menial housework; her mistress, on the other hand, performed
the spiritual work in the house.

A scene from the hit movie *The First Wives' Club* provides a contemporary example of the spiritual housewife's relationship to menial housework. The character played by Diane Keaton complains to her friends
about the work she did for her ex-husband: "I washed his shorts, I ironed
them, and I starched them." "You did?" her friends respond in amaze-
ment. "Well, I *supervised*," Keaton clarifies. The affluent housewife main-
tains her spiritual stature by supervising the menial labor of less privileged women.

Even more devastating than having to do the dirty work is the dominant society's denial that these minority women are capable of spiritual
housework. Dominant images have long depicted Black mothers as unfit,
uncaring, and immoral—just the opposite of a spiritual mother. All the
mythical figures of Black womanhood—Mammy, the sexually licentious
Jezebel, the home-wrecking matriarch, the cheating welfare queen—
were incredibly bad mothers. The evening news typically reports stories
about the depravity of the class of mothers who are assigned menial
household tasks, not their valuable care of their own children and homes.
With welfare reform, the very right of these women to be mothers at all
is increasingly under attack.

The availability of a class of menial workers, sustained by race and class
subordination, makes the division of women's housework possible. In addition to the ideological forces that distinguish between menial and spiritual domestic workers, welfare policy reinforces the racialized division of
housework. Domestics were excluded from the New Deal social welfare
laws. Northern Democrats struck a deal with their Southern brethren
that systematically denied Blacks eligibility for social insurance benefits.[14] During the 1960s, congressional debate over adding mandatory
work provisions to the welfare laws included white people's interest in
keeping poor Black mothers available for cheap domestic service. As Sen-

13. See Elizabeth Fox-Genovese, *Within the Plantation Household: Black and White Women of the
Old South* (Chapel Hill: University of North Carolina Press, 1988): 292.
14. See Jill Quadagno, *The Color of Welfare: How Racism Undermined the War on Poverty* (New
York: Oxford, 1995): 20–22.

ator Russell Long argued in 1967, "[E]ither I do the housework or Mrs. Long does the housework, or we get somebody to come in and help us, but someone has to do it, and it does seem to me that if we can qualify these people to accept any employment doing something constructive, that is better than simply having them sitting at home drawing welfare money."[15] Five years later, Southern white politicians similarly helped to defeat the Family Assistance Plan, which provided for a guaranteed income, by arguing, "There's not going to be anybody left to roll these wheelbarrows and press these shirts."[16]

The new welfare reform policies perpetuate this trend. They continue to devalue welfare mothers' spiritual work in their homes and to push these women into menial housework for others. At the same time that welfare reform rhetoric disparages welfare mothers' spirituality, it proposes that poor women take up menial housework for others. A recent cartoon by Wasserman in the *Boston Globe* suggests this motivation behind work requirements. It shows a politician holding a document labeled "Welfare Reform" while talking to a woman accompanied by her two young children:

Politician: "You are a bad mother."
Welfare mother: "Why?"
Politician: "You hang around the house taking care of the kids. We'll cut you off if you don't take a job."
Welfare mother: "Doing what?"
Politician: "Taking care of someone else's kids."[17]

Putting welfare mothers to work in day care centers was proposed as the new welfare law was debated. A 1995 *Washington Times* editorial suggested that welfare mothers with small children "can work in day care centers, tending their own children while caring for the children of other working mothers."[18] The National Governors Association's policy statement on welfare reform recommended that welfare recipients work in child care facilities as one of several transitional jobs used to move these women into private, unsubsidized work.[19] Mothers receiving benefits under Temporary Assistance to Needy Families (TANF) may meet their

15. Quoted by Judith Olans Brown et al., "The Mythogenesis of Gender: Judicial Images of Women in Paid and Unpaid Labor," 6 *UCLA Women's Law Journal* (1996): 457, 487 n. 134.
16. Quadagno, 130.
17. "Wasserman's View," *Boston Globe*, September 25, 1995, 10.
18. "How to Reform Welfare Sensibly and Humanely," *Washington Times*, March 23, 1995, A18.
19. Andrew Mollison, "Feds Go Back to the Drawing Board for Welfare Reform," *Austin American-Statesman*, January 7, 1995, A19.

work requirements by caring for the children of other TANF mothers who are participating in community service activities.[20] So many states have adopted this idea of using welfare reform to fill child care needs that a third of child care centers surveyed in five cities now employ welfare recipients who are satisfying work requirements.[21] Eighty percent of the for-profit chains, which pay the lowest wages, employed welfare recipients.

Of course, child care is an important and potentially fulfilling job. But there are several troubling aspects of the transition of mothers from welfare into paid care giving work. Child care workers are one of the lowest-paid professions in the nation: family day care providers earn an average of $13,000 per year and the mean annual salary for child care workers is only $12,058.[22] Entry-level child care jobs pay an even lower rate of $6.00 per hour, or $10,500 per year.[23] A third of child care programs, moreover, offer no health insurance to their employees. Unskilled women receiving welfare are typically hired as the lowest-paid assistants at day care centers offering the lowest wages.[24] Most centers that hire welfare recipients do not provide any on-site training. The more prestigious and well-paid teaching positions are reserved for women with college degrees and professional training.

What happens to the children of welfare recipients who leave home for paid employment? Welfare programs typically do not provide adequate child care services for mothers who move off welfare by taking child care and other jobs. The only work available to women on welfare is often the night shift at faraway locations, compounding the difficulty of finding child care. And they are the clients of child care chains that hire other untrained, low-paid women as workers with high turnover rates. Underlying this arrangement is the assumption that children from poor families, unlike those with affluent parents, do not deserve or require supervision by child care providers who are trained in early childhood education or who have chosen child care as their vocation.

In fact, the new welfare law affirmatively made finding affordable child care more difficult for poor women. The PRA eliminated the federal statutory guarantee for three important child care programs—entitlement programs that had ensured child care assistance to recipients of

20. Gong, 1053.
21. Tamar Lewin, "From Welfare Roll to Child Care Worker," *New York Times*, April 29, 1998, A14.
22. Gong, 1053.
23. Lewin, "From Welfare Roll to Child Care Worker."
24. Ibid.

Aid to Families with Dependent Children (AFDC) participating in work programs, to employed parents transitioning off AFDC, and to low-income working parents at risk of becoming dependent on AFDC if child care were not subsidized.[25] Federal funds for child care are now capped, and states have broad discretion to determine which families qualify for child care benefits under the federal block grant. The increase in federal spending on child care will not match the influx of poor mothers entering the workforce.

THE THREAT TO PARENTAL RIGHTS

Welfare reform not only demeans poor mothers ideologically; it also concretely threatens their relationships with their children. To be sure, some mothers will leave the welfare rolls for paid employment that improves their children's living conditions. But new measures make it more difficult for many other mothers to take care of their children in several ways: they reduce the amount of cash assistance to families; they cut off payments altogether to some families; and they require mothers to work and to participate in job training, counseling, and other programs without adequate child care. What will happen to the children of mothers who fail to meet new work rules because of child care or transportation problems, who are unable to find work within the two-year time limit, or who leave their children at home without adequate care while they participate in required work programs? It is likely that many of them will be removed from their mother's custody and placed in foster care.[26] One California county imposes "full family" sanctions for a mother's failure to comply with program requirements, cutting off payments for the children. The termination of benefits, in turn, triggers a mandatory home visit by a welfare caseworker, who may then notify child protective services.[27]

Some advocates of work requirements anticipated welfare mothers' loss of custody by promoting the use of institutional arrangements for poor children. Indeed, depriving poor women of parental rights appeared to be the goal of some politicians. Republican Speaker of the

25. Jo Ann C. Gong, "Child Care in the Wake of the Federal Welfare Act," 30 *Clearinghouse Review* 1044, 1044 (January–February 1997).
26. Jean Tepperman, "Welfare to Foster Care?" *Children's Advocate* (November–December 1998): 3.
27. Personal Communication with Martha Matthews, Staff Attorney, National Center for Youth Law (January 1998).

House Newt Gingrich, for example, argued that government funds going to children born to welfare mothers should be diverted to programs
that would put their babies up for adoption or place them in orphan-
ages.[28] These suggestions promoted the notion that poor children are
better off under state supervision than under their parents' care.

Black children, already overrepresented in the foster care population,
are at greatest risk for removal. Almost half the children in foster care are
Black, and the percentages are even higher in major cities such as Chicago and New York. Black children enter foster care at higher rates and
remain there longer than white children. Racism and cultural bias have
long led case workers to misinterpret Black family patterns as neglect.
The historic disrespect for the integrity of Black families helps to make
reform efforts that favor removing poor children from their homes and
placing them in institutions seem to be natural solutions to children's
poverty.

In addition to the provisions that throw many children deeper into
poverty, the PRA contains a number of features that appear calculated to
separate poor children from their families. Under the TANF block grant,
states are no longer required to pay benefits to relatives who care for poor
children. Like parents, relatives may be cut off from aid if they fail to find
work in time. Some recipients caring for a relative's child may return the
child to foster care rather than undergo the added burdens of job-related
requirements or community service. Curley Barron was forced to send
her niece and nephew back to foster care when she refused to participate
in a mandatory work program and lost the $435 in cash payments and
food stamps Mississippi had paid her.[29] Barron's care for her ailing
mother and brother, in addition to the children she took in, made it impossible to perform the thirty-five hours of weekly service the state demanded. Mississippi now spends more money—$510 a month—to sup-
port the children in foster care. Agencies may now be more reluctant to
place children with relatives who are not economically self-sufficient.[30]

Welfare reform also makes it more difficult for mothers who have lost
custody of their children to get them back. TANF cuts off aid to parents
for children who are away from home for more than forty-five days. This
hardly gives mothers whose children are temporarily placed in foster care

28. "GOP Welfare Plan Would Take Cash from Unwed Mothers to Aid Adoptions," *Chicago Trib-
une,* November 14, 1994, A7.
29. Jason DeParle, "Welfare Law Weighs Heavily on Delta, Where Jobs Are Few," *New York Times,*
October 16, 1997, A1.
30. Mark Hardin, Sizing up the Welfare Act's Impact on Child Protection, 30 *Clearinghouse Review* (January–February 1997): 1061, 1066.

time to correct the neglect that led to the removal. If anything, the loss of benefits may cause the mother to be evicted from her home, run out of food, and lose other resources needed for reunification with her children.

Along with work requirements and benefit reductions that make children vulnerable to child welfare intervention, the new welfare law contains provisions that affect funding of child welfare programs. Some of the new funding policies also promote disruption of poor families. The PRA leaves federal funds for foster care and adoption assistance as an uncapped entitlement while reducing and capping federal funds for cash assistance to families and for child protective services that support families.[31] The availability of federal matching funds for foster care may provide a financial incentive for state agencies to move children into foster care. As Jean Tepperman of the Action Alliance for Children warns, "If an economic downturn caused more families to seek welfare, federal funds might run out. Then putting a child in foster care would be the only way the state could get money for the child's support."[32] A child welfare agency faced with a family whose TANF benefits have expired may choose to place the children in out-of-home care rather than find the funds needed to preserve the family.

Consider the effect of this funding scheme on welfare offices' treatment of teen mothers who need public assistance. TANF denies aid to teen mothers not living with parents, adult relatives, or legal guardians. When these homes present a danger to the child, however, the public welfare agency must place the mother in an another adult-supervised arrangement. Federal matching funds may tempt agencies to place these teen mothers in foster care.[33] The TANF provision also increases the need for agencies to investigate teen mothers' homes.

Poor mothers' rights to their children are jeopardized further by the interaction of the new welfare law and other recent state and federal reforms concerning poor parents. A year after the PRA was enacted, President Clinton signed the Adoption and Safe Families Act, designed to double the number of children adopted annually by 2002. The new adoption law represents a dramatic shift in federal child welfare philosophy from an emphasis on the reunification of children in foster care with their biological families toward the adoption of these children into new

31. Rob Green and Shelley Waters, *The Impact of Welfare Reform on Child Welfare Financing* (Washington, D.C.: The Urban Institute, 1997).
32. Jean Tepperman, "Foster Care: The Last Entitlement," *Children's Advocate* (November–December 1998): 4.
33. Hardin, 1065.

families. The federal law directs state authorities to make the health and safety of children in foster care their priority rather than reuniting families. The rejection of family reunification is implemented through swifter timetables for terminating the rights of biological parents to free children for adoption and the removal of other barriers to adoption. The act requires states to begin termination proceedings if a child has been in state custody for fifteen of the last twenty-two months. Thus, the new law shortens the time allowed for parents to regain custody of their children to accelerate adoptions of children.

Of course, the state should facilitate adoptions of children where there is no hope of family reunification. The act's impact, however, may be to permanently separate poor children from families that might have been preserved with adequate state resources. The combination of welfare reform's decimation of the federal safety net for children and adoption reform's abandonment of the commitment to family preservation escalates the assault on poor mothers.

A local development is also likely to penalize poor mothers forced to work outside the home with inadequate support. In the last decade, a number of states and municipalities have enacted criminal statutes that punish parents for failing to prevent their children from becoming delinquent.[34] The first of these laws, passed by California in 1988 as part of an effort against gang violence, imposes criminal liability on parents who fail to exercise "reasonable care, supervision, protection, and control over their minor child."[35] Some jurisdictions hold parents strictly liable for their children's delinquency. Parental responsibility laws blame mothers for the deprived conditions and the profound race and class biases that make poor minority children more vulnerable to criminal sanctions than youth from white, middle-class families. Perversely, welfare reform further hampers poor mothers' ability to spend time with their children and to protect them from the hazards that often plague poverty-stricken communities.

CREATING A JUST WELFARE SYSTEM

Is it an exaggeration to say that welfare reform bans poor motherhood? Welfare and related laws do not prohibit poor women from having chil-

---

34. Naomi R. Cahn, "Pragmatic Questions about Parental Liability Statutes," 1996 *Wisc. L. Rev.* 399, 405; Paul W. Schmidt, "Note, Dangerous Children and the Regulated Family: The Shifting Focus of Parental Responsibility Laws," 73 *N.Y.U. L. Rev.* 667 (1998).
35. Cal. Penal Code § 272 (West. Supp. 1996).

dren, nor do the laws automatically deprive them of parental rights. Most mothers receiving public assistance will continue to raise their children under the new regime. Yet the convergence of policies that deter mothers on welfare from having more children, that make it more difficult for them to take care of their children, and that shift child welfare resources away from family preservation toward out-of-home placement and adoption constitutes an all-out assault on these mothers. The current welfare system treats poor women, especially those who are Black, as less deserving to become mothers and to have a secure relationship with their children. Creating a welfare system that abolishes the racialized division between women fit only for menial housework and women entitled to do spiritual housework and that values all mothers equally must be a priority for feminists and progressives in the new millennium.

III

Toward a New Welfare Politics?

Aren't Poor Single Mothers Women? Feminists, Welfare Reform, and Welfare Justice

Gwendolyn Mink

When the Personal Responsibility Act of 1996 transformed welfare, it also transformed citizenship. Flouting the ideal of universal citizenship, the act distinguishes poor single mothers from other citizens and subjects them to a separate system of law. Under this system of law, poor single mothers forfeit rights the rest of us enjoy as fundamental to our citizenship—family rights, reproductive rights, and vocational liberty—just because they need welfare. The law continues to injure poor single mothers' rights even after time limits end their access to benefits, for it directs them to forsake child raising for full-time wage earning. Both while they receive benefits and after they lose them, the Personal Responsibility Act (PRA) taxes poor women who have chosen motherhood and endangers their care and custody of children.

The PRA was the most aggressive assault on women's rights in this century. Yet it provoked only scanty protest from the millions of women who call themselves feminists. In fact, during three years of concerted debate leading up to enactment of the new welfare law, most feminists actually supported many of the restrictions contemplated by both the Clinton and the Republican versions of welfare reform. In their various roles as constituents, members of movement organizations, and even elected officials, they endorsed the core principles of welfare reform: child support rules that require welfare mothers to identify and associate with biological fathers even when they do not want to and work requirements that mandate work outside the home even at the expense of children.

The PRA's child support provisions exchange poor single mothers' income support from government with income support from individual men. Forwarding its statutory purpose of "encourag[ing] the formation and maintenance of two-parent families,"[1] the provisions compel each mother to associate not just with any man, but with *the* man the government tells her to: the biological father of her children. In addition to imposing potentially unwanted associations on mothers who need welfare, mandatory sperm-based paternal family headship impairs their sexual and family privacy. Under the PRA's child support provisions, mothers must help government identify biological fathers and locate their whereabouts so that government can collect child support from them. Where a mother is married, the establishment of paternity does not involve too much: paternity is a matter of public record, because the law assumes that a mother's husband at the time of her child's birth is the father, whether or not he is biologically related to the child.[2] Where a mother has not been married, though, it means having to tell a welfare official or a judge about her sex life.[3] It also means that government decides who belongs to welfare mothers' families and what those families should look like.

The PRA's work requirements further injure poor mothers' rights. For one thing, they deny poor mothers' parental choices about whether and how much outside employment is compatible with the needs of children. Further, like the child support provisions, the PRA's work requirements promote mothers' economic dependence on men, not independence through their own income. Sanctioning extramarital child raising, the act provides that where there are *two* parents, one may stay at home to care for children.[4] Where there is only *one* parent, in contrast, the act says she *must* leave her home and children to work for wages. This means that if a poor single mother can't find reliable child care, or wants to raise her own children—if she needs or wants to work *inside* the home—she would be well-advised to get married.[5]

What the new law means by "personal responsibility," then, is not per-

---

1. P.L. 104–193 (The Personal Responsibility and Work Opportunity Act), Title I, Sec. 401 (4).

2. See, e.g., *Michael H. v. Gerald D.* 491 U.S. 110 (1988), discussed in Gwendolyn Mink, *Welfare's End* (Ithaca: Cornell University Press, 1998), 87–93.

3. Renee A. Monson, "State-ing Sex and Gender: Collecting Information from Mothers and Fathers in Paternity Cases," *Gender and Society* 11 (June 1997): 279–296; Lisa Kelly, "If Anybody Asks You Who I Am: An Outsider's Story of the Duty to Establish Paternity," *Yale Journal of Law and Feminism* 6 (Summer 1994), 297–305.

4. P.L. 104–193, Title I, Sec. 407 (c)(1)(B).

5. The Personal Responsibility Act requires states to ease work requirements where "appropriate and affordable" child care is not available. P.L. 104–193, Title I, Sec. 407 (e)(2). However, as the suitability of care is decided by the welfare agency, not the mother, some mothers are compelled to work outside the home even though they do not find their child care arrangements to be acceptable.

sonal responsibility at all. The Personal Responsibility Act makes *government* responsible for how poor mothers lead their lives. Under the act, government tells poor single mothers with whom to associate, under what conditions to have and raise children, and what kind of work is appropriate. These instructions invade poor single mothers' freedom of association and freedom of vocation. They curtail their fundamental rights to sexual privacy and to make parenting decisions about their own children. Association, vocation, privacy, and parenting are basic constitutional rights—rights that are strictly guarded for everyone except mothers who need welfare.

The Personal Responsibility Act contradicts basic feminist axioms about the conditions for women's equality. Feminists long have argued that women's equality pivots on our ability to make independent choices. Constitutionally anchored liberties protect our choices, but we often cannot make them without having the means to do so. For thirty years, welfare was the currency for poor single mothers' choices, however constrained those choices may have been.[6] Once the Supreme Court recognized welfare as an entitlement—a guarantee—to mothers and children based on economic need, poor mothers had the means to decide to not be dependent on particular men or to not risk their own or their children's safety. For these reasons, during the late 1960s and early 1970s, some feminists hailed welfare rights as part of their agenda for women's equality. The connections between welfare rights and women's rights were never widely appreciated, however.

Hence, when the Personal Responsibility Act directly invaded poor single mothers' rights, few feminists regarded that invasion as a problem for *women*. After discussing this observation with an audience at a midwestern university not long ago, I was denounced by a white feminist who called me "the Camille Paglia of welfare reform." She charged me with holding feminists to a higher standard than "other interest groups" and wondered whether I demand "altruism" of feminists because we are women. I was stunned, at first, that a feminist would reduce the women's movement to an "interest group," separate the interests of feminists from those of poor single mothers, and attribute feminist support for poor single mothers to altruism rather than solidarity. As I considered how to respond, however, I realized that my challenger's words recapitulated the position of many feminists during the war against welfare.

6. On the emergence of certain welfare rights and their implication for welfare policy, see Mink, *Welfare's End*, chap. 2.

FEMINISTS AND THE POLITICS OF WELFARE REFORM

Feminists' role in recent welfare politics helps explain the success of reform initiatives, particularly those that substantially curtail the rights of poor mothers. Punitive welfare reform was not accomplished by one political party or by one side of the ideological spectrum. Republicans and Democrats, conservatives and liberals, patriarchalists *and feminists* were in consensus about basic elements of reform, including measures that interfere with the decisional liberties of poor women. Moreover, many feminists agreed with welfare reformers in both parties that welfare isn't "good for" women.

Not all feminists joined the welfare reform consensus, of course. Leaders of many national women's and feminist organizations—groups ranging from the American Association for University Women to the National Organization for Women—loudly and unwaveringly opposed the Personal Responsibility Act. They called press conferences, participated in vigils, appealed to their memberships, and lobbied Congress. Some leaders—like Patricia Ireland—even engaged in dramatic acts of civil disobedience. Other nationally visible feminists—including Gloria Steinem and Betty Friedan—joined the Women's Committee of One Hundred, a feminist mobilization against punitive welfare reform that was organized by feminist scholars and activists. As the cochair of the Women's Committee of One Hundred, I know firsthand that some feminists raised their voices in defense of poor single mothers' rights, including their entitlement to welfare. But I also know that feminist voices were relatively few.

The only national political group focused on welfare reform as problem for women's rights, the Women's Committee of One Hundred tried very hard to mobilize feminists against the PRA. But the millions of women who have made feminism a movement were either indifferent or hostile to our pleas. Sometimes by their silence and sometimes in their deeds, many feminists actually collaborated with punitive welfare reformers.

The feminists I'm talking about form the movement's mainstream. Most are middle-class and white. Many have ties to formal organizations, contributing to NARAL or to Emily's List and participating in local NOW chapters. Others march for abortion rights, work for feminist candidates, or simply vote feminist. Some have high political positions—one is a cabinet secretary, several are members of Congress. Although feminism has many iterations, these feminists often speak for all of feminism. When mobilized, they can wield impressive political clout—creating gender gaps in elections and saving abortion rights, for example. Yet when it came to welfare, for the most part they sat on their hands. Ignoring appeals from sister feminists and welfare rights activists to defend "welfare as a women's issue" and to oppose "the war against poor women" as if it were "a war against *all* women," many even entered the war on the antiwelfare/antiwoman side.[7]

Some examples: on Capitol Hill, all white women in the U.S. Senate —including four Democratic women who call themselves feminists— voted *for* the new welfare law when it first came to the Senate floor in the summer of 1995. In the House of Representatives in 1996, twenty-six of thirty-one Democratic women, all of whom call themselves feminists, voted *for* a Democratic welfare bill that would have stripped recipients of their entitlement to welfare.[8] Meanwhile, across the country, a NOW-Legal Defense and Education Fund appeal for contributions to support an economic justice litigator aroused so much hate mail that NOW-LDEF stopped doing direct mail on the welfare issue.[9]

Feminist members of Congress did not write the Personal Responsibility Act, of course. Nor did members of the National Organization for Women or contributors to Emily's List compose the driving force behind the most brutal provisions of the new welfare law. My claim is not that feminists were uniquely responsible for how welfare has been reformed. My point is that they were uniquely positioned to make a difference. They have made a difference in many arenas across the years, even during inauspicious Republican presidencies. They undid damaging Supreme Court decisions, for example, by helping to win the Civil Rights Restoration Act of 1988 after the Court gutted Title IX in *Grove City College v. Bell*.[10] They even expanded women's rights while George Bush was president: in the Civil Rights Act of 1991, they won women's right to economic and punitive damages in sex discrimination cases. So they certainly could have made a difference under a friendly Democratic president who both needs and enjoys the support of women. Indeed, such feminists as were opposed to welfare reform did make a difference ini-

7. This was the slogan of the Women's Committee of One Hundred. See, e.g., "Why Every Woman in America Should Beware of Welfare Cuts," *New York Times*, August 8, 1995 (full-page ad).
8. Castle-Tanner substitute amendment to H.R. 3734, "The Personal Responsibility and Work Opportunity Act of 1996," *Congressional Record*, July 18, 1996, H7907–H7974.
9. Felicia Kornbluh, "Feminists and the Welfare Debate: Too Little? Too Late?" *dollars and sense* (November/December 1996): 25.
10. *Grove City College v. Bell* 465 U.S. 555 (1984).

tially, in concert with antipoverty groups and children's advocates: President Clinton vetoed the first Republican version of the Personal Responsibility Act in November 1995. Had greater numbers of feminists cared that welfare reform harms poor mothers, we could have pressured the president to repeat his veto when a second bill crossed his desk in August 1996.

But welfare reform did not directly bear on the lives of most feminists and did not directly implicate their rights. The new welfare law did not threaten middle-class women's reproductive choices, or their sexual privacy, or their right to raise their own children, or their occupational freedom. So middle-class feminists did not raise their voices as they would have if, say, abortion rights had been at stake. This gave the green light to feminists in Congress to treat welfare reform as if it didn't affect women. No self-identified feminist in Congress would dare to ignore issues deemed important for women. Just watch C-Span whenever abortion rights are on the table: dozens of congresswomen crowd the well, each eager to prove her mettle as a defender of reproductive choice. By contrast, although many anguished over the fate of poor children, few rose to defend poor single *mothers* against welfare reform, notwithstanding its impact on poor women's right to choose motherhood.

Silence among feminists was not the only problem. At the same time feminists were generally silent about the effects of new welfare provisions on poor women's rights, some were quite outspoken about the need to reform welfare so as to improve the personal and family choices poor single mothers make. When feminists did talk about welfare as a women's issue, it often seemed that they were more concerned with reconciling welfare with feminism than with defending poor single mothers' right to receive it. Feminists I've talked to in communities and feminists I've listened to in Congress often reiterated the assumptions of welfare reformers: that welfare has promoted single mother's dependency on government rather than independence in the labor market; that it has discouraged poor women from practicing fertility control; and that it has compensated for the sexual and paternal irresponsibility of individual men.

Without a doubt, welfare never has been very nice to women, or congruent with feminism. Its goal never has been to enhance women's independence or to honor the full range of women's choices. Benefits always have been conditional and stigmatized, forcing poor mothers both to conform to government's rules and to suffer suspicion that they cheat on those rules. Critiques of social control are not what lie behind most feminists' reservations about defending poor women's entitlement to welfare, however.

The welfare debate focused on the deficiencies of welfare mothers, rather than on the deficiencies of the welfare system. It trafficked in the tropes of "illegitimacy," and "pathology," and "dependency," and "irresponsibility," to deepen disdain toward mothers who need welfare. Feminists did not dispute the terms of the debate, although many tried to soften it. In Congress, feminists called for more generous funding for child care, for example. This would ease the effects of mothers' wage work on many poor families; but it did not contest the premise that poor single mothers should be forced to work outside the home. Hence, feminists did not fight for a policy that would enable poor mothers to make independent and honorable choices about what kind of work they will do and how many children they will have and whether they will marry. If anything, many feminists agreed with conservatives that welfare mothers do not make good choices.

Feminist reservations about welfare mothers' choices strengthened the bipartisan consensus that there's something wrong with mothers who need welfare and that cash assistance should require their reform. The two pillars of the new welfare law—work and paternal family headship—were born from this consensus. The harshness of the law's work requirements and the brutality of its sanctions against nonmarital child rearing by mothers may be Republican and patriarchal in execution. But the law's emphasis on women's labor market participation and on men's participation in families were Democratic and feminist in inspiration.

PATERNITY ESTABLISHMENT AND CHILD SUPPORT

Feminists left their boldest imprint on the paternity establishment and child support provisions of the Personal Responsibility Act. For quite some time, feminists in Congress, like feminists across the country, have been emphatic about "making fathers pay" for children through increased federal involvement in the establishment and enforcement of child support orders.[11] When Republicans presented a welfare bill with-

11. Congresswoman Barbara Kennelly (D-Connecticut) played a crucial role in winning strengthened child support enforcement provisions in welfare law in the mid-1980s. She and other feminist congressmembers also have sponsored stand-alone child support enforcement bills, especially to improve collections across state lines and to toughen penalties on delinquent fathers.

out child support provisions, several feminist congresswomen embarrassed Republicans into adopting them.[12]

The child support provisions impose stringent national conditions on nonmarital child rearing by poor women. The first condition is the mandatory establishment of paternity. Welfare law stipulates that a mother's eligibility for welfare depends on her willingness to reveal the identity of her child's father. Since the purpose of paternity establishment is to assign child support obligations to biological fathers, the second condition is that mothers who need welfare must cooperate in establishing, modifying, and enforcing the support orders for their children. The law requires states to reduce a family's welfare grant by at least 25 percent when a mother fails to comply with these rules and permits states to deny the family's grant altogether.[13]

The "deadbeat dad" thesis—the argument that mothers are poor because fathers are derelict—is quite popular among middle-class feminists, as it is among the general public. Finding the costs of child bearing that fall disproportionately on women a wellspring of gender inequality, many feminists want men to provide for their biological children. Incautious pursuit of this objective aligned middle-class feminists behind a policy that endangers the rights of poor single mothers.

Paternity establishment rules compel nonmarital mothers to disclose private matters in exchange for cash and medical assistance—to answer questions like with whom did you sleep? how often? when? where? how? Meanwhile, child support rules require nonmarital mothers to associate with biological fathers, and in so doing to stoke such fathers' claims to parental rights. In these and other ways, paternity establishment and child support provisions set poor single mothers apart from other mothers, subjecting them to stringent legal requirements because of their class and marital status. The provisions beef up services that deserted middle-class mothers may *choose* to enlist—hiring registries and interstate enforcement mechanisms, for example. But they *impose* such services on—and compel intimate revelations from—poor mothers who have chosen to parent alone.

Middle-class feminist interest in vigorous child support enforcement is part of a vision of gender justice. According to this vision, men ought to be held responsible for the procreative consequences of their access to women's bodies. The quest for fairness in procreative relations drives

---

12. See, e.g., "Remarks of Mrs. Kennelly," *Congressional Record,* January 31, 1995, H895; "Remarks of Mrs. Woolsey," *Congressional Record,* February 1, 1995, H1031.
13. P.L. 104–193, Title I, Sec. 408 (a) (2).

the increasingly punitive proposals designed to force fathers to meet their obligations to children. But it doesn't explain why middle-class feminists think that coercing mothers is an acceptable way to make fathers responsible.

We can look to congressional debates about welfare and child support for some clues. The debates show that most feminist legislators didn't really notice that the child support provisions are coercive for poor, never-married mothers. When they spoke about child support they either referred to their own class and marital experiences or to the experiences of women like them. When middle-class women think of the circumstances that might lead them to welfare, they think of divorce—from middle-class men who might have considerable financial resources to share with their children.

California Congresswoman Lynn Woolsey is a case in point. Something of a Beltway icon during the welfare debate, she described herself and was described by others as "a typical welfare mother." Thirty years earlier, she had had to turn to welfare following her divorce from a man she describes as "very successful." [14] Though she had a support order, she "never received a penny in child support." [15] So she had had to turn to welfare. Despite this, she built a successful career and was elected to Congress. Woolsey's story provided a useful strategic intervention into the welfare debate, countering the stereotypic image of welfare mothers as Black and unmarried. But her story, however uplifting, is not representative of most mothers who need welfare. Treating it as representative permitted feminists in Congress to either miss or ignore the very serious ways in which the PRA's child support and paternity provisions sacrifice poor mothers' rights.

The compulsory features of paternity establishment and child support enforcement may be unremarkable to a divorced mother with a support order: she escapes compulsion by choosing to pursue child support, and what matters to her is that the support order be enforced. But some mothers do not have support orders because they do not want them. A mother may not want to identify her child's father because she may fear abuse for herself or her child. She may not want to seek child support because she has chosen to parent alone—or with someone else. She may know her child's father is poor and may fear exposing him to harsh penal-

14. Congresswoman Lynn Woolsey (D-California), "Remarks," in Gwendolyn Mink, ed., *Women and Welfare Reform: Women's Poverty, Women's Opportunities, and Women's Welfare*, Conference Proceedings, Institute for Women's Policy Research (October 23, 1993).
15. "Remarks of Mrs. Woolsey," H1031.

ties when he cannot pay what a court tells him he owes.[16] She may consider his emotional support for his child to be worth more than the $100 the state might collect and that she will never see.[17]

"Making fathers pay" may promote the economic and justice interests of many custodial mothers. But *making mothers* make fathers pay means making mothers pay for subsistence with their own rights—and safety. The issue is not whether government should assist mothers in collecting payments from fathers. Of course it should. Neither is the issue whether child support enforcement provisions in welfare policy help mothers who have or desire child support awards. Of course they do. Nor is the issue whether it is a good thing for children to have active fathers—of course it can be. The issue is coercion, coercion directed toward the mother who doesn't conform to patriarchal conventions—whether by choice or from necessity. It is also coercion directed toward the mother whose deviation from patriarchal norms has been linked to her racial and cultural standing.

Paternity establishment and child support became strategies for welfare reform not because of the unjust effects of divorce on mothers but because of the allegedly unsavory behavior of mothers of nonmarital children. It is nonmarital childbearing, not divorce, that has been blamed for social pathologies like crime and dependency. The preamble to the new welfare law legislates precisely this point of view. Such patriarchal reasoning leaches into racial argument, as welfare discourse specifically correlates nonmarital childbearing rates among African Americans with social and moral decay.[18]

The coercive aspects of paternity establishment and child support policy are aimed against single mothers in general. However, they have decidedly racial effects. The mandatory maternal cooperation rule targets mothers who are not and have not been married, as well as mothers who do not have and do not want child support. Nonmarital mothers are

16. In 1989, the average annual child support award for poor mothers was only $1,889. Ellen L. Bassuk, Angela Browne, and John C. Buckner, "Single Mothers and Welfare," *Scientific American* (October 1996): 62.

17. The Personal Responsibility Act ended the $50 "pass-through," the amount of collected child support state governments were required to share with mothers enrolled in the Aid to Families with Dependent Children program.

18. On the "implicit stories of race and gender" in welfare politics, see Nancy E. Dowd, "Stigmatizing Single Parents," *Harvard Women's Law Journal* 18 (1995): 19, 26, 45–46; Regina Austin, "Sapphire! Bound," *University of Wisconsin Law Review* (1989), reprinted in Patricia Smith, ed., *Feminist Jurisprudence* (New York: Oxford University Press, 1993), 575–594; Martha Fineman, *The Neutered Mother, The Sexual Family* (New York: Routledge, 1995) chap. 5; and the works of Dorothy Roberts, especially *Killing the Black Body* (New York: Pantheon, 1997).

the bull's-eye, and among nonmarital mothers receiving welfare, only 28.4 percent are white.[19] This means that the new welfare law's invasions of associational and privacy rights will disproportionately harm mothers of color. Inspired by white feminist outrage against middle-class ex-husbands, the paternity establishment and child support provisions both reflect and entrench inequalities among women.

WORK REQUIREMENTS

Feminists' general support for the claim that poor mothers need "work, not welfare" proceeded more from the internal logics of the late-twentieth-century women's movement than from specific policy goals. Feminists have long fought for women's right to work outside the home, and to do so on terms equal to men. Rather than demand honor and equity for all forms and venues of work, our bias has been toward work performed in the labor market. We've even been a little suspicious of the woman who doesn't work in the labor market—as if by working inside the home full-time she somehow undermines feminism. Often, we have demeaned her as "just a housewife."

The feminist work ethic made sense for the white and middle-class women who rekindled feminism in the 1960s. They politicized their own lived experiences, experiences that enforced their inequality. Heading the list of oppressive experiences was domesticity, which had confined middle-class white women to the home and had ensured their economic dependence on fathers and husbands. Middle-class feminists understandably keyed on work outside the home as the alternative to domesticity—and therefore as the defining element of women's full and equal citizenship.

As we entered the labor market in ever larger numbers during the 1970s and 1980s, women did not abandon care giving work. Rather, we found our energy doubly taxed by the dual responsibility of earning and caring—even in families with two parents. Accordingly, by the 1980s, many feminists began calling for labor market policies that address the care giving responsibilities that fall disproportionately on women—especially caring for children. The concern has been that care giving obligations impede women's opportunities and achievements in the labor market. Following this, we have sought labor policies that relieve women's family re-

19. *1996 Green Book*, Table 8-2.

sponsibilities so that we may participate equally in the labor market. Take child care policy, for example. We have been far less interested in winning social policies that support women where we do our care giving work: in the family. We have not focused on how wage work impedes care giving work.

Feminists of color have struggled alongside white feminists for equality in the workplace—for better pay, improved benefits, and due recognition of our merit. However, the idea that liberation hinges on work outside the home historically has divided feminists along class and race lines. Women of color and poor, white women have not usually found work outside the home to be a source of equality. To the contrary, especially for women of color, such work has been a site of oppression and a mark of inequality. Outside work has been required or expected of women of color by white society, though white society does not require or expect outside work of its own women. It also has been necessary for women of color because often their male kin cannot find jobs at living wages, if they can find jobs at all. And it has been exploitative because women of color earn disproportionately low wages. Since women of color have always worked outside their own homes—often raising other people's children—the right to care for their own children (to work inside their own homes) has been a touchstone goal of women of color struggles for equality.

For their part, white, middle-class feminists have been reluctant to make equality claims for women as family care givers. Still, they have never denied that women's family work has social value. During the early 1970s, for example, some feminists argued that the gross national product should include the value of women's work in the home.[20] Many radical and socialist feminists challenged the sexual division of labor, illuminating connections between women's unpaid labor in the home and their gender-based inequality. Some on the feminist left drew the conclusion that "women's work" should be remunerated—that women should be paid "wages for housework."[21] But across ideological divisions, most white, middle class feminists found the home to be the prime site of women's oppression and accordingly stressed the liberating potential of leaving it—for the labor market.

Accordingly, second-wave feminism has given us a fairly monolithic

20. Ann Crittenden Scott, "The Value of Housework: For Love or Money?" *Ms.* (July 1972): 56–59; John Kenneth Galbraith, "How the Economy Hangs on Her Apron Strings," *Ms.* (May 1974): 74–77.
21. This position was most famously developed by Marianosa Dalla Costa (with Selma James) in "The Power of Women and the Subversion of the Community," *Radical America* 6 (1972): 67–102.

emphasis on winning rights in the workplace. This has been accompanied, *sotto voce*, by a feminist expectation that all women *ought* to work outside the home and an assumption that *any* job outside the home— including caring for other people's children—is more socially productive than caring for one's own. Although feminism is fundamentally about winning women choices, our labor market bias has put much of feminism not on the side of vocational choice—the choice to work inside or outside the home—but on the side of wage earning for all women. In the Personal Responsibility Act, the feminist *right* to work outside the home has become poor single mothers' *obligation* to do so.

The labor market focus of second-wave feminism has accomplished much for women—most important, establishing equality claims for women as wage earners. Contemporary feminist calls for further labor market reforms—for an increased minimum wage, for comparable worth, and for child care—rightly point out the persisting impediments to women's equality in the labor market. The problem is not with the specific content of feminist agendas but with their one-sidedness and prescriptivity. Feminists' singular emphasis on equality where men work —outside the home—has left us with few precedents and rhetorical tools to challenge the new welfare paradigm.

To be sure, many feminists have fought ardently to attenuate the PRA's harshest provisions. For example, the NOW-Legal Defense and Education Fund has been working hard to get states to adopt the Family Violence Option, which exempts battered women from some of the most stringent welfare rules. Lucille Roybal-Allard in the U.S. House and Patty Murray in the U.S. Senate have fought hard to broaden the domestic violence exemption to include exemption from the PRA's strict time limit for welfare eligibility. Patsy Mink in the U.S. House has battled to secure vocational education funds for single mothers. At the local level, grassroots feminists and welfare rights activists have been struggling to enforce fair labor standards in welfare mothers' jobs.

If successful, all of these efforts could improve some women's fate in the new welfare system. But they do not disturb the principles behind the welfare law: they do not refute the idea that poor single mothers *should* seek work outside the home. Except among welfare rights activists and a handful of feminists, no one has defended poor mothers' right to raise their children, and no one has questioned the proposition that poor single mothers should *have to*—should be compelled by law to—work outside the home.

Nor has anyone paid serious attention to the racial effects of welfare principles. Although work requirements aim indiscriminately at all poor single mothers, it is mothers of color who bear their heaviest weight. African American and Latina mothers are disproportionately poor and, accordingly, are disproportionately enrolled on welfare. In 1994, adult recipients in AFDC families were almost two-thirds women of color: 37.4 percent white, 36.4 percent Black, 19.9 percent Latina, 2.9 percent Asian, and 1.3 percent Native American.[22]

So when welfare rules indenture poor mothers as unpaid servants of local governments (in workfare programs), it is mothers of color who are disproportionately harmed. And when time limits require poor mothers to forsake their children for the labor market, it is mothers of color who are disproportionately deprived of their right to manage their family's lives, and it is children of color who are disproportionately deprived of their mothers' care.

FEMINIST WELFARE

What can we do now for poor mothers who need welfare? A big part of the answer lies at the local level, where struggles over labor standards, child care, education, and transportation are currently playing out. Another part of the answer takes us to the courts, where we need to defend recipients' basic rights against provisions that exchange rights for welfare. Specifically, we need to defend the right to have children as a basic reproductive right; and we need to defend the right to raise one's own children as basic to family privacy as well as to associational and vocational freedom. But we also must argue further, that women's basic constitutional rights depend on a right to welfare—that a right to welfare is a condition of women's equality.

What kind of welfare policy *would* promote poor single mothers' equality? During the welfare debate, feminists who did mobilize against punitive reforms found common ground in opposition to the initiatives proposed by the Republicans, as well as to some proposed by President Clinton. But we were far from united behind a common vision of welfare justice. While we could all agree on the urgency of child care and health care and jobs, we were less certain about what social policy should say to single mothers who want to or need to care for their own children in their own homes—namely, mothers who need *welfare*. Even feminist welfare scholars, who spend much of our time debating what equality and justice mean and how both might be achieved, could not agree on

22. U.S. House of Representatives, Committee on Ways and Means, *1996 Green Book*, Table 8-32.

the elements of a welfare policy that forwards feminist goals. This was in part because we hadn't given much attention to the ideal of welfare justice; rather, we generally had confined our scholarly debates and inquiries to whether and how welfare had subordinated women. Blindsided by Bill Clinton's pledge to end welfare, we were ill-prepared to defend welfare as an element of gender justice.

Our collective uncertainty about the design of welfare justice didn't matter during the welfare debate, however, for the terms of debate were so narrow. No one was asking "What should welfare be for?" or "How might welfare work *for* women?" Although I don't think we're likely to be blindsided by such questions in the near future, one lesson from the campaign to end welfare is that feminists need to work among ourselves so that we can seize opportunities to affirm the relationship between welfare rights and women's equality.

One way to affirm that relationship is to recognize that poor single women who give care to their children are mothers whose care giving *is work*.

We all know that care giving work—household management and parenting—takes skill, energy, time, and responsibility. We know this because people who can afford it *pay* other people to do it. Many wage earning mothers pay for child care; upper-class mothers who work outside the home pay for nannies; very wealthy mothers who don't even work outside the home pay household workers to assist them with their various tasks. Moreover, even when we are not paying surrogates to do our family care giving, we pay people to perform activities in the labor market that care givers also do in the home. We pay drivers to take us places; we pay nurses to make us feel better and help us get well; we pay psychologists to help us with our troubles; we pay teachers to explain our lessons; we pay cooks and waitresses to prepare and serve our food.

If economists can measure the value of this work when it is performed for other people's families, why can't we impute value to it when it is performed for one's own? In 1972, economists at the Chase Manhattan Bank did just that, translating family care giving work into its labor market components—nursemaid, dietitian, laundress, maintenance man, chauffeur, food buyer, cook, dishwasher, seamstress, practical nurse, gardener. The economists concluded that the value of family care givers' work was at least $13,391.56 a year (1972 dollars)—an amount well above the poverty line![23]

Once we establish that *all* care giving is work and that it has economic

---

23. Scott, "The Value of Housework: For Love or Money?"

value—whatever the racial, marital, or class status of the care giver and whether or not it is performed in the labor market—we can build a case for economic arrangements that enable poor single mothers to do their jobs. In place of stingy benefits doled out begrudgingly to needy mothers, welfare would become an income owed to nonmarket, care giving workers—owed as a matter of right to anyone who bears sole responsibility for children (or for other dependent family members).

This would not require a radical restructuring of social policy, or an unprecedented departure from past practice. The survivors' insurance system—which has been around since 1939—does for widowed parents and their minor children exactly what I'm advocating for poor single mothers.[24] Survivors' insurance is an entitlement and does not involve stigma and social control. Mothers who are eligible for survivors' insurance do not have to submit to governmental scrutiny to receive benefits and do not have to live by government's moral and cultural rules. Benefits are nationally uniform and are paid out automatically—much like social security benefits are paid out to the elderly.

Every parent who receives survivors' insurance is a single parent. The only difference between a survivors' insurance parent and a welfare parent is that the former was married. Because she was once married to her children's father, a survivors' insurance mother is not required to work outside the home—though she may take a job and still receive benefits. Because she was once married to her children's father, a survivors' insurance mother gets to make *her own* choices about care giving and wage earning. Survivors' insurance says that for once-married mothers, at least, care giving is a socially necessary and valuable activity, deserving of social assistance.[25]

In my view, if widowed mothers are entitled to public benefits, poor single mothers should be, too. In fact, all family care givers are owed an income in theory, for all care giving is work. However, a care giver's income should redistribute resources to mothers without means, for their capacity to sustain families and to make independent choices hangs on their ability to provide. The cardinal purpose of such an income should be to redress the unique inequality of solo care givers—usually mothers—who shoulder the dual responsibilities of providing care for children and financing it. While some single mothers may be able to af-

---

24. This discussion focuses on survivors' insurance provisions for widows/widowers and their minor children. Survivors' insurance also provides for widow(er)s of insured workers who are age 60 or older.
25. *Weinberger v. Wiesenfeld* 95 S. Ct. 1225, 1230 (1975); *Califano v. Boles* 443 U.S. 282, 289 (1979).

ford both responsibilities, most cannot, because they are time poor, cash poor, or both.

A care giver's income would relieve the disproportionate burdens that fall on single mothers and in so doing would lessen inequalities among women based on class and marital status and between male and female parents based on default social roles. But although paid to single care givers only, this income support should be universally guaranteed, assuring a safety net to all care givers if ever they need or choose to parent—or to care for other family members—alone. The extension of the safety net to care givers as independent citizens would promote equality, as it would enable adults to exit untenable—often violent—relationships of economic dependency and to retain reproductive and vocational choices when they do.

We need to end welfare in this way to enable equality—in the safety net, between the genders, among women, and under the Constitution. Income support for all care givers who are going it alone would permit solo parents to decide how best to manage their responsibilities to children. It might even undermine the sexual division of labor, for some men will be enticed to do family care giving work once they understand it to have economic value. Offering an income to all solo care givers in a unitary system—to nonmarital mothers as well as to widowed ones—would erase invidious moral distinctions among mothers and eliminate their racial effects. Further, universal income support for single parents would restore mothers' constitutional rights—to not marry, to bear children, and to parent them, even if they are poor. It would promote occupational freedom, by rewarding work even when work cannot be exchanged for wages. So redefined, welfare would become a sign not of dependency but of independence, a means not to moral regulation but to social and political equality.

Ending welfare this way will remedy inequality where it is most gendered—in the care giving relations of social reproduction. Yet, it will not be enough to end welfare by replacing it with a care givers' income. The end of welfare—the goal of feminist social policy—must be to enhance women's choices across their full spectrum. We need to improve women's opportunities as *both* nonmarket and market workers, so that care givers' choice to work inside the home is backed up by a real possibility of choosing not to.

Middle-class feminists were right to reject *ascribed* domesticity, and they have taught us well that fully independent and equal citizenship for women entails having the right *not* to care. So we must also win labor market reforms to make outside work feasible even for mothers who are parenting alone. Unless we make outside work affordable for solo care givers, a care givers' income would constrain choice by favoring care giving over wage earning.

The end of welfare, then, includes "making work pay," not only by remunerating care giving work but also by making participation in the labor market equitable and rewarding for women, especially mothers. Thus, for example, we need a minimum wage that provides a sustaining income—so that poor mothers can afford to work outside the home if they want to. We need comparable worth policies that correct the low economic value assigned to women's jobs. We need unemployment insurance reforms covering women's gendered reasons for losing or leaving jobs—such as pregnancy or sexual harassment. We need paid family leave so that the lowest paid workers can take time off to care for sick kids or new babies just as better paid workers do. We need guaranteed child care so that a parent's decision to work inside the home is truly a decision—not something forced on her because she can't find affordable and nurturing supervision for her children. We also need universal health care; full employment policy; a massive investment in education and vocational training; and aggressive enforcement of antidiscrimination laws.

This end to welfare will take us down many paths, in recognition of women's diverse experiences of gender and diverse prerequisites for equality.

Welfare, Dependency, and a Public Ethic of Care

—Eva Feder Kittay

There is every reason to react with alarm to the prospect of a world filled with self-actualizing persons pulling their own strings, capable of guiltlessly saying "no" to anyone about anything, and freely choosing when to begin and end all their relationships. It is hard to see how, in such a world, children could be raised, the sick or disturbed could be cared for, or people could know each other through their lives and grow old together.

—Naomi Scheman [1]

"Welfare is a Women's Issue" [2]—
The Subtext of Welfare "Reform"

A strange cacophony of justifications and rebuttals dominates contemporary discussions of welfare and welfare reform. While the right speaks of "family values," "unwed mothers," "family breakdown," and "teenage pregnancy," the left responds with appeals to "structural unemployment," "creating jobs," and "ending poverty." "Welfare policies encourage dependency," the right insists. "Provide jobs" answers the left. "Provide 'values'," the right retorts. Is this the mismatch in call and response it seems to be, or do these two stances share certain philosophical underpinnings? Both positions, in different ways, assume a conception of

A revised version of this article is reprinted in Eva Feder Kittay, *Love's Labor: Essays on Women, Dependency and Equality* (New York: Routledge, 1999).
1. Naomi Scheman, "Individualism and Psychology," in *Discovering Reality: Feminist Perspectives on Epistemology, Metaphysics, Methodology, and Philosophy of Science*, Sandra Harding and Merrill Hintikka, eds. (Dordrecht, Holland: Reidel Publishing, 1983).
2. The title of this section is borrowed from Johnnie Tillmon, "Welfare is a Woman's Issue," in *America's Working Women: A Documentary History—1600 to the Present*, Rosalyn Baxandall, Linda Gordon, and Susan Reverby, eds. (New York: Vintage Books, 1976), 356.

the citizen based on a male model of the "independent" wage earner. Both see the person on welfare as someone who can be incorporated as a full citizen only by fulfilling the role of the "independent" wage earner. And neither questions the conception of social cooperation that presumes, but does not credit, women's unpaid labor as caretaker.[3] Feminists, meanwhile, see welfare and the welfare state as a women's issue: as a patriarchal control over the lives of poor women, but also as an essential safety net for all women.[4] Paraphrasing Johnnie Tillmon, in a recent talk[5] on welfare Kate Millet remarked, "The Man walked out—he quit." But poverty remains, and it is poverty with a woman's face.

Although most of the recipients of the now-defunct Aid to Families with Dependent Children (AFDC) program were children, 90 percent of the adults benefiting from the program, which we called "welfare," were women. The new welfare program established under the Personal Responsibility and Work Opportunity Act of 1996, Temporary Assistance to Needy Families, similarly affects mostly women and their children. Clearly, welfare is not *only* a poverty issue, it is a women's issue. Moreover, the thrust of welfare reform threatens *feminist* gains. It is, first, a challenge to the reproductive rights of women—poor women's right to bear children. Also, despite some pious calls for ending violence against women in the home, the constriction of aid to solo mothers deeply affects women's exit options in abusive relationships. As some current studies indicate, more than half the women who make use of public assistance are coming out of situations of domestic violence.[6] Furthermore, the new welfare law makes a mockery of feminist demands for fulfilling

3. Iris Young, "Mothers, Citizenship, and Independence," *Ethics* 105, no. 3 (April 1995): 535–57; Carol Pateman, "The Patriarchical Welfare State," in *The Disorder of Women*, Carol Pateman, ed. (Cambridge: Polity, 1989).

4. For some examples of these analyses see Abramovitz, Mimi, *Regulating the Lives of Women* (Boston: South End Press, 1996); Sassoon, Ann Showstack, ed., *Women and the State* (London: Hutchinson, 1987); Skocpol, Theda, *Protecting Soldiers and Mothers: The Political Origins of Social Policy in the United States* (Cambridge: Harvard University Press, 1992); Linda Gordon, ed., *Women, the State and Welfare* (Madison: University of Wisconsin, 1990); Linda Gordon, *Pitied But Not Entitled: Single Mothers and the History of Welfare* (New York: Free Press, 1994); Mink, Gwendolyn, *Wages of Motherhood* (Ithaca: Cornell University Press, 1995). Many of these feminist writers see welfare in terms of both gender and race.

5. Johnnie Tillmon, "Welfare is a Woman's Issue," p. 356, paraphrase by Millet at the Teach-In on Welfare at SUNY Stony Brook, Stony Brook, N.Y., March 1997. Tillmon was a welfare mother and National Welfare Rights Organization leader. She spoke of welfare as "a supersexist marriage" in which we trade in "a" man for "the" man.

6. A recent study released by the McCormack Institute and the Center for Survey Research, both at the University of Massachusetts, Boston, found that among a representative sample of the Massachusetts Transitional Aid to Families with Dependent Children (TAFDC) caseload, 65 percent would be considered victims of domestic violence by a current or former boyfriend or husband using the Massachusetts state law definition of abuse.

and well-paying nonfamilial labor. To be *compelled* to leave your child in a stranger's care or with no care at all and to accept whatever work is offered is another form of subordination, not a liberation. And it devalues the work women traditionally have done.

The issue of welfare, then, is a women's issue both in the sense that it affects primarily women *and* that it pertains to feminist goals. The end of AFDC, which guaranteed women with children a basic level of income if they fell below a certain level of poverty, must be a siren call to understand why "a war against poor women is a war against all women" (as the slogan of a feminist advocacy group, the Women's Committee of One Hundred, declares). This moment, however, should also be grasped as the occasion to reconsider the basis of welfare. We need to muster the political will to shape and support welfare policies that can serve women raising families without stigmatizing those in need. Such policies are necessary for the consolidation of feminist gains and for the achievement of full citizenship for women, especially in the context of modern industrial economies.[7]

TRADITIONAL JUSTIFICATIONS OF WELFARE

To aid in forming the requisite political will, we need to be clearer about the justification for welfare generally, and the justification for welfare targeted at the needs of women in particular. The contemporary right/left debate reflects a number of different understandings of the bases for welfare and the welfare state by those who endorse it and by those who oppose it.

The welfare state, and especially those policies directed at the poor are, by one account, based on the need to protect against failures of the market and to eliminate poverty. Within a market economy, the satisfaction of needs, the creation of needs, and the negotiation of what constitutes need is tied to one's participation in a relation of reciprocity between the production of wealth and its consumption. This participation is marked first and foremost by labor that is compensated in wages or salaries. It defines *independent*. To stand outside these reciprocal arrangements re-

7. Nancy Fraser, "After the Family Wage: A Postindustrial Thought Experiment," in *Justice Interruptus: Critical Reflections on the "Postsocialist" Condition*, Nancy Fraser, ed. (New York: Routledge, 1997), 41–68; Young, "Mothers, Citizenship, and Independence"; Selma Sevenhuijsen, "Feminist Ethics and Public Health Care Policies," in *Feminist Ethics and Social Policy*, Patrice DiQuinzio and Iris Marion Young, eds. (Bloomington: Indiana University Press, 1996); Gwendolyn Mink, *Wages of Motherhood*; Ann Shola Orloff, "Gender and the Social Rights of Citizenship," *American Sociological Review* 58 (June 1993): 303–328.

duces one to the status of *dependent*, someone dependent on an individual, a charity, or the state.[8]

Yet as even the earliest proponents of a market economy saw, a market economy, in and of itself, will not guarantee that all who can and want to work will be adequately employed. The dynamism of a capitalist economy produces great wealth, but also great poverty. Such poverty is morally unacceptable in the midst of wealth and is politically destabilizing. But efforts at redressing the inequity encounter what Donald Moon[9] has called "Hegel's dilemma," a dilemma articulated but never resolved by the philosopher in his *Philosophy of Right*. For while the redistribution of wealth can mitigate the poverty, such redistribution (through cash transfers or the provision of goods and services in kind) may, on the one hand, undermine a citizen's sense of participation in community and so undermine the citizen's sense of self-worth. If, on the other hand, the state steps in to create jobs, such action interferes with the autonomous functioning of the market and so disrupts the machine that generates wealth.

The creation of the welfare state is a compromise between capitalism and democracy. Some welfare programs have been developed to skirt the offense to self-respect.[10] Populist policies, such as progressive taxation or free public education, have as their goal redistribution in the service of community and equality. Social insurance policies are another compromise that avoids the offense to self-respect. These benefits are understood as "earned entitlements" intended to "protect citizens against the "predictable risks of modern life."[11] Although redistribution is not the goal of social insurance, it, too, redistributes wealth, since what is received as a benefit by a participant normally exceeds what is paid in by that individual. Two other visions of welfare, residualism and behaviorism, are aimed at the poor. Residualism establishes a safety net—a floor beneath which individuals must not fall. Behaviorism attempts to alter the behavior of the poor. Behaviorism makes explicit the view that pov-

8. For an excellent discussion of how the term *independent* came to be associated with wage labor and *dependent* became attached to those who were excluded from wage labor, see Nancy Fraser and Linda Gordon, "A Genealogy of Dependency: Tracing a Keyword of the U.S. Welfare State," *Signs* 19, no. 2 (Winter 1994): 309–336. They point to three groups that epitomized a dependent status: paupers, slaves, and women. As they narrate the semantics of dependency, children, the disabled, and the frail elderly do not figure in the primary use of the term.

9. Donald J. Moon, "The Moral Basis of the Democratic Welfare State," in *Democracy and the Welfare State*, Amy Gutman, ed. (Princeton: Princeton University Press, 1988), 27–53.

10. See Theodore R. Marmor, Jerry L. Mashaw, and Philip L. Harvey, *America's Misunderstood Welfare State: Persistent Myths, Enduring Realities* (New York: Basic Books, 1990), for a discussion of the distinctions between social insurance, residualist, behaviorist, and populist welfare policies.

11. Theodore R. Marmor, Jerry L. Mashaw, and Philip L. Harvey, *America's Misunderstood Welfare State*.

erty is the fault of those who are impoverished. Residualism, as practiced in the United States today, makes such an assumption implicit in its treatment of beneficiaries. While populist and social insurance policies avoid one horn of Hegel's dilemma, residualist and behaviorist policies do not spare their recipients a goring. The scar marks them as "dependent." And as Fraser and Gordon argue, dependency, which in preindustrial times was seen as a structural social feature, has in industrial society and still more strikingly in postindustrial society come to be seen as a characterological feature of the poor who rely on public assistance, and poverty itself is viewed as a characterological flaw.[12]

Welfare debates today are most often between residualists on the left and behaviorists on the right.[13] The right, emphasizing the evils of dependency on state support, has pushed workfare, or work outside the home in exchange for benefits. The left does not question the "debilitating effects of dependency" and does not dispute the premise that a job is preferable to a "handout." It insists that if some persons are employable but not employed, there is a need for job creation. That is what is implied in the question "Where are the jobs?" to which the welfare "dependents" are to turn in their newly forged (and forced) independency.

Supporters and foes alike nonetheless recognize that not *everyone* in a society is able to perform waged work, even if jobs are limitless. Individuals may lack the capacities required for employment, suffering ill health or disabling conditions or having inadequate education or training. Nor does any society expect *everyone* to work. Within most industrial societies, we exempt and even prohibit children from working and don't presume that those over a certain age will continue to work.

Welfare policy initially assumed that solo mothers would not work outside the home. Aid to Dependent Children (ADC), the forerunner of AFDC, was, in the words of the 1937 Committee on Economic Security, "designed to release from the wage-earning role the person whose natural function is to give her children the physical and affectionate guardianship necessary not alone to keep them from falling into social misfortune, but more affirmatively to make them citizens capable of contributing to society."[14] It was aimed precisely at those women who were *justifiably*

---

12. Nancy Fraser and Linda Gordon, "A Genealogy of Dependency."
13. Even as the left tries to protect residualist programs from being eviscerated, the target of the right is broader. Many programs such as social security, progressive taxation, and even public education are targets. By restricting a defense of welfare to residualism, supporters of the welfare state may lose the opportunity to respond adequately to both the narrow and the broad attack.
14. Cited in Mimi Abramovitz, *Regulating the Lives of Women.*

not engaged in wage labor. ADC, like its predecessor Mothers' Pensions, was supposed to be doled out to mothers—though only to "deserving" mothers, that is, widowed or abandoned domestic mothers.

The 1962 amendments to the Social Security Act stressed the twin goals of strengthening the family and family self-sufficiency. "For the first time in 1962, federal law permitted states to require adult recipients to work in exchange for benefits."[15] These amendments, which altered the name of the federal welfare program from Aid to Dependent Children to "Aid to *Families* with Dependent Children," also permitted two-parent families to receive assistance where the breadwinner was unemployed. Congress and welfare rules expressed general ambivalence about forcing mothers to find employment rather than care for their children, focusing work expectations on fathers as family providers.

Since 1962, women's increased poverty and dependence on public assistance has, paradoxically, coincided with our entry into the workforce and our greater equality of opportunity. Shifting expectations and opportunities have significantly altered the understanding of mothers' dependency on state aid. The declarations of 1937 and the debates of 1962 are scarcely conceivable today, when nearly half the women with children of preschool age are in the workforce, at least part-time.

As systematic, formal barriers to social goods are removed, injustices that remain become less visible and those who are unable to take advantage of new opportunities are blamed for their own distress.[16] So while previous social policies attempted to distinguish "deserving" from "undeserving" poor women, the removal of obstacles to women's employment has opened the door to characterizing all unemployed poor women as undeserving. Nonetheless, not all poverty, even in postindustrial society, has been viewed as a character flaw. When the disabled are poor, we either fix the working environment to enable employment, or we look to supplemental income for those so disabled that they cannot maintain employment even with altered work environments. We do not say to them "work or lose benefits." When, in our recent past, the aged constituted the majority of the poor, our nation looked for solutions that were adapted to that population. The solution was not to force every able-

15. Abramovitz, *Regulating the Lives of Women.*
16. In an environment of equal opportunity rhetoric, victims of social circumstances not infrequently blame *themselves* especially harshly. As Sandra Bartky remarks: "It is itself psychologically oppressive to both believe and at the same time not to believe that one is inferior. . . . I may [inconsistently] live out my membership in my sex or race in *shame*; . . . Or, somewhat more consistently, . . . I may locate the cause squarely within myself . . .—a character flaw, an 'inferiority complex,' or a neurosis." Bartky, Sandra Lee, *Femininity and Domination* (New York: Routledge, 1990).

bodied elderly person to get a job, but to provide old-age insurance, to peg benefits to inflation, and to provide medical care for the elderly.

In reading the literature by men, and some women, one comes to wonder why, when *women* are poor, theorists and social scientists fail to ask if there are not particular causes of women's poverty.[17] Why are the conditions faced by women, especially those caring for dependents, not highlighted? There is a presumption that when it comes to getting jobs there is no gender inequity and that the joblessness of women is independent of the gender-related vulnerabilities they face at home, in the family, and in the economic sphere. There is no talk of gendered wage inequity, of the gendering of familial caretaking responsibilities, of gendered susceptibility to spousal abuse and sexual abuse in the workplace.

The inattention to the gender issues behind women's poverty should be of special concern to feminists, not only for the obvious reason that feminists must always be alert to analyses that ignore gender, but also feminist gains for some women may jeopardize other women, especially those least benefited by equal opportunity gains and reproductive rights legislation. For example, reproductive rights currently least benefit those women who are poorest, as they often lack the means to procure contraception or obtain abortions. But they are held accountable for each pregnancy and birth as if they had the same choices that middle-class women do. Even feminist women will say of poor women, "Why do they have children if they can't afford them."[18] With respect to the expectation that even women with children will be employed, Linda Gordon points out, "The fact that most mothers today are employed . . . nurtures resentment against other mothers supported (if only you could call it 'support') by AFDC."[19] Naomi Zack,[20] in another context, warns, "You must dismount a tiger with great care." The efforts of some better situated women to dismount the tiger of patriarchy may well have left other women—less well situated—in mortal danger. In particular, feminist successes have facilitated an analysis that ignores the gendered concerns of women who have turned to welfare to support their families.

17. Diana Pearce put this point in this fashion at a panel on women and welfare at Yale University, May 1995. I borrow my formulation from her.
18. I have heard this remark time and again from women who considered themselves "liberal" and "feminists." One officer of NOW Legal and Educational Defense Fund remarked that she had rarely seen so much negative mail and threats to withdraw support as when the organization took up the fight against the "family cap" provision of state welfare plans. The family cap provision prohibits the use of public assistance for any child born while the mother was receiving welfare.
19. Linda Gordon, ed. *Women, the State and Welfare.*
20. Naomi Zack, "Mixed Black and White Race and Public Policy," *Hypatia* 10, no. 1 (Winter 1995): 120–132.

THE MATERNALIST JUSTIFICATION OF WELFARE

As noted, at the inception of U.S. social policy, the poverty of women was thought to be distinctive. Feminist scholars have documented the influence of women in building the welfare state in the United States and in drafting the policy that was to become AFDC.[21] The story of how a welfare program initiated by women for women became the despised program we now call simply "welfare" is a fascinating, if depressing, story. At best, it is a story of a "progressive maternalism," which gained power through the efforts of well-educated upper- and upper-middle-class women even before women had gained the vote. At worst, it is a story about how these same women, mostly white, used the social benefits conferred to women to "Americanize" (and thus erase the native ethnic identities of Eastern and Southern European women), even at the cost of preventing those benefits from being extended to Black women and non-European immigrants.

The progressive maternalists, adopting a philosophy of "social housekeeping," saw their role as bringing maternal virtues into the public sphere. Along with establishing a Children's Bureau within the executive branch of government, the Sheppard-Towner Act, and Mothers' Pensions, they were also responsible for administrative rules, which monitored mothers' sexuality, reviewed the women's housekeeping standards, and intervened in feeding and rearing customs retained from the Old World. These policymakers were *maternalists* in that they wanted to bring women's values into the public sphere. But as the city housekeepers, the eyes of the well-meaning reformers were primarily directed at the end result—the child. They bypassed the mother as a citizen in her own right. Gwendolyn Mink writes: "The fruits of maternalist social policy research were policies designed to improve motherhood through cultural reform. The beneficiary of these policies was the child, the conduit her mother, the social goal the fully Americanized citizen."[22]

The maternalists' feminist vision resonates with certain feminist visions today, especially those that are associated with the feminist morality of care.[23] Although there are doubtless many significant differences

21. Linda Gordon, *Pitied But Not Entitled: Single Mothers and the History of Welfare*; Theda Skocpol, *Protecting Soldiers and Mothers*.

22. Mink, *Wages of Motherhood*, 27.

23. It also resonates with questions relevant to "the public household." Bell, Daniel, *The Cultural Contradictions of Capitalism* (New York: Basic Books, 1976). Michele Moody-Adams points to social policy "that seeks to use . . . the vast resources of the public household to legislate against certain behavior rather than to provide positive social support. . . ." Moody-Adams, Michelle, "The Social Construction and Reconstruction of Care," in *Sex, Preference, and Family: Essays on Law and Nature*, David Estlund and Martha Nussbaum, eds. (New York: Oxford University Press, 1997),

between the historical case and feminists today, the historical example alerts us to some of the dangers lurking in the otherwise worthwhile project of bringing women's value of care, of concern for children, and so forth to the public arena. For how, and in what spirit, we try to import these values makes all the difference.

DEPENDENCY REVISITED

The question before us today is whether, and how, we can conceive of welfare that addresses women's lives. How, that is, can we fashion policy that does not insist that all women must fit the Procrustean bed of the male wage worker, that recognizes the demise of the "family wage," and that recognizes the dependency of those for whom mothers care but does so without subjecting the mothers themselves to dependency and control? Another way to pose this question is to ask if we can conceive of social welfare policy that extends social citizenship to all women?[24] As feminists have argued, women's social citizenship requires social recognition and support for the caring labor done by women. Can we develop policies that meet this goal?[25]

We need to shift our attention on dependency away from the social, political, economic, and moral registers that Fraser and Gordon explicate. For there is another deployment of the term that gets lost and that

---

3–17. While such "reactive" policies are inimical to truly liberal democratic institutions, I propose elsewhere [Eva Feder Kittay, "Human Dependency and Rawlsian Equality," in *Feminists Rethink the Self*, D. T. Meyers, ed. (Boulder, Colo.: Westview Press, 1996)] that noteworthy principles of liberalism are inadequate for the more positive policies implied by the notion of the public household.

24. For the notion of social citizenship with respect to women see, for example, Francis Fox Piven, "Women and the Welfare State," in *Gender and the Life Course*, Alice Rossi, ed. (New York: Aldine, 1985), 265–287; Birte Siim, "Toward a Feminist Rethinking of the Welfare State," in *The Political Interests of Gender*, K. Jones and A. Jonasdottir, eds. (Newbury Park, Calif.: Sage, 1988), 160–186; "The Patriarchal Welfare State," in *The Disorder of Women*, Carole Pateman, ed.; *Women, the State and Welfare*, Linda Gordon, ed.; Ann Shola Orloff, "Gender and the Social Rights of Citizenship;" Theda Skocpol, *Protecting Soldiers and Mothers*.

25. See also Ann Shola Orloff, "Gender and the Social Rights of Citizenship," offering a gendering of the "power resources" school of analysis, who argues that social citizenship for women is not centrally about the decommodification of labor, as it is for men within a market economy. Instead, she argues, social citizenship for women involves both women's ability to be economically independent of men and their capacity to form and sustain autonomous families. This is an argument that can motivate feminists, but one still needs to show that the corresponding condition disadvantages women unfairly—that is, that it amounts to an inequitable distribution of the benefits and burdens of social cooperation between men and women and that this condition benefits the larger social group and simultaneously disadvantages women. That is the point of the argument in this section of the chapter.

we can retrieve in the acronym AFDC—Aid to Families with *Dependent*
Children. Human development, disease, disability, and decline result
in "inevitable dependencies."[26] I have called the relationships in which
these dependents are cared for, "dependency relations." Dependency relations, as I conceive of them, have as their core, a dependent (or charge)
and a dependency worker (one who cares for the charge). Dependency
relations require support from additional sources to be sustainable. I call
this support "the provider."[27]

The Derived Dependency of Dependency Workers

Dependency relationships, which are all too easily eclipsed when society is understood as an association of independent equals,[28] constitute
the fount of all social organization.[29] The bonds of political association
among equals, however binding they may be, are not as powerful as those
created by caring relationships. These intimate ties allow individuals at
different stages of life to withstand the forces that act upon them.[30] As
Virginia Held has argued, the intimate bonds of dependents and their
caretakers make civic order and civic friendship possible.[31] With the solo
mother and her children, we find the distillation of these founding social
relations. But in caring for the dependent, the dependency worker herself is in need of support wherever and whenever caring for dependents
is incompatible with producing the material support needed to sustain
those in the relationship. In more highly developed economies care giving is rarely compatible with wage earning.

26. Martha Albertson Fineman, *The Neutered Mother: The Sexual Family, and Other Twentieth
Century Tragedies* (New York: Routledge, 1995).
27. Eva Feder Kittay, "Taking Dependency Seriously: The Family and Medical Leave Act Considered in Light of the Social Organization of Dependency Work and Gender Equality," *Hypatia*
10, no. 1 (Winter 1995): 8–29; Kittay, "Human Dependency and Rawlsian Equality." See also Eva
Feder Kittay, *Love's Labor*.
28. See Jack P. Greene, *All Men Are Created Equal: Some Reflections on the Character of the American Revolution* (Oxford: Clarendon Press, 1976) for a discussion of the role of independence and
manhood in the consideration of who were the persons deemed equal by the authors of the Declaration of Independence and the United States Constitution. Also see Iris Young, "Mothers, Citizenship, and Independence," and Kittay, "Human Dependency and Rawlsian Equality," for the
relation between independence/dependence and equality.
29. Virginia Held, "Non-Contractual Society: A Feminist View," *Canadian Journal of Philosophy*
13 (1987): 111–137; Annette Baier, "The Need for More Than Justice," in *Science, Morality and Feminist Theory*, Marsha Hanen and Kai Nielsen, eds. (Minneapolis: University of Minnesota, 1987),
41–56; Pateman, "The Patriarchal Welfare State"; Kittay, "Human Dependency and Rawlsian
Equality."
30. Kittay, "Human Dependency and Rawlsian Equality."
31. Held, "Non-Contractual Society: A Feminist View."

The welfare "dependency" which so exercises the critics of welfare is not the dependency of the children, but that of their mothers. Yet these two dependencies are linked. Feminist research has established that "in all industrialized Western countries, welfare—tending to children, the elderly, the sick and disabled—is largely provided in private households by women without pay, rather than by states, markets, and voluntary nonprofit organizations."[32] That is, women not only do most of the dependency work, they do it without pay. Having dependents to care for means that without additional support, you cannot—given the structure of our contemporary industrial life and its economy—simultaneously provide the *means* to take care of them and to do the caring for them (to use a useful distinction in the term *caring* that Joan Tronto[33] has introduced). This also means that without additional support a person cannot participate in the reciprocal arrangements of production and consumption, as defined within a market economy. The requirement for support, then, constitutes a condition of a derived dependency for dependency workers, especially those who do unpaid dependency work. The dependency of the dependency worker is derivative, not inevitable—it is structural, not characterological.

Even dependency workers who are paid incur a special vulnerability to derived dependency, because this dependency is, in large measure, due to the nature of dependency work and the relation to the dependent. Three features of this labor are together responsible for this vulnerability. First, because dependency work involves the charge of one who is in many important regards helpless without the caretaker, there is a moral obligation that transcends the bounds of most jobs. Second, because dependency work requires a responsiveness to needs, often an anticipation of needs, the dependency work, when done well, requires a degree of emotional attachment to the charge. We want a caretaker who *cares*.[34] Third, the work of dependency care is "functionally diffuse" rather than "functionally specific."[35] That is to say that a caretaker has not a fixed set of tasks, but has to address the individual's general state of well-being and do whatever

32. Orloff, "Gender and the Social Rights of Citizenship."

33. Joan C. Tronto, *Moral Boundaries: A Political Argument for an Ethic of Care* (New York: Routledge, 1993).

34. A striking instance of this is indicated by an infant's need for high-quality interaction with his or her caretaker to develop well cognitively. Such interactions are most likely to be found in ongoing relationships with caretakers. See Sandra Blakeslee, "Studies Show Talking with Infants Shapes Basis of Ability to Think," *New York Times*, April 17, 1997, D21.

35. Rosalyn Benjamin Darling, "Parental Entrepreneurship: A Consumerist Response to Professional Dominance," *Journal of Social Issues* 44, no. 1 (1988): 141–158.

is needed to ensure that her charge's needs are met. Such responsibilities often override the needs of the caretaker herself, except where meeting her own needs are crucial to meeting the needs of her charge.

The moral and emotional commitments, then, which are part of the very work of dependency care, mean that the dependency worker's own needs are too often left unattended. As Joel Handler has argued, the regulatory models and legal rights that govern citizen-state or citizen-citizen interactions serve poorly to adequately protect the dependent and to limit the obligations, as well as properly compensate the labor of dependency workers.[36] It is for these reasons that the dependency worker is liable to incur a dependency that has a character different from the dependency on the economic and governmental to which all workers are subject.

Patriarchal family structures, whether the nuclear family prevalent in industrial societies or the extended family forms of agrarian societies and peasant communities, have been a response to the requirement that dependency relations require support. As feminist critiques of the patriarchal family have shown, however, they are neither the only nor the best response. Within these structures, dependency work is assigned by gender, not by skill or disposition, and the dependency of the dependency worker is the condition of her vulnerability to exploitation, abuse, and all the ills against which feminists have fought. Patriarchal state support in the form of welfare has been the response to the solo mother in need in capitalist welfare states.[37] Again, it has been a poor response—better than none, but too little, too stigmatized, and too intrusive. The welfare repeal, called "reform," is no response at all. The demand that women on welfare "work" not only fails to value the unpaid dependency work of the women using welfare to support themselves and their children, but, by imposing on these women the model of the male breadwinner, it also fails to recognize the dependency work of mothering. In the name of fostering a fictive "independence," it refuses to acknowledge "the obligation of the social order to attend to the well-being of dependents *and* of their caretakers, and to the *relation* of caretaker and dependent upon which all other civic unions depend."[38]

36. Joel Handler, *Dependent People, the State, and the Modern/Postmodern Search for the Dialogic Community*, Special Publications, The Institute for Legal Studies, University of Wisconsin—Madison, Special Publications (Madison: University of Wisconsin—Madison, Law School, 1987).
37. For a comparative study of welfare and family assistance in the different economic systems of the United States, Sweden, and China, see Carolyn Teich Adams and Kathryn Teich Winston, *Mothers at Work: Public Policies in the United States, Sweden, and China* (New York: Longman 1980).
38. Kittay, "Human Dependency and Rawlsian Equality."

Political theories (on which social policy depends for its justifications) are intended to capture the conditions for justice, and the relationships of dependency and care have been seen as standing outside these "public" domains. Since the publication of Gilligan's *In a Different Voice*, feminist theorists have pointed to the distinction between principles of justice and principles of care. They have taken political philosophies to task for ignoring the principles of care. Perhaps we should say, with Susan Okin and Marilyn Friedman, that the distinction between care and justice should not be overdrawn.[39] We should say that justice itself is not served if principles of care are not incorporated within the social order and that care is not served if it is meted out without reference to principles of justice. For dependents to receive care, they must be able to be cared for by one who can focus on their particular needs. Good caring requires a relationship between the one cared for and the one caring. But the one caring must herself not be treated without justice or caring. Her needs must themselves be met if a just caring is to be possible. A society that refuses to support this bond absolves itself from its most fundamental obligation—its obligation to its founding possibility.

The Citizen and Social Goods

Theories of the just state tend to neglect these considerations. The result is that they fail to include among the social goods those that bear on the needs of dependency workers, dependents, and the relations of dependency. Because of its power and influence, Rawls' theory of justice serves as a good starting point for a discussion of how to reconceive of the welfare state by centering the concerns of dependency.

Consider the conception of the citizen as the free, independent equal to whom rights attach. This is the citizen who enters freely into exchanges with equals with a sense of justice, but also with a conception of his own good. He both benefits from social cooperation with equals and partakes of the burdens of such cooperation. Within this conception of society as an association of equals, however, neither interactions with dependents nor the dependencies that result from caring for dependents figure. They vanish from the considerations of what are the moral features of citizens, the social goods that are crucial to their citizenship, or the conception of social cooperation.

39. Susan Okin, "Reason and Feeling in Thinking about Justice," *Ethics* 99, no. 2 (January 1989): 229–249; Marilyn Friedman, "Beyond Caring: The De-Moralization of Gender," in *Science, Morality and Feminist Theory*, Marsha Hanen and Kai Nielsen, eds. (Calgary: University of Calgary Press, 1987).

Consider for a moment Rawls's characterization of free and equal citizens. The moral features of the citizen are those that contribute to political and civic participation with equals. Rawls speaks of citizens as having two moral powers: an ability to form and revise one's conception of one's own good and a sense of justice. These give rise to the political and civil rights that are given prime consideration under liberal democracies. When the exigencies of life in a market economy are figured in, the social rights not to have all of life's interactions commodified are included. These two moral capacities call for a set of social goods necessary for their exercise. This set of goods, which Rawls calls "primary goods," serves as an index for making comparative assessments of interpersonal well-being.

The list, unaltered through the many revisions of Rawlsian theory, includes (1) the basic liberties (freedom of thought and liberty of conscience), (2) freedom of movement and free choice of occupation against a background of diverse opportunities . . . as well as [the ability] to give effect to a decision to revise and change them, (3) powers and prerogatives of offices and positions of responsibility, (4) income and wealth, and finally (5) the social bases of self-respect. . . .[40] Examining this list one may identify the first as given by political rights, the second and third by civil rights, and the final two as social rights. Omitted from the list are just the sort of social goods that are critical for women's social citizenship. These are the goods of dependency care and relationships of caring.

That is to say, a conception of a just state must include an understanding of the citizen as having not two, but three moral powers, including the capacity for responding to those in need with care.[41] The exercise of this moral power requires additional social goods, namely, (1) the understanding that we will be cared for if we become dependent, (2) the support we require if we have to take on the work of caring for a dependent, and (3) the assurance that if we become dependent, someone will take on the job of caring for those who are dependent upon us. Without these social goods, all persons, but women especially, cannot assume their rightful role as citizens. If we can possess basic liberties, freedom of movement and choice of occupation, the powers and prerogatives of public office, even income and wealth, we are provided with the po-

---

40. John Rawls, "Social Unity and Primary Choice," in *Utilitarianism and Beyond*, Amartya Sen and Bernard Williams, eds. (Cambridge: Harvard University Press, 1980).

41. For an argument that this moral capacity is not reducible or included within Rawls's other two moral powers, see Kittay, "Human Dependency and Rawlsian Equality," in *Feminists Rethink the Self*. Also see Sybil Schwarzenbach, "The Concept of the Person in Hegel and Rawls." Lecture. American Philosophical Association, Pacific Division, San Francisco, March 3, 1990.

litical and civil rights of citizenship. But if we do not have the assurance that when we are called on to do the work of caring for a dependent—when we focus our energies and attention on another—we will not lose the ability to care for ourselves (and so for our charge as well), we have not yet attained the powers and capacities to function as free and equal citizens. These, then, are the social goods all citizens, but particularly women, require for social citizenship. We have yet to discuss how these might translate into demands for particular social policies.

REVISIONING WELFARE

Social Cooperation and the Principle of Doulia

I have claimed that the ideal of the independent citizen presumes an equality and reciprocity of social relations that is blind to the inherent dependencies in which we all are immersed. To incorporate dependency and the dependency relation into social relations, we need a concept of interdependence that recognizes what is not precisely a relation of reciprocity but a relation that I characterize as "nested dependencies."[42] These link those who need help to those who help and link the helpers to a set of supports. If we look at women's poverty and the social response to "welfare" from a perspective of the dependency relation, and we attempt to reconstruct our understanding of social goods and cooperation from this perspective, we get, I believe, a conception of and argument for welfare, as it pertains to women especially, that is different from either antipoverty considerations (the residual model) or social control justifications (the behaviorist model).

If we agree that the care of dependents takes place within a dependency relation,[43] then a principal ethical justification of welfare, and indeed of the welfare state, is to support dependency relations. The purpose of welfare needs to be at once to care for dependents and to mitigate the costs to dependency workers for their participation in the dependency relation. But to be politically viable, this welfare must not be restricted to the poor, but extended to cover dependency work more generally.

As we look for a way to bring a care ethic to the public arena, the contemporary version of social housekeeping, we need both a conception of

---

42. Kittay, "Taking Dependency Seriously: The Family and Medical Leave Act Considered in Light of the Social Organization of Dependency Work and Gender Equality"; Kittay, "Human Dependency and Rawlsian Equality"; and Kittay, Love's Labor.
43. And, as I argue in Kittay, Love's Labor, needs take place within dependency relations.

social goods and a notion of social cooperation that acknowledges dependencies and the need for care and that employs a notion of reciprocation appropriate to a situation in which one member of the relation is incapable of reciprocating. Such a concept of social cooperation I have called *doulia*, adopting a term that derives from the Greek word for a service,[44] which I have adapted from the name of a type of care giver, the doula, who assists the postpartum woman.

Some families within the United States have traditionally availed themselves of a paid care provider, the "baby nurse," who displaces the mother by taking over care of the infant. The doula, instead, assists by caring for the mother as the mother attends to the child.[45] We can extend this notion of service and shift it from the private circumstance of postpartum care to a public conception of care by calling for an arrangement whereby those who become needy by virtue of tending to those in need can be cared for as well. *Doulia*, the *practice* of the doula, can be captured in the colloquial phrase: "What goes round comes round."[46] If someone helps another in her need, someone, in turn, will help the helper when she is needy—whether the neediness derives from her position as caretaker or from circumstances that pertain to health or age. We are each implicated in a set of dependency relations at some point in our lives, either as the one who needs care, as one called on to care, or as one responsible for obtaining care for another. We may reciprocate the caring we received by ourselves caring for the same person or seeing that this person is cared for. But we also may reciprocate by assuring care for still another individual who must depend on us in the way we depended on another. The circles of reciprocity move outward to the larger social structures of which we are a part and on whom we depend. We can articulate a principle of doulia: *"Just as we have required care to survive and thrive, so we need to provide conditions that allow others—including those who do the work of caring—to receive the care they need to survive and thrive."* [47]

While the doula who served as our paradigm is engaged in private interactions, the idea of *doulia* extends to the public domain. Just as the caretaker has a responsibility to care for the dependent, the larger society

44. I wish to thank Elfie Raymond for helping me to search for a term with the resonance necessary to capture the concept articulated here.

45. Ina Aronow, "Doulas Step in when Mothers Need a Hand," *New York Times*, Sunday, August 1, 1993, 1, 8.

46. The importance of this ethic within the African American community is documented in Carol B. Stack, *All Our Kin: Strategies for Survival in a Black Community* (New York: Harper and Row, 1974).

47. Kittay, "Human Dependency and Rawlsian Equality."

has an obligation to attend to the well-being of the caretaker. Only so can the caretaker fulfill responsibilities to the dependent without being subject to an exploitation some have called "compulsory altruism."[48]

Robert Goodin writes that the justification for the welfare state is, ultimately, an ethical one, namely, to address the needs of dependents.[49] His argument is that "those who depend on particular others for satisfaction of their basic needs are rendered, by that dependency, susceptible to exploitation by those upon whom they depend. It is the risk of exploitation of such dependencies that justifies public provision—and public provision of a distinctively welfare state form—of those basic needs."[50] There is much to be said for an understanding of welfare as the protection of the vulnerable. The vulnerability in need of protection, however, is not only the dependent who is disadvantaged by age, illness, or disability.[51] I have already addressed vulnerability of the dependency worker which the work itself incurs. We need to add that the dependency worker is not only economically vulnerable, but is also less able to make her social and political voice heard, especially when it goes against the provider of the material support that helps to sustain her and her charge.[52] Furthermore, because the dependent requires a relationship, not only the caretaking itself, to thrive, and because the dependency worker to be a caring worker requires the recognition that only a genuine relationship provides, the relationship itself requires protection. What I am suggesting is that the concept of *doulia* can serve as a justification for welfare extended to the solo mother, but that it is a justification that calls for a much broader implementation. Not only must welfare be extended to impoverished solo mothers, but it should also be extended to all dependency workers, on a model that moves away from residualism and approaches the universalistic models of social insurance and populism.

---

48. Peter Taylor-Gooby, "Welfare State Regimes and Welfare Citizenship," *Journal of European Social Policy* 1 (1991): 93–105. Cited in Orloff, "Gender and the Social Rights of Citizenship."
49. Robert Goodin, *Reasons for Welfare* (Princeton: Princeton University Press, 1988).
50. Goodin, *Reasons for Welfare*.
51. In David Schmidtz and Robert E. Goodin, *Social Welfare as an Individual Responsibility: For and Against* (New York: Cambridge University Press, 1997). In a later work, Goodin takes these matters into account. His is a superb defense of the notion of collective responsibility against those who maintain the primacy of "personal responsibility."
52. The question can be raised, "What happens when the government is the provider?" But where the provider is not privatized and individualized as it is in families, the dependency worker has an option that is available to other workers, and that is to organize. This doesn't mean that the dependency worker should take the option of strikes and walk out on dependents. But they have available mobilization strategies used by other politically organized groups. The model of the National Welfare Rights Organization is perhaps useful here.

A Vision of Welfare Based on *Doulia*

The concept of *doulia* itself suggests that the dependency worker must be involved in what Fraser has called "the struggle over needs interpretation." The feminist theorist and advocate must be careful not to follow the model of the invasive baby nurse rather than the assisting doula. Nonetheless because dependency work does partially deprive the dependency worker of political voice, interventions are crucial. With these caveats in mind, I would like to say a few things about what basing welfare policies on a concept of *doulia* entails.[53] First, it requires that all dependency work, whether it is care for children, the ill, the aged, or the disabled, be recognized as social contributions that require reciprocation, not by the cared for but by a larger social circle in which the dependency relation is embedded; that the social goods and burdens to be distributed and shared must include the goods of caring relations. There are a number of possible ways in which such goods and reciprocation can be recognized.

As we've already noted, the traditional family, with its breadwinner and caretaker, forms one such embedding nest at least for the care of young children. Because it does, many conservatives, but also some liberals, have seen the "two-parent" family as the best solution to welfare dependency. Is it? Let us presume the viability of the traditional family— ignore for the moment the social forces that have hammered away at it and at the questionable justice of its gendered division of labor. Let us imagine a family form and an economy in which one breadwinner can produce income sufficient to support a spouse, who does the domestic labor and caring work, and a couple of children; and let us suppose that this family is not governed by traditional gender divisions of labor. The dependency worker cares for the dependents; the breadwinner, whom we'll also call "the private provider," supports the dependency relation with resources sufficient to maintain all. This is then a private arrangement which presumably calls on no additional social supports and so is "self-sufficient."[54]

53. Nancy Fraser, "After the Family Wage" listed a number of criteria by which to evaluate proposals for the welfare state. The criteria are guided by an ideal of gender parity. I invite the reader to consider the proposals put forward here in terms of these criteria.

54. This is a close to the vision articulated by 1996 vice presidential candidate Jack Kemp in one of the vice presidential debates. He envisioned an economy that could support a family with one breadwinner and one stay-at-home parent, although he was quick to add that the stay-at-home parent would not have to be the woman! It is interesting to have the ideal of the "family wage," a concept fought for by the left in this country, reemerge as a proposition by the right, at the same time

There are at least three problems with this analysis. The first is conceptual, the second is economic, and the third is ethical and a matter of justice. First, it is an obfuscation to think of such a structure as "self-sufficient." Although dependency work results in the dependency worker's derived dependency, all employment involves some dependency. The provider is dependent on an employer and still more significantly dependent on an economy whose skills, services, or products are marketable. The waged worker is him/herself in nested dependencies—dependent on an employer, who is dependent on a market and on a particular configuration of economic structures and forces, such as interest rates, global competition, and so forth. A private provider does not lend "self-sufficiency" to the dependence relation, because this self-sufficiency is a conceptual chimera in a capitalist economy. The appropriate contrast between a dependency worker and other workers is not between those who are self-reliant and those who are dependent, but between those whose labor results in some sorts of vulnerabilities rather than others.[55]

Second, an economically self-reliant provider/caretaker model requires a rate of compensation that makes it viable for a provider to support a family. The fact of structural unemployment, as we all know, means that not all providers can find employment, and especially employment adequate to support a family. The rates of poverty among families with two adults present indicate that this goal is not achievable within the current economy for large numbers of families.[56] The reality for most two-parent families today is a wife who has primary responsibility for both domestic work and dependency work, but who also holds down a job, often part-time, almost always not paying as well as her husband's. The pure provider/caretaker model has been hybridized. The change comes in part out of women's aspirations and in part out of economic necessity since the average weekly inflation-adjusted earnings have declined

when they are legislating the entrance of women (usually without male support) on welfare, even those raising children as young as two, into the labor force at minimum wage salaries.

55. Ann Shola Orloff, "Gender and the Social Rights of Citizenship," points out that one way to characterize the difference between welfare programs geared to men and those targeted at women is that the former are meant to shield the citizen against the worst effects of market failures, while the latter are meant to shield against familial failures. In this respect it is important to see that when the benefits are intended to deal with familial failures, it is the fate of the children rather than the adult women that is most likely to garner public sympathy. Women again come to be seen as conduits rather than as persons and citizens in their own right.

56. According to the *Current Population Surrey* of March 1994, 9 percent of married coupled were poor, and single mothers comprised 46 percent of the poor; of all poor families 12 percent had at least one year-round, full-time worker and 32 percent had at least one member who worked at least 30 weeks during the year. These figures are based on a rate of poverty that all experts agree are set too low.

by 19 percent since 1973 (U. S. Department of Labor, Bureau of Labor Statistics).

Dependency work and provision can be so divided that each of two partners engage in each of the two forms of labor and relationship. But more often, even the hybridized model follows many of the same structural features as the pure model.[57] The hybridized dependency worker continues to assume primary responsibility for dependents and remains largely (though not totally) dependent on the income of the hybridized breadwinner partner. If the marriage falls apart, the financial suffering falls largely to the one who bears the major responsibility for dependency work. It is often the demands of the dependency work that prevent that partner from pursuing financially more advantageous situations.

Third, as we have suggested, the work of dependency care disadvantages the dependency worker with respect to her (or his) exit options if the relationship with the breadwinner becomes fragile. Orloff has argued that the social right that women need to demand is the capacity to form and sustain autonomous families. Only such a right would adequately address the vulnerability of the dependency worker. Her vulnerability to the good graces of the private provider means that she has what Sen terms a disadvantage of bargaining power in relations of "cooperative conflict."[58] This handicap is a source of the myriad injustices that pervade the intimate relations of family life and consequently deprive woman of the social citizenship that the welfare state affords the male worker by "decommodifying" his labor.[59] The consequences of cooperative conflict and the economic dependency on an individual man are aggravated by women's subordinate position in the larger society, that is, by the likelihood that she will receive a smaller paycheck, that she is susceptible to sexual intimidation on the job, and so forth. But the injustices of intimate life, particularly when one is responsible for the well-being of a dependent would continue to be present (albeit to a lesser degree) even if many of the public injustices were corrected. Furthermore, even if de-

57. Why this is so is an interesting sociological question. It is also interesting to contemplate the possibilities for gender equity within the family if such an arrangement within the home is coupled with genuine gender equity in the public domain of paid employment and political and social power. But despite all of women's advances, this remains a utopian vision, whose possibility of realization remains in the realm of speculation. I suspect that the sorts of considerations with respect to dependency work that I bring forth here would be relevant to the realization of this more private instantiation of genuine gender equality and sharing of dependency responsibilities and dependency work.

58. Amartya Sen, "Gender and Cooperative Conflict," in *Persistent Inequalities*, Irene Trinker, ed. (New York: Oxford University Press, 1989), 123–149.

59. Orloff, "Gender and the Social Rights of Citizenship."

pendency work were not *gendered*, the disadvantage in cooperative conflicts such as in the family would itself be a consequence of the dependency work on a private provider model.

This means that a just reciprocation for dependency work could not
presume the so-called private arrangement of the traditional bread-
winner/caretaker model—or even the hybridized model. This urges a
universalization of benefits for dependency work. Just as workman's compensation and unemployment insurance became programs that were universally[60] available to workers, with benefits rationalized and routinized
(and extended without stigma), so must compensation for dependency
work.[61] I can envision a payment for dependency work, which could be
used to compensate a mother for her time caring for her child or to allow
her to use the money to pay for child care, or payments to a son or daughter to care for an ailing parent or to pay someone else to perform the service. The level of reciprocation, furthermore, must allow the dependency
worker not only to survive, but also to have the resources to care for the
dependent as well as herself. This means considering what else a dependency worker requires: health coverage (as all workers and all dependents
should get); certain in-kind services or goods or their monetary equivalent; housing. But again, specifying these must be a work in which dependency workers are themselves engaged.

The conception of *doulia* respects not only the nature of dependency,
but also the caretaker as a dependency *worker*. Like other workers they
need vacations, exit options, retraining when they are no longer needed
at their employment. And like all work, dependency work must be de-
gendered, in fact, not in name only. This suggests public programs of educating for dependency work—especially for young boys and men.

But workers normally are accountable to those who pay their wages.
One problem with having public support for dependency work may be
that when the state pays for the labor of caring for one's own children, or
one's aging parents, then the state can claim that it has the right to over-
see the quality of work and the input of the worker. Such intrusion into
the "private domain" runs counter to much liberal thought. Can we

---

60. Strictly speaking, universality is too strong a claim, for occupational exclusions and eligibility
rules restrict who can receive these benefits. Nonetheless, all workers within those limits are eligible
and their eligibility is not income dependent. When writers on welfare and the welfare state speak
of "universal" programs, they mean either that all citizens receive the benefit or that all with a certain category do. The contrast is generally with programs that depend on income or, sometimes,
occupation. For example, neither AFDC nor farm subsidies are universal benefits.
61. Kari Waerness, "On the Rationality of Caring," in *Women and the State*, Ann Showstack Sassoon, ed. (London: Hutchinson, 1987), 207–234.

justifiably say to the state, "be the 'public' provider, be the one who pays the dependency worker her salary, but then, except of course when the dependency worker violates the trust of her charge and begins to be abusive or negligent, stay out of the 'private' dependency relation"? Putting the matter this way may rely too much on the dichotomy of public and private that feminist theorists have urged us to reconsider. But state oversight of personal relations, except to protect against abuse and the perpetuation of sexist oppression, seems to run counter to most feminist liberatory goals as well.

I believe that the concept of social cooperation inherent in the concept of *doulia* offers a resolution to this dilemma. Ordinary concepts of reciprocation dictate that if I provide you with a product or a service, you compensate me for the product or the labor I poured into that product or service. Lines of accountability follow the lines of reciprocation. If you do not pay me, I do not receive the benefits for which I labored, and so I hold you accountable, and it is my right to do so. If you pay me but I do not deliver the goods, I do not receive the benefits for which I labored, and I hold you accountable and, again, it is my right to do so. No third party is affected by the transaction, and each party is accountable to the other, except that the state may have a duty to ensure that both parties honor their agreements. But the labor of the dependency worker flows to the dependent. If I do a good job as a dependency worker, the dependent is the beneficiary. I am accountable, first and foremost, to the direct beneficiary of my actions, that is, to my charge. Just as any other worker, I have a right to demand compensation for my labor. But because the dependent, virtually by definition, is not in a position to compensate, the compensation comes from another source (e.g., the provider). The right to demand that the work be well done, however, is the right of the dependent. The duty of the state, whether it is a provider or not, is to be sure the work is well done and that the dependency worker is compensated. The duty of the state is especially significant in the case of a party as vulnerable as the charge. The point is only that when a larger social structure is the provider, being such a provider is not the same as being the employer to whom a worker is responsible. Such a duty is not an open ticket to intrude on the relationship or to regulate the life of the dependency worker. The duty of the public provider remains the duty of the state at present: to ensure that a child is not neglected or abused or denied provisions of a fundamental sort. Such a duty is consonant with the obligation of the state to protect its citizens against abuses from other citizens. Just as we do not want the "private relation" of spouses to be exempt, so we cannot want dependency relations to be exempted.

Adequate public support of dependency work, then, would significantly alter the dependency workers' bargaining position, making both them and their charges better able to respond to abuse within the family and less subject to intrusive state regulation. Even the miserly AFDC program was primarily a boon to women with children escaping abusive relations. A welfare program that universalizes compensation for dependency work, whether or not another able adult were present in the home, would allow women to leave abusive relations without the stigma of current welfare participation.

Within our own society, dependency workers—paid or unpaid—are generally poorer than others. Paid dependency workers, such as child care workers, are the most poorly paid workers relative to their level of education and skill.[62] In hospitals and nursing homes, orderlies and aides, those who do most of the hands-on dependency care of patients and clients, are the lowest paid staff. Female-headed households account for the poorest families in the United States. *Doulia* requires that dependency work which is currently paid work be well-paid. It is not enough that women be able to have affordable child care. We are not adhering to a principle of *doulia* when we exploit other women to care for our children.

Finally, a concept of *doulia* would be accepting of any family form in which dependency work is adequately realized. It would honor different familial forms of caring, a child caring for an elderly parent; a gay man caring for his partner with AIDS; a lesbian woman caring for her lover, and her lover's children, through a bout of breast cancer; a single-parent household or a multiple-adult household in which children are being raised. A concept of *doulia* only recognizes need and the vulnerability arising from the responsiveness to need—not family form or forms of sexuality, gender, class, or race.[63]

Underlying the debate over AFDC has been the question of the visibility and the social responsibility for the dependency work of women. By keeping the responsibility private, poor women will stay poor and those not poor will be impoverished if they try to raise families without support of a man. It is a category in which the interests of women of dif-

62. Heidi I. Hartman and Diana Pearce, *High Skill and Low Pay*. Report prepared for child care action campaign, Institute for Women's Policy Research (Washington, DC: Institute for Women's Policy Research, 1989).
63. But it also recognizes that all these specificities are called into play when in discursive matters of need interpretation—so again, how the need is defined and how it is to be satisfied are things that must be negotiated by those in the dependency relation. (See Nancy Fraser, "Women, Welfare and the Politics of Need Interpretation," *Hypatia* 2, no. 1 (Winter 1987): 103–121.)

ferent races or classes can be turned against each other. White women benefit from the dependency work of women of color, for example, and wealthy women benefit from the dependency work of poorer women. Glenn points to the difficulties that await an effort to unite women around issues of care. She writes:[64]

> With the move into the labor force of all races and classes of women, it is tempting to think that we can find unity around the common problems of "working women." With that in mind, feminist policy-makers have called for expanding services to assist employed mothers in such areas as child care and elderly care. We need to ask, Who is going to do the work? Who will benefit from increased services? The historical record suggests that it will be done by women of color . . . and that it will be middle-class women who will receive the services. (p. 36)

Applying this scenario to the needs of employed middle-class women and regulations insisting that women on welfare find employment, she wryly points out that the apparent coincidence of interest comes apart when one recognizes that, at current wages, child care work will not suffice to bring the welfare mother out of poverty, and if wages are raised the middle-class woman will not be able to afford the less advantaged women's services. Feminism will come apart unless women speak and think together about how to forge policies that will benefit both sets of women and will lessen the increasing disparity between them.

The call for a concept of *doulia* and universal policies is not to smooth over these difficult issues between women with different interests and from different races and classes. Nor is it to reinstate universalism as if none of identity politics, postmodernism, and critical race theories mattered. But the call for universal policies is not universalism. Universal policies do not pretend that we are all alike in some designated characteristic. They maintain only that if anyone should have access to a given resource, everyone should have access to such a resource, because such a resource comes to us by virtue of our membership within a given community, often because it is believed that such a resource is needed for each to function as a full member of such a community.

As I indicated earlier universal policies have had their critics. They have been criticized as not sufficiently redistributive and as benefiting most

---

64. Evelyn Nakano Glenn, "From Servitude to Service Work: Historical Continuities in the Racial Division of Paid Reproductive Labor," *Signs: Journal of Women in Culture and Society* 18, no. 1 (Autumn 1992): 1–43.

those who need them least. But universal policies that are formed from the perspective of the least well-off and formed to serve their needs first are least likely to be deficient in this respect. A good example is provided by the case of disability. The ramps and modified sidewalks meant to serve the disabled, but available for all to use, have benefited many populations for whom they were not envisioned without diminishing their usefulness to the disabled. The universal policies advocated on a conception of *doulia* derive from the need that women have to function as full citizens in a postindustrial world. To function, free of vulnerability to exploitation due to paid or familial dependency work, to be free to engage with the full resonance of their voices, women must have access to universal provision that recognizes their indispensable function as dependency workers and the importance of their participation as full citizens.

Toward a Framework for Understanding Activism among Poor and Working-Class Women in Twentieth-Century America

Mimi Abramovitz

"The more closely one looks at the record the less comfortable one becomes with reducing the tens of thousands of people . . . who participated" in local activism "to faceless masses . . . marching in the background. If we are surprised at what these people accomplished, our surprise may be a commentary on the angle of vision from which we view them." [1]

The passage of the Personal Responsibility and Work Opportunity Act of 1996 has spawned many useful critiques of welfare "reform." As a result we know more about how individual women negotiate the welfare system. We also are learning about the impact of welfare reform on women forced to leave the rolls. However, we know very little about the ways in which low-income women—the majority of social welfare clients—have tried, as a group, to shape social welfare policy on their own behalf. The reporters and politicians who recently discovered middle-class "soccer" moms and working-class "waitress" moms regarded these politicized mothers as a new phenomenon.[2] This contrasts with an emerging series of case studies which show that throughout the twentieth century, if not before, poor and working-class women in the United States have pressed their claims on employers, merchants, landlords, and the welfare state to improve or defend the typically precarious standard of living of their families and communities.

---

1. C. M. Payne, *I've Got the Light of Freedom: The Organizing Tradition and the Mississippi Freedom Struggle* (Berkeley: University of California Press, 1995), 3, 5.
2. M. Henneberger, "Want Votes with That? Get the 'Waitress Moms,'" *New York Times*, October 25, 1998, Sec. 4, 3.

Unfortunately, poor and working-class women rarely benefit from the sense of power that stems from knowing their own history. With the exception of the welfare rights movement in the 1960s, we lack a comprehensive history of low-income women's social welfare activism. The existing case studies on low-income women's activism provide fascinating snapshots of specific people, organizations, and events. However, these singular studies inevitably leave the long history of activism individualized, time-bound, and largely unknown. Fortunately, in the aggregate the same studies provide a way to convert the currently fragmented data into a cohesive historical account.

This chapter presents concepts for such a history of poor and working-class women's activism during the twentieth century in the United States. However, uncovering this history has required new approaches to the study of politics and collective action. More specifically, the standard understandings of the forces that shape political participation—politics, consciousness, and contradictions in the political economy—were too narrow and too singularly reflective of the experiences of men to effectively capture the lives and activism of low-income women. The definitions used had to be both broadened and gendered.

In this chapter I first reconfigure notions of activism. To bring women into view I reconsider both the ways in which poor and working-class women become active and the sites of their activism. Next I synthesize recent efforts by scholars to reconceptualize definitions of political consciousness in ways that account for the class experiences of low-income women. Then I explore the conflicts/contradictions in the wider political economy that appear to activate low-income women. The following section notes the importance of the wider social context. Finally I discuss impacts and outcomes. The discussion that synthesizes and recasts the existing case studies of low-income women's activism and feminist histories of the welfare state represents the beginnings of a framework for a planned book on the history of activism among poor and working-class women. It focuses on activism directed toward economic security and racial justice—issues that have consistently preoccupied low-income women. It is limited to Black and white low-income women, given the greater amount and availability of historical studies of activism by women in these two groups.

The project grows from a wider effort within the academy to give voice and visibility to underrepresented groups. It has been fueled by the still small but growing resurgence of social welfare activism among low-income women who since the mid-1980s have fought welfare reform as it swept across the country. It also builds from the increased number of case studies on grassroots women's collective action, as well as from my prior work on the impact of social welfare policy on the lives of women.

Except for the courage and stamina of poor and working-class women activists, there would be no story to tell at all. From the outset they have longed for both "bread and roses"—a slogan popularized by women during the 1912 strike against the owners of the Lawrence, Massachusetts, textile mills. Like the textile mill workers, low-income women have had to battle for "bread" to feed their families. However, they have also fought for "roses," that is, beauty, dignity, respect, and a better quality of life.

RECONFIGURING ACTIVISM TO BRING WOMEN INTO VIEW

Poor and working-class women mobilized around a wide range of issues during the twentieth century. Although they became active in various venues and engaged in various activities, their collective actions remained largely invisible in the media, the academy, and wider society. For years, most researchers ignored women of all classes and races altogether. They dismissed white middle- and working-class women, whom they presumed were passive, apolitical, and confined to the home. They especially ignored African Americans whom they did not see as women at all.

The standard definition of *politics* also rendered women invisible. Informed by narrow notions of what is political and what is worthy of study, scholars have favored formal political actors, established political structures, and organized social movements—the very political institutions that barred women. The researchers also tended to overlook the distinctive form of politics created by women who overcame or otherwise negotiated the socially imposed constraints of womenhood to become politically active.

These practices, combined with other gender, race, and class biases, effectively obliterated women, especially low-income women, from the researchers' radar screen. However, when we include identifiable women's "spaces"[3] and gendered modes of activism, the concealment nearly evaporates.

3. S. M. Evans, *Born for Liberty: A History of Women In America* (New York: Free Press, 1989); S. M. Evans, *Personal Politics: The Roots of Women's Liberation in the Civil Rights Movement and the New Left* (New York: Vintage Book, 1980).

The "Spaces" Inhabited by Women

Women occupy specific if not exclusive "spaces" in the welfare state but also in the workplace and the community. The concentration of women in these "female" spaces reflects the gender division of labor, which assigns women and men to different roles and spheres. The resulting isolation of women as a group has fostered the development of gendered grievances, consciousness, and organizational capacity that have enabled them to engage in collective action directed toward the state as well as toward private enterprise.

The Welfare State. The welfare state has always been a major focus of women's social welfare activism. The historic poverty of women, the predominance of women among welfare state recipients and workers, and the state's role in providing for family support ensured that the welfare state became a women's "space." Feminist scholars have shown that white and Black middle-class women reformers played a significant role in the origins of the U.S. welfare state.[4] This research revised much of U.S. history and shattered the stereotypes of middle-class women as apolitical and confined to the home.

However, poor and working-class women have developed their own relationship to the welfare state based on their shared experiences as a low-paid workers, community members, and social program clients. Before the development of state and federal social welfare provision, low-income activist women organized so that landlords, merchants, and employers would not deprive families and communities of basic necessities such as an adequate income, affordable food, and decent housing. These early confrontations with private business exposed the inability

---

4. J. Brenner and B. Laslett, "Gender, Social Reproduction and Women's Self-organization: Considering the U.S. Welfare State," *Gender and Society* 5, no. 3 (September 1991): 311–333; T. Skocpol, *Protecting Soldiers and Mothers: The Political Origins of Social Policy in the U.S.* (Cambridge: Harvard University Press, 1992); S. Koven and S. Michel, *Mothers of a New World: Maternalist Politics and the Origins of Welfare States* (London: Routledge, 1992); S. Lemons, *The Woman Citizen: Social Feminism in the 1920s,* (Charlotteville: University Press of Virginia, 1973); R. Muncy, *Creating a Female Dominion in American Reform* (New York: Oxford University Press, 1991); L. Gordon, Black and White Visions of Women's Welfare Activism, 1890–1945, *Journal of American History,* 78 (September 1991): 559–590; E. Boris, "The Power of Motherhood; Black and White Activist Women Redefine the Political," *Yale Journal of Law and Feminism* 2(Fall 1989): 25–491; S. Ware, *Beyond Suffrage: Women in the New Deal* (Cambridge: Oxford University Press, 1981); B. Robnett, *How Long? How Long? African American Women in the Struggle for Civil Rights* (New York: Oxford University Press, 1994); J. G. Robinson, *The Montgomery Bus Boycott and the Women Who Started It* (Knoxville: University of Tennessee Press, 1987); T. W. Hunter, *To 'Joy My Freedom: Southern Black Women's Lives and Labors' after the Civil War* (Cambridge: Harvard University Press, 1997).

of the market economy to adequately meet basic human needs. The women's demands also prefigured the goods and services that the government would eventually have to provide to sustain families, to ensure a healthy, productive, and properly socialized work force, and to quiet social unrest.

With the advent of state and then federal government programs, poor and working-class women became consumers of cash benefits, public housing, food programs, and other social services. As the welfare state grew and expanded, low-income women—often with the help of middle-class women activists from feminist organizations, trade unions, and left political parties—insisted that the state meet their needs more adequately. The welfare state expanded from 1935 to 1975, due to population growth, economic fluctuations, and pressure from social movements. The increased scale and scope of government benefits, services, and protections available to low-income families and communities held out the promise of an economic cushion and emboldened women to make individual but also collective claims on the state. Some of the more obvious campaigns included the cost-of-living protest in the 1930s,[5] the welfare rights movement in the 1960s and 1970s,[6] and war on poverty activism in the 1970s and 1980s.[7] More recently, faced with an assault on social welfare programs, some poor and working-class women became discouraged and silenced. Others, including many women on welfare, mobilized to defend what their foremothers had previously won.

It turns out, however, that the welfare state is only one site of social welfare struggle for low-income women. Indeed, looking at activities not usually thought of as social welfare activism uncovers considerable social welfare activism elsewhere. Most studies of low-income women's activism center on labor and community events. Given this focus, the social welfare implications of this work often go unnoticed. Yet another look at the workplace and the community reveals that both working women and community-based housewives have had a strong social welfare agenda. The short economic distance between the family on welfare

5. A. Orleck, *Common Sense and a Little Fire: Women and Working-Class Politics in the United States, 1900–1965* (Chapel Hill: University of North Carolina, 1995).
6. G. West, *The National Welfare Rights Movement: The Social Protest of Poor Wopmen* (New York: Praeger, 1981); S. H. Hertz, *The Welfare Mothers Movement: A Decade of Change for Poor Women* (Washington, D.C. University Press of America, 1981); N. Kotz and M. Kotz, *A Passion For Equality: George Wiley and the Movement* (New York: W.W. Norton, 1977).
7. N. Naples, *Grassroots Warriors: Activist Mothering, Community Work and the War on Poverty* (New York: Routledge, 1998); I. Susser, *Norman Street: Poverty and Politics in an Urban Neighborhood* (New York: Oxford University Press, 1982).

and the working-poor household creates the basis for social welfare activism among both groups. The social welfare agenda of low-income working women and community-based homemakers without a direct need for economic assistance can be seen in their regular demands that local, state, or federal authorities assist, protect, and regulate workplace and community conditions.

The Workplace. Poor and working-class women have regularly engaged in social welfare activism on the job. Low-income white women and especially African American mothers and wives have a long history of employment—be it in factories, offices, fields, stores, or in other people's homes. Indeed, many households rely on the income of mothers for survival. Even more than middle-class women, in most workplaces low-income women have found themselves confined to traditional women's jobs. This segregation of occupations by sex and race and the concentration of women at the bottom of most job ladders created shared grievances and networks that at times became the basis for women's workplace activism.

Throughout the twentieth century low-income working women led militant labor uprisings. They waged lengthy strikes for better wages and working conditions, fought hard for union protection, and otherwise protested exploitation.[8] Although poor and working-class women did not typically rally around the feminist demand for equal rights with men, they did react strongly when sexism barred them from improving the quality of life in their families and communities. When unions and employers continued to ignore their demands, the women frequently turned to the government to replace their lost income; to regulate wages and working conditions; to prohibit race discrimination, sex discrimination, and sexual harassment; and to otherwise protect their dignity and standard of living. That is, they engaged in social welfare activism from the job.[9]

The Community. Contrary to popular stereotypes, however, community-based homemakers have also mobilized regularly on behalf of their standard of living. By defining women's place as in the home (even when they work outside it), the societal gender division of labor concentrates

8. M. W. Greenwald, "Working Class Feminism and the Family Wage Ideal: The Seattle Debate on Married Women's Right to Work, 1914–1920," *Journal of American History* 76, no. 1 (1989): 118–149.
9. Z. Eisenstein, *Radical Future of Liberal Feminism* (New York: Longman, 1981).

women in local neighborhoods. Having learned that electoral politics and other mainstream institutions often fail to represent their best interests, poor and working-class women, and especially women of color, historically exercised what power they had in the community from the bottom up.[10]

White and Black women from poor and working-class communities have made their voices heard in many ways—the long tradition seemingly unknown to the media given its surprise, noted earlier, at the existence of the politically interested "soccer" and "waitress" moms. Since the turn of the century, low-income women have organized or participated in rent strikes (1900s), cost-of-living protests (1930s), civil rights drives (1940s, 1950s, and 1960s), welfare rights demonstrations (1960s and 1970s), neighborhood improvement projects (1970s and 1980s) and antiretrenchment campaigns of all kinds (1980s and 1990s). They have boycotted stores, blocked evictions, sat in at welfare offices, picketed public schools, formed cooperatives, and supported striking husbands— to name just a few of the tactics used by social welfare activists to achieve greater economic security and racial justice.

In addition to securing access to food, shelter, and welfare state services, low-income African American women faced many manifestations of the often unbridled racism which posed endless threats to self, household, and the overall well-being of the African American community. Given that the survival of African American families and communities depended on both economic security and racial justice, low-income Black women activists have always targeted individual prejudice, organizational discrimination, and institutionalized racism—whether in the form of racial stereotyping, employment discrimination, or racial violence. Indeed, racial justice and economic security cannot be separated for persons of color—or, for that matter, for the white community.

WAYS OF BECOMING ACTIVE

Although women of all classes regularly violated gender expectations of passivity and dependence to become politically active, low-income women's activism is especially difficult to document because of, among other things, a scarcity of easily accessible data. Unlike their better-off sisters, poor and working-class women rarely left a paper trail of letters, di-

---

10. R. Feldman and S. Stall, "The Politics of Space Appropriation: A Case Study of Women's Struggles for Homeplace in Chicago Public Housing." Unpublished manuscript, 1992.

aries, or organizational records needed to retell their story. The media's long-standing preference for large events, famous people, and national issues also deprived investigators of reports of local working-class struggles.[11] When the media did cover community actions, they often failed to note the presence of women in the crowd. The American political process itself also discouraged collective action among poor and working-class people. Indeed, political parties favor those with money, while business and the state periodically stymie the organizational efforts of poor people, deprive them of resources, crush their mobilizations, and allow them to die without a trace.[12] These obstacles suggest that to document the history of low-income women's activism, it becomes important to identify and include more than one type or level of politics. While standard studies of politics focus on individual actions of resistance or social protests or social movements, all three types must be considered to bring forth the long history of low-income women's activism.

Individual acts of resistance are the small, personal, daily strategies resorted to by the most marginalized members of society. Locked outside of established institutions and deprived of power, subordinated people frequently cannot afford the risks of visible collective action. Instead, they create a hidden politics of life to protect their personal dignity and economic interests. This includes oppositional talk, walk, and dress; dissident messages embedded in songs, jokes, and folklore; as well as absenteeism, foot-dragging, evasive actions, and petty theft, including so-called welfare "fraud."[13] These measures may not constitute activism in the standard sense of the word.[14] Yet they represent one of the means

---

11. For example, the recent national actions organized by the Kensington Welfare Rights Union of behalf of its parent organization, the National Welfare Rights Union (NRWU), went largely unreported. In June 1998, in town after town, NWRU's suporters welcomed the NWRU's Freedom Bus as it toured the country holding poor people's tribunals. The tour ended in New York City on July 1, 1998, where it held an International Tribunal at the United Nations. In October 1998 a follow-up Poor People's Summit in Philadelphia was attend by some 300 poor women and men. Most of the mainstream media did not consider these unique and spirited events worthy of coverage.

12. Francis Fox Piven, Preface, in L. N. Ballis, *Bread or Justice: Grassroots Organizing in the Welfare Rights Movement* (Lexington, Mass.: D.C Heath, 1974).

13. R. D. Kelly, *Race Rebels: Culture Politics and the Black Working Class* (New York: Free Press, 1994); T. W. Hunter, *To 'Joy My Freedom: Southern Black Women's Lives and Labors after The Civil War* (Cambridge: Harvard University Press, 1994); J. Jones, *Labor of Love, Labor of Sorrow: Black Women Work and Family, From Slavery to the Present*, New York: Basic Books, 1985); D. Katzman, *Seven Days a Week: Women and Domestic Service in Industrializing America*, (New York: Oxford University Press, 1978).

14. N. S. Perl, "Resistance Strategies: The Routine Struggle for Bread and Roses," In K. B. Sachs and D. Remy, eds., *My Troubles Are Going to Have Trouble with Me* (New Brunswick: Rutgers University Press, 1984), 193–209; V. R. Seitz, "Class, Gender, and Resistance in the Appalachian Coalfield"; in N. Naples, ed. *Community Activism and Feminist Politics Organizing across Race, Class and Gender* (New York: Routledge, 1989), 213–236.

used by poorly positioned persons to fight back.[15] Women rank high among such poorly positioned persons given the large numbers of female slaves, domestic servants, low-paid women workers, and welfare state clients. The record of this type of resistance reminds us that fear of losing one's job or one's life can deter collective action. But it cannot completely silence the voice of protest among the most disadvantaged women. The conditions that provoke individual resistance also highlight the sources of exploitation and oppression that at other times have mobilized low-income women for collective protest.

Social protest refers to the conscious and common actions taken by a group of people who pool their energies, resources, and opportunities. Collectively they seek positive change or oppose developments that will bring them harm. Some social protests remain sustained over a period of time. More often they remain sporadic, spontaneous, minimally organized, and largely unseen. This holds especially true for low-income women, whose activism tends to be local, community-based, and short-lived—and, as noted earlier, devalued. Many observers have dismissed this form of collective action, much of it targeted to the welfare state, as inconsequential and not worthy of notice. Others see it as a rational and political means of challenging the status quo.[16] Yet, it was just this kind of social protest by groups of local women on welfare that sparked the welfare rights movement in the 1960s and again in the 1990s. The French historian George Rudé suggests that under certain conditions, such everyday collective actions may have far-reaching effects, may pave the way for wider social movements, and may create unanticipated possibilities for social change.[17]

Social movements are organized groups designed to bring about or resist change by means of various strategies. The most widely studied type of activism, social movements typically involve key elements. These include formal organizations governed by rules and regulations, influential leaders, large numbers of people, an identified membership, and a degree

15. N. S. Perl, "Resistance Strategies: The Routine Struggle for Bread and Roses," in K. B. Sachs and D. Remy, eds., *My Troubles Are Going to Have Trouble with Me*, 193–209. D. E. Janiewski, *Sisterhood Denied: Race, Gender and Class in a New South Community* (Philadelphia: Temple University Press, 1985); A. Cameron, "Bread and Roses Revisited: Women's Culture and Working Class Activism in the Lawrence Strike of 1912," in R. Milkman, ed., *Women, Work and Protest: A Century of U.S. Women's Labor History*. (Boston: Routledge and Kegan Paul, 1985), 42–61.
16. F. F. Piven and R. Cloward, *Poor People's Movements: Why They Succeed, How They Fail* (New York: Vintage Books, 1977).
17. George Rudé, *The Crowd in History: A Study of the Distribution of Power*, (New York: Wiley, 1964.

of longevity. When studying low-income women's social welfare activism the temptation exists to write off the trade union, civil rights, and women's liberation movements because they historically dismissed poor and working-class women as unimportant players and seemed to ignore social welfare issues. The civil rights and trade union movements typically barred women from participation or relegated them to minor roles and rarely took up welfare rights. The feminist movement often failed to address the needs of women of color and low-income white women and thus did not attract them. Most women's organization also failed to support the welfare rights movement in the 1960s and the 1990s, further increasing their distance from their low-income sisters.

However, a second look reveals that these large national movements did involve low-income women. Looking at the particular "spaces" inhabited by women rendered them visible. When one considers that most of the daily activism of social movements takes place at the local level, one instantly sees the poor and working-class women who for years have volunteered as quiet supporters, street-level organizers, and local leaders. Indeed, some of the movements may not have survived without the unheralded female foot soldiers who forged links between national organizers and local residents. Yet few commentators give credit to these "bridge" women whom Robnett refers to as "micromobilizers."[18] The male leaders and the media ignored them during the heyday of the movements. Most scholars disregarded them afterward. Most important, most social movement scholars did not notice or simply ignored the social welfare implications in their research. Yet, it is well known that the demands of these movements helped to fuel the expansion of the U.S. welfare state after World War II.

THE CLASS CONSCIOUSNESS OF POOR AND WORKING-CLASS WOMEN

It is widely accepted that social welfare activism reflects the interplay of consciousness, objective conditions, and the wider social context. These concepts are hardly new. But they need to be reconfigured to take into account the ways in which gender and race as well as class shape the realities of women's lives.

18. B. Robnett, *How Long? How Long? African American Women in the Struggle for Civil Rights* New York: Oxford Univesity Press, 1997).

Consciousness

The standard accounts of political consciousness have focused singularly on class dynamics, and they associate class conflict with men and waged work. This view presumes that women lacked class consciousness because they did not work for wages outside the home. Alternatively it was assumed that women's class experience mirrored that of men. Both explanations marginalize women and fail to account for any unique ways in which the experience of class shapes the consciousness of women, both white and Black. In recent years, to capture the gendered and racialized experience of women as members of the working class, efforts have been made to modify these presumptions.

The dictionary defines *consciousness* as having knowledge of what is happening around oneself.[19] Harstock adds that consciousness reflects the limits of human understanding set by the daily experience and social position of individuals and groups.[20] Political consciousness additionally entails a critique of prevailing power relations that emerges from communal association and social/economic conflict.[21] In other words, an individual's or group's "place" in society, shared experiences, and legacy of community struggle shapes their ideas, actions, and "standpoint."

The original standpoint theory held that the class structure of society yielded two key groups: the owning and the working class. Based on their dominant or subordinated position, each developed a unique view of the world. Through associations with other workers on the job and collective struggles against employers, the perceptions of at least some laborers turned into a powerful critique of capital. The movements they formed called for changes ranging from unionization to the creation of worker's political parties to a more equal redistribution of wealth and power. However, beyond calling for a family wage for men to support their wives and children, these trade unions and political parties rarely acknowledged the needs of women or allowed them to express their political voice.

Harstock has expanded standpoint theory to include women.[22] She posits that, along with class location, the gender division of labor shapes

19. N. Webster, *Webster's New Universal Unabridged Dictionary* (New York: Simon and Schuster, 1983).
20. N. Harstock, "The Feminist Standpoint: Developing the Ground for a Specifically Feminist Historical Materialism" in S. Harding, ed., *Feminism and Methodology* (Bloomington: Indiana University Press, 1987), 150–180.
21. T. Kaplan, "Class Consciousness and Community in Nineteenth Century Andalusia," *Political Power and Social Theory.* 2: 21–57.
22. N. Harstock, "The Feminist Standpoint."

women's place and options in society. Among other things, the gender division of labor assigns women to homemaking and caretaking and gives rise to an ideology of gender roles that rationalizes the social arrangements that hold women down.[23] Like class divisions, those of gender create opposing visions of reality for women and men. Based on their subordinated position in the wider social order, women develop a unique view of the world. The segregation of women into female spaces led women to develop shared grievances and organizations on the job, in the community, and within the welfare state. Through these associations and their conflicts with men for a fair, if not a controlling share of resources and power, the perceptions of at least some women turned into a powerful critique of patriarchy and male domination. Through struggles to gain voice, visibility, and power activist women have generated a "feminist" standpoint and a women's movement. Its critique of male supremacy and patriarchal society led to calls ranging from women rights to women's liberation.

The racial divide in the United States leaves Blacks and whites living in what political scientist Andrew Hacker has referred to as two separate, unequal, and often hostile nations.[24] The segregation of African Americans on the job, in urban neighborhoods, and in social welfare programs led them to develop shared grievances and organizations. Through these associations and their conflicts with white people for a fair, if not a controlling share of resources and power, the perceptions of at least some African Americans turned into a powerful critique of racism and white domination. Through their struggles to gain voice, visibility, and power, activist Blacks have generated an African American "standpoint" that has underpinned civil rights and Black power movements since at least 1900.

The diversification of standpoints along the fault lines of class, gender, and race inequality broadens our understanding of consciousness and collective action. However, the specific standpoints tend to "splinter human agency"[25] by ignoring how all three levels of experience—class, gender, and race—interact to shape low-income women's group identity, interests, and struggles. Nor can they account for social welfare activ-

23. J. Brenner and M. Ramas, "Rethinking Women's Oppression," *New Left Review* 144: 33–71; K. B. Sacks, "Ethno-European Working Class Women's Community Culture," *Frontiers* 14, no. 1: 1–23.
24. A. Hacker, *Two Nations: Black and White, Separate, Hostile, Unequal* (New York: Charles Scribner's Sons, 1992).
25. S. Morgen and A. Bookman, "Rethinking Women and Politics: An Introductory Essay," in A. Bookman and S. Morgen, eds., *Women and the Politics of Empowerment* (Philadelphia: Temple University Press, 1988), 3–29.

ism which also reflects the combined dynamics of gender, class, and race. To overcome this problem, scholars have labored to define the world-view, standpoint, or consciousness of poor and working-class women activists based on the unique constellation of low-income women's life experiences.[26]

A gendered understanding of women's consciousness argues that it stems from and reflects the experiences created by the gender division of labor and the ideology of women's roles as well as by the social structures of class and race. This reconfiguration challenges the long-standing be-liefs that women lack class consciousness and that class consciousness de-rives solely from exploitation at the "point of production."[27] It suggests instead that, once industrialization severed the home from the work-place, the family and community became important agents in structur-ing perceptions of the class experience which included exploitation at the "point of consumption" as well as the "point of production."[28] The emphasis on consumption included class- and race-based definitions of a satisfactory standard of living and of women's "proper" roles. Indeed families and communities expected women as caretakers and consumers to help them secure what they needed.[29] Poor and working-class women, in turn, identified survival needs as a prime class concern mediated by the imperatives of gender and race.[30]

The terms "female consciousness," "womanism," and "working-class feminism" discussed next represent recent efforts to depict the meaning and specification of class-driven "gendered obligations" that have shaped both the consciousness and the social welfare activism of poor and work-ing-class women.

Female Consciousness. Kaplan coined the term "female consciousness" to explain a gendered class consciousness among working-class women based on their gendered participation in the process of consumption.[31]

26. S. Eisenstein, *Give Us Bread But Give Us Roses: Working Women's Consciousness in the United States, 1890 to the First World War* (London: Routledge and Kegan Paul, 1983). M. W. Greenwald, "Working Class Feminism and the Family Wage Ideal: The Seattle Debate on Married Women's Right to Work, 1914–1920," *Journal of American History* 76, no. 1 (1989): 118–149.

27. T. Kaplan, "Class Consciousness and Community in Nineteenth Century Andalusia."

28. D. Frank, "Gender, Consumer Organizing, and the Seattle Labor Movement, 1919–1929" in A. Baron ed., *Work Engendered: Toward a New Labor History* (Ithaca: Cornell University Press, 1991), 273–295.

29. K. M. Blee, "Family Patterns and the Politicization of Consumption Relations," *Sociological Spectrum.* 5, no. 4 (1985): 295–316.

30. S. Morgen, & A. Bookman, "Rethinking Women and Politics."

31. T. Kaplan, "Female Action and Collective Action: Barcelona," *Signs: A Journal of Women, Culture, and Society,* 7: 4–56.

In her studies of early nineteenth century Barcelona working-class house-wives, Kaplan noticed that women became active when high prices or other market forces prevented them from buying what their families needed to survive. They and other women who become active on behalf of their own class, race, ethnic, religious, or national group express a solidarity with others, including men. Unlike feminists who became active to challenge the gendered status quo by securing equal rights with men, these poor and working-class women seemed to accept and work within the gendered status quo. Indeed they became active to fulfill their socially defined wife and mother roles, which included helping to defend or improve the standard of living of their families and communities. The terms "communal consciousness,"[32] "proxy activism,"[33] activist mothering,[34] and "practical gender needs"[35] have been used along with "female consciousness" to describe activism by low-income women targeted to family subsistence and community needs, rather than to female subordination. Put in other words, the women seek to fulfill what I have termed their "gendered obligations."

Researchers have applied expanded views of consciousness to the study of community-based, low-income women's activism in the United States. Their work suggests that since the eighteenth century women have regularly converted their commitments as wives and mothers into an oppositional ideology on behalf of the wider community to which they belonged. That is, when faced with threats to communal well-being, low-income women became active to assert their right to sustain their families and to have the resources that their class and race-based gendered obligations entailed.

According to historian Annelise Orleck, women's activism on behalf of a "just price" for food and housing has transcended time and place. In only a few countries, she adds, has it occurred as frequently or over such a long period as in the United States.[36] The historical record in the United States reveals that under certain conditions, when women cannot feed, cloth, shelter or otherwise maintain their families and communities, they protest collectively at grocery stores, in housing markets, and at welfare state offices. During the American Revolution, for example,

32. N. F. Cott, "What's in a Name? The Limits of 'Social Feminism' or Expanding the Vocabulary of Women's History," *Journal of American History* 76, no. 3 (1989): 809–829.
33. V. R. Seitz, "Gender and Resistance in the Appalchian Coal Fields," in N. Naples ed. *Community Activism and Feminist Politics*, 213–236.
34. N. Naples, *Grassroots Warriors*.
35. N. F. Cott, "What's in a Name?"
36. A. Orleck, *Common Sense and a Little Fire: Women and Working-Class Politics in the United States, 1900–1965*.

crowds of women seized essential goods from merchants whom they believed to be hoarding.[37] Housewives conducted flour riots during the economic crisis of the 1830s. In the early twentieth century, immigrant women organized milk, bread, and meat strikes.[38] Homemakers in many cities organized local meat boycotts in 1935, 1948, 1951 (their demands included government regulation of the meat trusts),[39] the Montgomery bus boycott in the mid-1950s,[40] and the welfare rights protests in the 1960s.[41] In the 1970s they participated in the antipoverty movement.[42] Beginning in the 1980s, women mobilized to defend their families against welfare state cuts and what became known as welfare "reform." Through their demands the women insisted that production and provision of goods be oriented to social needs.[43]

The gendered version of class consciousness is most often used to explain women's community-based activism, which includes many women on welfare. However, the notion of a gendered class consciousness also illuminates the thinking of women workers and their workplace activism. It helps to explain why, throughout much of the nineteenth and twentieth centuries, so many poor, white, immigrant, and African American housewives violated the gender norms of wider society to work for wages outside the home and why they participated in labor struggles. Married women took in boarders and sewing or went to work in the fields, factories, stores, or other people's homes. They worked for wages despite the fact that the definition of manhood and womanhood in their communities rested on having women stay at home and despite the fact that their families and communities endorsed the "family wage" ideal

37. S. Foner Philip, *Women and the American Labor Movement: From Colonial Times to the Eve of World War I*, vol. I, (New York: Free Press, 1979).

38. D. C. Hine, "The Housewives League of Detroit: Black Women and Economic Nationalism," in C. C. Hine, ed., *Hine Sight: Black Women and the Reconstruction of American History* (Brooklyn: Carlson Publishing, 1994), 129–146; P. E. Hyman, "Immigrant Women and Consumer Protest: The New York City Kosher Meat Boycott of 1902," *American Jewish History* 70 (1980): 91–105.

39. A. Orleck, *Common Sense and a Little Fire*.

40. J. A. Robinson, *The Montgomery Bus Boycott and the Women Who Started It* (Knoxville: The University of Tennessee, 1987).

41. G. West, *The National Welfare Rights Movement: The Social Protest of Poor Wopmen* (New York: Praeger, 1981); S. H. Hertz, *The Welfare Mothers Movement: A Decade of Change for Poor Women* (Washington, D.C.: University Press of America, 1981); N. Kotz, and M. Kotz, *A Passion for Equality: George Wiley and the Movement.* New York: W. W. Norton, 1977).

42. N. Naples, *Grassroots Warriors*; I. Susser, *Norman Street: Poverty and Politics in an Urban Neighborhood.*

43. B. Weinbaum, and A. Bridges, "The Other Side of The Paycheck: Monopoly Capital and the Structure of Consumption," in Z. Eisenstein, ed., *Capitalist Society and the Case for Socialist Feminism* (New York: Monthly Review Press, 1979), 190–205.

which held that male breadwinners should earn enough so that wives and children could remain at home. Indeed, the family wage ideal coexisted with the expectation in many communities that the "good wife" contribute to family income.[44]

Poor and working-class married women worked for wages because their husband's paycheck rarely covered basic household needs. That is, women's income along with their unpaid household labor became essential to family survival. The paid work of women, like that of other family members, reflected female consciousness embedded in a broader strategy designed to sustain, if not raise, the family and communal standard of living. Likewise for the participation of low-income women in labor struggles. During the first half of the twentieth century before suburbanization dispersed them, workplaces were located in or in near proximity to neighborhoods and employed many family members and community residents.[45] Thus, economic struggles often involved the entire community. In urban areas when low wages, union drives, and dangerous factory conditions sparked battles with employers, gender obligations mobilized women either to improve their own wages and working conditions or to build local support for striking or unionizing family members. In Appalachia and other rural communities miners' wives often helped to meet the practical needs of their families by activating the women's auxiliary of the union to rally the community behind striking husbands.[46] Once mobilized, the women's actions resonated throughout the family and the neighborhood. Indeed, the women frequently aroused working-class men, alerted the community that something was terribly wrong, and otherwise determined the outcome of conflicts with employers, merchants, landlords, and the state.[47] That is, the women often became pivotal figures in the development of both class consciousness and community action.

Womanism. Given that African American women live in a society dominated by white people, racial dynamics inevitably shape the standpoint and consciousness of poor and working-class women of color.

44. K. B. Sacks, "Ethno-European Working Class Women's Community Culture," *Frontiers* 14, no. 1 (1993): 1–23.
45. M. Greenwald, "Women and Pennsylvania Working-Class History," *Pennsylvania History* 63, no. 1 (1996): 5–16.
46. V. R. Seitz, "Gender and Resistance in the Appalchian Coal Fields" in N. Naples, ed., *Community Activism and Feminist Politics*, 213–236.
47. B. Laslett, "Production, Reproduction, and Social Change: The Family in Historical Perspective," in J. Short Jr., ed., *The State of Sociology: Problems and Prospects* Beverly Hills, Calif.: Sage, 1981), 239–258.

Collins, a Black feminist sociologist, suggests that living as a Black woman in the United States has produced "an enduring and shared Black women's standpoint."[48] The experience of racial oppression, the legacy of Black struggles, and the capacity to survive in two contradictory worlds at the same time have left Black women with a unique angle of vision on self, community, and society.

Alice Walker and Elsa Barkely Brown have revived the term "womanist consciousness" to capture the ways in which race and gender intersect in the lives of Black women. Like the more widely used term *Black feminism*, womanism brings a racialized meaning to the gendered experience suggested by feminism. Often linked to middle-class Black women, in fact it applies across the board to African American women. The experience of class, however, complicates analysis of the African American community. For most of the twentieth century, white society did not treat middle-class Blacks as middle class. It denied them the privileges of class even whey they could afford payment for them.[49]

The terms "womanism," "Black women's standpoint," and "Black feminism" have been used to depict the consciousness of African American women as it has been shaped by the dynamics of race. The language has also been used to characterize Black women's tradition of courage, independence, and pragmatism under the brutal conditions of slavery and institutionalized racism.[50] Unlike the feminism linked to white, middle-class women, the notions of womanism, Black women's standpoint, and Black feminism emphasize the simultaneity of oppressions that affect Black women and other women of color.

Some definitions of womanism parallel the communal or female consciousness noted above. O'Delight Smith, a white female labor organizer, actually coined the term "womanism" in the early 1900s.[51] She used it to convey her own conviction that women's progress was inseparable from that of the larger community, which in this case meant the trade union movement. As used by African American scholars, "womanism" assumes that women, in this case African American women, carry out their gen-

48. P. H. Collins, *Black Feminist Thought: Knowledge, Consciousness, and the Politics of Empowerment* (London: Harper Collins, 1990).
49. E. B. Higginbottham, "African American Women's History and the MetaLanguage of Race," *Signs: A Journal of Women, Society and Culture* 17, no. 1992) 2: 251–275, cited in G. Steinem, and D. Hayes "Womanism," in W. Mankilller, G. Mink, M. Navarro, B. Smith, and G. Steinemn, eds., *The Reader's Companion to US Women's History* (New York: Houghton Mifflin, 1992), 639–642, B. Smith, "Black Feminism," in W. Mankiller, et al, eds., *The Reader's Companion to U.S. Women's History*.
50. E. B. Higginbottham, "African American Women's History."
51. J. D. Hall, "O. Delight Smith's Progressive Era: Labor Feminism and Reform in the Urban South," in N. Hewitt and S. Lebsock eds., *Visible Women: New Essays on American Activism* Urbana: University of Illinois Press, (1993), 166–198.

dered obligations on behalf of family and community well-being. Collins argues that Black women's standpoint stemmed from and gave rise to two kinds of activism: one based on a culture of resistance, the other aimed at fundamental social change. The first type of activism, the "struggle for group survival" parallels Kaplan's notion of "female consciousness" in that it refers to ways devised by Black women to protect family and community from the daily assaults of racism. However, the activities of activist Black women also include preserving African customs, rejecting anti-Black, antifemale ideologies, and otherwise building a culture of resistance to protect the community from white and male domination. Like women with "female consciousness" they work within the race and gendered status quo. The second struggle, the "struggle for institutional transformation," moves beyond protective resistance to calls for change in the racialized structures of the wider society.

Both white and Black poor and working-class women fought with and on behalf of their entire communities. For Black women this meant taking on issues of race as well as class. These twin oppressions typically intersected and overlapped, as did Black women's community and workplace hardships. At the turn of the century the Black women's club movement adopted the slogan "lifting as we climb." The language and specific issues changed over the years; however, racial uplift continued to include struggles for better economic conditions and opposition to racial segregation and discrimination, whether lynching, job discrimination, redlining, or lack of welfare rights. Black women also fought to refute the harmful stereotypes of Black women as lazy or sexually available. While the latter struggle preoccupied middle-class Black women in particular, it resonated throughout the Black community. Winning respect for Black women became part of the wider strategy for improving the life of the entire African American community. Although low-income African American women, like many low-income white women, typically became active in their own "spaces," in many cases their respective social landscapes included the needs of kin, neighbors, and coworkers who were themselves marginalized and exploited.[52]

Like female consciousness, womanism can be applied to the consciousness of both working and community-based women. Deep and persistent poverty, the by-product of institutionalized racism, forced many African American wives to work for wages at a time when many of their white working-class counterparts managed to remain at home. Since before the turn of the century, Black domestics and laundresses

---

52. J. D. Hall, "O. Delight Smith's Progressive Era"; G. Steinem, and D. Hayes, "Womanism," in W. Mankiller et al. *The Reader's Companion to U.S. Women's History*.

(the main jobs open to urban Black women) engaged in acts of individual resistance. They also struggled collectively to unionize and otherwise improve their jobs.

For these housewives/working women, trying to ensure the survival of their families and communities could not be separated from protecting the race. Likewise, the Black women who participated in the Montgomery bus boycott in the mid-1950s fought to desegregate the buses that they and the rest of the community used to get to work. The boycott against laws forcing Black men, women, and children to sit in the back of the bus also typified the struggle for dignity amidst the injuries of race. Throughout the 1950s and 1960s, hundreds of low-income Black women worked as liaisons and leaders in community-based voting rights and other civil rights campaigns. Since it was often safer (but not safe) for women than men to take the enormous risks involved in opposing white supremacy, Black wives, mothers, sisters, and daughters with "womanist consciousness" entered the battle for racial justice on behalf of their race and class. Like women with female consciousness, they often mobilized the rest of the community and became central forces for the development of a racialized class consciousness.

Working-Class Feminism. The employment of women gave birth to a distinct new consciousness which some refer to as "trade union,"[53] "industrial feminism,"[54] or "working-class feminism."[55] Mildred Moore coined the phrase "industrial feminist" in 1915 to characterize the white middle-class members of the Women's Trade Union League, a Progressive Era labor-oriented women's reform organization. Evidence of industrial or working-class feminism also exists among poor and working-class women. This working-class feminism does not represent a formally articulated ideology or an independent social movement. Rather it reflects a class-based feminism that evolved from working women's own experiences—a consciousness that combines female and womanist consciousness and an attack on gender and race barriers at the work place.

Eisenstein has concluded that employment had the potential to politicize women and change their worldview.[56] Paid work outside the home

53. R. Milkman, "Women Workers, Feminism and the Labor Movement Since the 1960s," in R. Milkman, ed., *Women, Work, and Protest: A Century of U.S. Women's Labor History*, 300–322.

54. A. Orleck, *Common Sense and a Little Fire.*

55. D. Frank, "Working Class Feminism in W. Mankiller et al., *The Reader's Companion to U.S. Women's History.*

56. Z. Eisenstein, *Radical Future of Liberal Feminism* (New York: Longman, 1981).

exposed women to exploitation by owners but also to workplace sexism. Once in the labor force, women saw that the democratic promise of equal opportunity for all did not always apply to them. Waged work taught women that they faced major difficulties in supporting themselves and their families and that securing a better standard of living often meant fighting hard to be treated equally with men.[57]

As noted earlier, many poor and working-class women equated work for wages with fulfilling their gender obligations. Some of those who be-came active effectively reconfigured their gendered obligations into a working-class feminism. Unlike women with female consciousness who worked within the gendered status quo, working-class feminists found it necessary to change gender relations at work and within the unions to preserve their dignity as women and to advance the class as a whole.[58] For much of the nineteenth and twentieth centuries gender norms, family responsibilities, and male hostility to working women made it diffi-cult for women to get well-paying jobs or to be admitted into the male-dominated trade unions. Nonetheless, labor historians have repeatedly noted that once organized, women workers often acted much more mil-itantly than men.[59]

The long history of working-class feminism dispels the myth that only middle-class women became active and developed a feminist conscious-ness.[60] Indeed, an industrial working-class women's consciousness ap-peared in 1840s and 1850s, among the young native-born women em-ployed by the earliest New England textile mills. The short-lived and spontaneous strikes (called *turnouts*) organized by these farmers' daugh-ters drew thousands of women who opposed wage cuts and the long ten-hour day.[61] Like their male counterparts, the strike leaders regularly at-tacked the "moneyed aristocracy." Influenced by Mary Wollstonecraft

57. M. W. Greenwald, "Working Class Feminism and the Family Wage Ideal: The Seattle Debate on Married Women's Right to Work, 1914–1920," *Journal of American History* 76, no. 1 (1989): 118–149.
58. D. Frank, "Working Class Feminism" in W. Mankiller et. al., *The Reader's Companion to U.S. Women's History*.
59. C. Turbin, Beyond Conventional Wisdom: Women's Wage Work, Household Economic Contribution, and Labor Activism in a Mid-Nineteenth Century Working-Class Community," in C. Groneman and M. B. Norton, eds., *"To Toil the Livelong Day": America's Women at Work, 1780–1980* (Ithaca: Cornell University Press, 1987), 47–67; A. Kessler-Harris, *Out to Work: A History of Wage Earning Women in the United States* (New York: Oxford Univesrity Press, 1982).
60. R. Milkman, "Gender and Trade Unionism in Historical Perspective," in L. Tilly and P. Gurin, eds., *Women, Politics and Change* (New York: Russell Sage, 1990), 87–107.
61. M. Frederickson, "I Know Which Side I'm on": Southern Women in the Labor Movement in the Twentieth Century," in R. Milkman, ed., *Women, Work and Protest: A Century of U.S. Women's Labor History*, 156–180.

and leading feminists of the day, they also called for "the rights of women" including equal pay with men.[62]

During the rest of the nineteenth century and for most of the twentieth, the exclusionary practices of employers and unions sparked repeated rounds of working-class feminism. In the mid-1800s, after working women failed to win entry into the skilled trade unions, they created separate women's locals and labor organizations, often with the help middle-class suffragists such as Susan B. Anthony and Elizabeth Cady Stanton who also hoped to win working-class women's support for the vote.[63]

By the early 1900s, when more than five million women over age ten were employed,[64] working-class women emerged as key leaders in the great garment industry strikes, such as the 1909–1910 strike of the New York shirtwaist makers, also known as the "Uprising of 20,000." The women activists in the garment trades also had to fight the union's resistance to women becoming members and shop leaders, not to mention top officials.[65] Devalued by both employers and unions, the women turned to the state. They campaigned for new laws such as protective labor legislation that would ensure better wages, a shorter workday, and other important changes. Reflecting a mix of female and feminist consciousness, they argued for government protection on the grounds that women were the potential mothers of the race (childbearer), needed more time for their families, and/or wanted to end their economic dependence on men. Once again the suffrage and feminist movements provided the strongest support for working women's demands—most notably, the white middle-class Women's Trade Union League (WTUL), which from 1903 to 1950 helped low-income women form unions, pass laws, and sharpen their working-class feminism.[66]

By the 1920s women had secured the vote, entered the labor force in large numbers and won occasional begrudging acceptance from unions. During the 1930s and 1940s, the newly formed Congress of Industrial

62. D. Balser, *Sisterhood and Solidarity: Feminism and Labor in Modern Times* (Boston: South End Press, 1987); S. E. Kennedy, *If All We Did Was to Weep at Home: A History of White Working Class Women in America* (Bloomington: Indiana University Press, 1981).
63. S. E. Kennedy, *If All We Did Was to Weep at Home*.
64. S. E. Kennedy, *If All We Did Was to Weep at Home*.
65. A. Kessler-Harris, "Problems of Coalition Building: Women and Trade Unions in the 1920s, in R. Milkman, ed., *Women, Work and Protest: A Century of U.S. Women's Labor History*, 110–138; M. Greenwald, "Women and Pennsylvania Working-Class History," *Pennsylvania History* 63, no. 1 (1996): 5–16.
66. A. Orleck, *Common Sense and a Little Fire*; A. Kessler-Harris, "Problems of Coalition Building."

Organizations (CIO) organized mass production industries. The CIO recruited thousands of women,[67] aided and abetted by the wartime mobilization of women workers. The rising number of women on the job emboldened a small but growing group of female labor leaders to decide to place women's issues—equal pay for equal work, nondiscriminatory seniority lists, protection of women's jobs during the postwar reconversion, and female representation in labor leadership—on the agenda of some unions.

The hostility of both employers and unions to these demands increased the awareness of sexism among more and more rank-and-file women.[68] In 1945, after many battles and under strong pressure from its women members, the United Auto Workers (UAW) established its own Women's Bureau. These women and working-class feminists in the United Electrical Workers (UE) and other trade unions began to educate their memberships about women's issues. They also increased women's visibility in the union and created formal women's networks. Their progress was slowed after the end of World War II by the continued hostility of male workers and union leaders, postwar conservatism, and the absence an active feminist movement. Nonetheless, the working-class feminists won some important policy changes and union leadership positions and paved the way for the growth of working-class feminism in the next decade.[69]

The explosive growth of the female labor force during the 1960s combined with the reemergence of a mass women's movement inspired a new gender consciousness among working women.[70] The idea of female equality gained further credibility in 1962 when Kennedy appointed the Presidential Commission on the Status of Women and when Congress passed both the 1963 Equal Pay Act and the 1964 Civil Rights Act. Contrary to popular wisdom, Kates and Dilseppe argue that women unionists with feminist consciousness actually played a fundamental, if

67. S. H. Strom, "'We're No Kitty Foyles': Organizing Offfice Workers for the Congress of Industrial Organizations, 1937–1950," in R. Milkman, ed., *Women, Work and Protest*, 206–234; S. M. Evans, *Born for Liberty: A History of Women in America* (New York: The Free Press, 1989).
68. C. Kates, "Working Class Feminism and Feminist Unions: Title VII, the UAW and NOW," *Labor History Journal* 14, no. 2 (1989): 28–45; L. Kannenberg, "The Impact of the Cold War on Women's Trade Union Activism: The UE Experience," *Labor History* 34, nos. 2–3 (1993): 309–323.
69. N. Gabin, "Women and the United Automobile Workers' Union in the 1950s," in R. Milkman, ed., *Women, Work and Protest*, 259–266.
70. R. Milkman, *Women Workers, Feminism, and the Labor Movement*, in R. Milkman, ed., "Women, Work and Protest," 300–323; V. R. Seitz, "Gender and Resistance in the Appalchian Coal Fields," in N. Naples, ed, *Community Activism and Feminist Politics*, 213–236.

uneven role in building the second wave of the feminist movement in the 1960s.[71] Women UAW leaders began building support for the ERA among working women as early as 1963. That same year two unions— the UAW and the Communication Workers of America (CWA)—helped to found the National Organization for Women (NOW), although most publicity went to the middle-class feminists.[72] During 1964, the UAW did most of NOW's clerical work.[73] From 1965 to 1975 union women fought for and supported the federal equal employment opportunity laws. To its surprise, the Equal Employment Opportunity Commission found itself flooded by complaints of sex discrimination from working women. The U.S. Congress sent an Equal Rights Amendment (ERA) to the states in 1972. Pressed by working-class feminists from within, the AFL-CIO eventually endorsed the ERA in 1973. Working women's support for women's issues helped to legitimize the feminist agenda of the middle-class women's movement, especially its strong call for the fair treatment of women on the job.[74]

By the early 1970s, a growing number of unions had formed their own women's departments and began to include some women's concerns when negotiating contracts. Meanwhile, working-class feminists around the country began to develop interunion coalitions. This included the Union Women's Alliance to Gain Equality in the San Francisco-Berkeley area (1971); United Union Women formed by women from thirty unions in Chicago in 1972; and Nine-to-Five, founded by Boston-area women in 1973 to organize office workers. Nine-to-Five later became District 925 of the Service Employees International Union.[75] In 1974, the Coalition for Labor Union Women (CLUW) convened 3200 delegates from 58 unions to hear Myra Wolfgang of the Hotel and Restaurant Employees' and Bartenders' International Union tell them," We didn't come here to swap recipes."[76]

Since the mid-1970s, downsizing, deindustrialization, and the export of production abroad has undercut women's improved status on the job and within trade unions. These factors combined with a major assault on

71. C. Kates, "Working Class Feminism and Feminist Unions: Title VII, the UAW and NOW"; D. Deslippe, "Organized Labor, National Politics, and Second-Wave Feminism in the United States, 1965–1975," *International Labor and Working Class History* 49 (Spring 1996): 143–165.
72. S. E. Kennedy, *If All We Did Was to Weep at Home*.
73. C. Kates, "Working Class Feminism and Feminist Unions."
74. D. Deslippe, "Organized Labor, National Politics, and Second-Wave Feminism in the United States, 1965–1975."
75. R. Milkman, "Women Workers, Feminism and the Labor Movement."
76. S. E. Kennedy, *If All We Did Was to Weep at Home*.

trade union movement has cost unions many of their members. Today only 14 percent of the civilian labor force belongs to a trade union. The failure to build a coalition between women and unions contributed to the weakness of the labor movement for much of this century. However, now that women comprise nearly half of the workers, the labor movement may have learned a lesson from its own past. Whether for reasons of principle or survival, organized labor has hired more women, recognized working-class feminist issues, and begun to pay considerably more attention to its female base.

Contradictions That Foster Collective Action

The gender division of labor provides a lens through which to identify the conditions that shape low-income women's activism as well as the sites of their activism, and the nature of their class consciousness. Designed to keep women at home, the societal gender division of labor paradoxically fostered collective action among women outside these confines—at the workplace, in the community, and within the welfare state.

The modern gender division of labor appeared with the rise of industrial capitalism in the early nineteenth century. It assigned men to breadwinning in the workplace and women to caretaking in the home. To inform men and women of their new roles and convince them to adhere to them, the emerging domestic code equated masculinity with waged labor and male domination and femininity with unpaid labor and female subordination to men. The arrangement became legitimized through social thought that viewed gender roles as biologically determined rather than socially assigned and by legal doctrine that defined women as the property of men. Legislation also barred women from working for wages, owning property, making contracts, and participating in politics. This domestic code placed white, middle-class women on a pedestal. But it offered no such support to enslaved women, free Black women, or poor, white native-born or immigrant women. These low-income women, both white and of color, were expected to work to help their families survive. African American women faced additional contradictions between the idealized version of white womanhood contained in the domestic codes and the realities of Black women's lives.

Despite the enormous gains made by women during the last 150 years, a reconfigured domestic code remains with us today. The age-old belief that assigns childbearing, child rearing, and homemaking to women no longer disqualifies them for work. However, the domestic code still holds that women's place is in the home even when they work for wages outside. It still justifies sex-segregated occupations and the unequal treatment of women on the job. The resulting economic insecurity leaves women financially dependent on men, marriage, or the welfare state and locked into traditional women's roles. The presence of women at home, in turn, "proves" that the home is women's natural "place," where women want to stay and where they belong.[77]

The structural contradictions created by the gender division of labor have contributed to low-income women's social welfare activism. As noted earlier, the gender division of labor isolated women in the home and in local communities. Designed to keep women down and out, the gender division of labor often bred its opposite—collective action for social change. Second, the inherent conflict between profitable economic production and successful family maintenance (also referred to here as social reproduction) periodically sparks low-income women's activism at the point of consumption because it undercuts their capacity to carry out their socially assigned female tasks. A third contradiction exists within the welfare state itself. The welfare state emerged in part to underwrite family maintenance because, left to its own devices, the market economy could not do the job. However, the capacity of the welfare state remained limited to ensure that it did not pose too great a threat to wage rates and patriarchal family structures. Thus, it, too, became a site of political struggle for poor and working-class women whose families often relied on government assistance for support and protection. Finally, low-income women's social welfare activism has been sparked by the democratic promise of equal opportunity for all and the continual reconfiguration of inequality based on the dynamics of race, gender, and class.

Social Isolation Breeds Activism

The gender division of labor confines women to separate female spheres at home, in the community, on the job, and within the welfare state. Paradoxically, by isolating women in these ways, the gender division of labor brought women together—a prerequisite for collective action. Racial segregation likewise bred activism in the Black community. The standard discussion of collective action typically focuses on men

77. M. Abramovitz, *Under Attack, Fighting Back: Women and Welfare in the United States* (New York: Monthly Review Press, 1996), 88.

in the workplace. It holds that the advance of the market economy created the possibility for collective action among workers at the "point of production." That is, centralization of production into ever larger mines and factories concentrated a large number of employees in one place. As workers recognized their shared exploitation and the power of owners they became more class conscious and motivated for collective action. Action included both unionization and the formation of labor-based political parties. Because the majority of workers in these jobs were men, this analysis could not account for collective action among women, especially those outside the paid labor force.

However, the female "spaces" created by the gender division of labor created the conditions for low-income women's activism "at the point of consumption."[78] Just as the rise of larger and larger factories concentrated male workers in one place and exposed conflicts between capital and labor, so the gender division of labor clustered women into female enclaves—housewives in neighborhoods, workers in women's jobs, and clients in social welfare programs. Collective awareness of the conflicts between economic production and adequate consumption increased the likelihood of joint responses. That is, the marginalization of women created the shared anger and conditions known to breed the motivation and consciousness for collective action among women.

The gender division of labor also generated the needed organizational capacity. Isolated in women's spaces, women shared common grievances as mothers, wives, shoppers, renters, workers, and community residents. Through their daily encounters in parks, churches, laundries, grocery stores, child care centers, and welfare offices, women develop strong ties that reappear in local organizations. The resulting network of clubs, associations, and alliances become the foundation for an infrastructure for protests on behalf of a better standard of living in the community and at the welfare office. Similarly, the shared experiences of women concentrated in low-paid women's jobs leads women workers to join forces on the job.

Racial segregation, designed to isolate African Americans and keep them down and out, created similar paradoxical effects. Many Blacks migrated north after World War II, where they found segregated neighborhoods and segregated jobs. Piven and Cloward argue that the isolation resulting from racial segregation created the possibility for collective

78. D. Frank, "Gender, Consumer Organizing, and the Seattle Labor Movement, 1919–1929," in A. Baron, ed., *Work Engendered: Toward a New Labor History* 273–295.

action.[79] As Black people became increasingly outraged by discriminatory policies that denied them access to decent jobs, voting booths, and most other mainstream institutions, their segregation in America's urban neighborhoods ironically created a potentially influential African American political bloc. Racial exclusion created the shared anger and conditions known to breed the motivation, consciousness, and organizational capacity for collective action in the Black community. It fueled the civil rights and Black power movements as well as considerable grassroots activism by African American women.

Conflicts between Economic Production and Social Reproduction

The second dynamic that creates the conditions for activism among poor and working-class women stems from the competing demands of economic production and social reproduction in families.[80] Economic production takes places in the market, where companies produce goods and services and sell them for a profit. Social reproduction takes places in the family, which carries out the tasks of procreation, socialization, nurturance, and the survival of individuals. It includes giving birth to the next generation; making food, clothing, and shelter available for immediate consumption; socializing family members to assume proper adult work and family roles; and providing for people who are too old, too young, or too sick to care for themselves. Some of this day-to-day care of people also occurs in schools, child care centers, nursing homes, and other social institutions staffed mostly by women. In light of the gender division of labor, social reproduction relies heavily on women's unpaid labor in the home, even when they work outside. Indeed, women's domestic labor converts the wages of paid workers into the means of subsistence for the entire household.

Business depends heavily on the family and other units of social reproduction both to reproduce the species and to maintain a healthy, productive, and properly socialized workforce. Women's work as consumers and caretakers keeps individuals fed, clothed, and sheltered. It also replenishes the energy of family members so that they can put in another

79. F. F. Piven and R. Cloward, *Regulating the Poor: The Functions of Public Welfare* (New York; Pantheon, 1971); F. F. Piven, and R. Cloward, *The New Class War: Reagan's Attack on the Welfare State and Its Consequences* (New York: Pantheon, 1982).
80. B. Laslett, "Production, Reproduction, and Social Change: The Family in Historical Perspective," in J. F. Short Jr., ed., *The State of Sociology: Problems and Prospects* (Beverly Hills: Sage, 1981), 239–258.

day of school or work. Business and wider society clearly rely on the family system and women's unpaid domestic labor to create future workers, sustain current workers, and care for those not in the labor force. At the same time, families depend heavily on what business and industry provide. At minimum, families need the jobs and income that business supplies and the material goods (e.g., clothing, shelter, other products) that companies produce to accomplish the family's socially assigned tasks.

Despite codependence, the market economy periodically fails to sustain families, who then cannot carry out the tasks of social reproduction. Business must accumulate enough capital both to invest in new plants, labor, and equipment and to yield a profit above these costs. To this end, companies favor high prices, lower labor costs, and increased productivity. As a result, the profit-driven market economy often does not generate the levels of income, employment, education, housing, and health care needed by the average family to reproduce and maintain itself.[81] Instead, workers face low income, unemployment, and enormous wear and tear. When the standard of living falls too far it weakens the productive capacity of individuals, increases the stress levels of families and communities, and limits the capacity of women to carry out their gendered obligations.

The conflict between the requirements of profitable economic production and the conditions for successful social reproduction can foster both individual and collective action. Historically, families have tried to defend their standard of living by trying to accumulate the resources they need for successful caretaking, homemaking, employment and consumption. Individually, families have reduced their size, sent additional family members to work, or invested more in education to upgrade their skills. Collectively, families have engaged in political action. They have supported workplace struggles to secure higher wages and better working conditions, organized in the community to bring down the cost of living, and demanded governmental programs.[82] According to British historian E. P. Thompson,[83] people become politically active when conditions violate widely held class or cultural norms for what the market should provide.

81. J. Brenner, and B. Laslett, "Social Reproduction and the Family," in Ulf Himmelstrand, ed., *The Social Reproduction of Organization and Culture* (London: Sage Publications, 1986), 116–131; J. Dickinson, and B. Russell, *Families, Economy and State* (New York: St. Martins Press, 1986).
82. J. Brenner, and B. Lasslett, "Social Reproduction and the Family."
83. E. P. Thompson, "The Moral Economy of the English Crowd in the Eighteenth Century," *Past and Present.* 50 (1971): 71–136.

When it comes to family maintenance, the activism becomes highly gendered. Over the years, more women than men have involved themselves in issues concerning the care of people, natural resources, and household consumption.[84] Given their role in social reproduction, as noted earlier, the ongoing conflict between maximizing profits and sustaining people has created the conditions for social welfare activism among low-income women at the "point of consumption" (as well as at the "point of production").

The Welfare State's Capacity to Enhance or Undercut Family Maintenance

The third dynamic that gives rise to low-income women's social welfare activism is the conflicting capacity of the welfare state to either enhance or undercut social reproduction. This contradiction falls heavily on women, who, as noted earlier, predominate among welfare clients and workers. Women's central role in caretaking and the welfare state's role in underwriting the maintenance of poor and working-class families have made the welfare state a target of low-income women's social welfare activism.

Throughout the nineteenth and the twentieth centuries, when the individual strategies that families devised to create a decent standard of living failed, they often turned to the government for help. Some families in need became clients of private charities or local, state, and then federal welfare programs. Others, often led by women with female, womanist, or working-class feminist consciousness, engaged in collective action to improve family caretaking capacities and to more effectively carry out their gendered obligations at home and in the community.

One way to understand the development of the welfare state is to think of it as a response to this tension between profitable economic production and social reproduction discussed earlier. The collapse of the economy during the 1930s underscored what many observers already knew: (1) that the market economy could not always provide jobs and income for all those ready and able to work and (2) that the federal government had to step in to save capitalism from itself. The Great Depression also

---

84. L. Tilly, "Paths of Proletarianization: Organization of Production, Sexual Division of Labor, and Women's Collective Action," *Signs: A Journal of Women, Society and Culture* 7, no. 2: 400 – 417; A. G. Jonasdotier, "On The Concept of Interest: Women's Interest and the Limitation of Interest Theory," in K. B. Jones and A. G. Jonasdottier eds., *The Political Interests of Gender* (London: Sage, 1988).

made it clear that people could lose their income and jobs "through no fault of their own." This explanation of economic insecurity provided powerful support for the idea that the government needed to ensure basic subsistence, as did the realization that business could not recover from the Depression or sustain profitability in the future without government programs that increased purchasing power; created a healthy, educated, and properly socialized labor force; and quieted the social unrest that market inequality produced.

The emergence and expansion of the welfare state from 1935 to the mid-1970s drastically altered the relationships among the family, the economy, and the state. By promising, among many other things, to underwrite costs of social reproduction, it created the conditions for social welfare activism among women. If the pre–World War I activism of low-income women prefigured what the government would have to provide to sustain families, activism during and after the Great Depression reflected what it actually offered. The income support programs established an economic floor below which no one would have to sink, thereby cushioning families against the loss of income due to low wages, unemployment, illness, old age, and death. Health, education, housing, and social services provided what families needed to care for members who were unable to care for themselves because of age, illness, lack of work, or the absence of breadwinner. Women increasingly targeted the welfare state because it now shared responsibility for family maintenance with them.

In its support for social reproduction, the welfare state has reflected a strong preference for caretaking in patriarchal families. Its rules and regulations have encouraged women to remain tied to marriage and have reinforced traditional gender roles in the family. They have rewarded families that conform to the traditional heterosexual, male breadwinner and female homemaker model and have punished those women who could not or chose not to follow the prescribed wife and mother roles.[85] Single mothers, abandoned women, or divorced wives have faced the lowest benefits, the most coercive rules, the closest supervision, and the most highly stigmatized programs.

The welfare state has created the conditions for low-income women's social welfare activism, but in contradictory ways. On the one hand, the welfare state often fails to deliver the goods. The creation of the welfare

85. M. Abramovitz, *Regulating the Lives of Women: Social Welfare Policy from Colonial Times to the Present* (Boston: South End Press, 1996).

state may have helped to save capitalism from itself. However, given the welfare state's long-standing relationship to both the labor market and the family system, generous benefits pose an implicit threat to capitalist profits and patriarchal family structures. Indeed, high benefits force wages up, make it easy for workers to resist the worst jobs, and otherwise interfere with profitable production based on the exploitation of labor. Likewise, decent cash assistance and access to reproductive rights and other services can advance women's autonomy and enable them to establish and maintain independent households. This in turn challenges the underpinnings of patriarchy.

Therefore, to uphold both the work and the family ethic, from the start, welfare state programs have deterred applicants, stigmatized recipients, and provided only minimal support. Since colonial times, social welfare policy has been designed to ensure that no one chooses government aid over work of any kind. To this end they have distinguished between individuals and families regarded as worthy or unworthy of aid based on the recipients' perceived willingness to work, created work tests to deter applications, and set the value of public assistance benefits below the lowest prevailing wage. As noted earlier, they also define women as deserving or undeserving of aid based on their marital status and use moralistic behavior standards to stigmatize husbandless women, especially never-married mothers, and limit their aid.

Welfare state critics justify these policies by claiming that access to benefits creates "dependency" on the state. However, the "dependency" critique obscures the underlying purpose of these policies. On the work side, meager cash assistance, strict work requirements, moralistic eligibility rules, and their reincarnation in contemporary welfare "reforms" channel poor and working-class women into the lowest rungs of the labor market or otherwise ensure their impoverishment. This increases the number of workers forced to compete for the same jobs. The enlarged supply of desperate people seeking work makes it that much easier for employers to pay lower wages and harder for unions to negotiate good contracts. When it comes to single motherhood, welfare state policies send a message to all women about what happens to those who do not play by the rules. These harsh policies and meager benefits undercut the capacity for successful social reproduction. When things go too far, poor and working-class women have risen up in anger. One of the most sustained examples of this has been the national welfare rights movement of the 1960s and 1990s.

Despite its constraints and limitations, the welfare state contains the potential to enhance women's autonomy and ability to fight back. In many ways, the provision of cash benefits operates as an alternative to the market wage or as what the British call a social wage. Like a strike fund, the social wage can embolden social activism. For one, it increases the leverage or bargaining power of male and female workers vis-à-vis employers and women vis-à-vis men. That is, the availability of cash assistance makes it possible for workers of both sexes to avoid the worst low-paid or unsafe jobs and for women to leave unhappy or dangerous relationships. More generally, the presence of such an economic backup makes it easier for women and men to take the risks involved in fighting against economic insecurity and racial injustice whether on the job, in the community, or within the welfare state. The social wage also enables women to fight for greater government investment in social reproduction.

Rather than foster laziness, inertia and "dependency," as welfare state critics insist, even the lowest cash assistance has the potential to alter the terms of political struggle between labor and capital,[86] between women and men, and between people and the state. Indeed, the rise of the welfare state and its expansion after 1935 generated a sense of felt needs and entitlement that encouraged many people in need both to use the programs and to engage in collective action to improve them. During the Depression, the early social welfare programs nurtured civil rights consciousness among African Americans.[87] The growth of the welfare state from 1945 to 1975 both reflected and fueled pressure from mass movements. Social security pensions stimulated claims-making among senior citizens. The political rights won by the civil rights movement in the early 1960s formed the basis for subsequent demands for social and economic rights. Access to Aid to Families with Dependent Children benefits, for example, gave rise to a welfare rights movement among single mothers in the late 1960s and early 1970s.

The postwar expansion of the welfare state came to an end in the mid-1970s. Faced with mounting competition from abroad and a deepening economic crisis at home, corporate America downsized its domestic workforce and searched for cheaper labor abroad. With a reduced stake in U.S. workers, CEOs turned against the welfare state. Arguing that social spending interfered with private investments, empowered the poor and working class, and undercut the traditional family, conserva-

86. F. F. Piven and R. Cloward, *The New Class War: Reagan's Attack on the Welfare State and Its Consequences.*
87. L. Gordon, *Share-Holders in Relief: The Political Culture of the Public Sector.* Working Paper #134. New York: Russell Sage Foundation, June 1998).

tive politicians pushed the federal government to reverse sixty years of social welfare policy. Devolution, privatization, tax cuts, and balanced budgets have returned many of the costs of social reproduction to states and cities, to private organizations, and most of all, to women in families. Once again, faced with threats to their living standards, women with "female" and "womanist" consciousness have begun to join forces to secure the essentials needed to form and maintain families. This time they must work to recapture, rather than to improve, their gains. The odds may be against them now. Yet, like thousands of others before them in the United States and around the world, low-income women continue to become active in order to fulfill their gender obligations, which include helping to defend the standard of living of their families and communities.

The Democratic Promise of Equal Opportunity for All

The fourth societal tension that has stimulated social welfare activism stems from the failure of democracy to fulfill is promise of equal opportunity for all, especially when it comes to racial equality. Observers from Alexis de Tocqueville[88] in 1840 to Gunnar Myrdal in 1944[89] to the National Advisory Commission on Civil Disorders in 1968 have found America beset by a social and moral paradox. "Of all the world's nations, the United States speaks eloquently of universal justice and equal opportunity. Yet its treatment of its principal minority belies this basic commitment."[90] From the end of the Civil War in 1865 to the Civil Rights Act of 1964, to increased Black representation in elected office since then, persistent and pervasive racism has kept African Americans and other persons of color out of the voting booth and locked into inferior jobs, housing, and schools. Instead of opening the door to give persons of color a chance to become full citizens, the slow progress toward greater equality in the United States has been accompanied by bitter white resistance, widespread violence, and minimal government support.[91] From slavery to Jim Crow to the attack on affirmative action, the nation has denied African Americans and other subordinated groups equal access to

---

88. Alexis de Tocqueville, *Democracy in America*. (New Rochelle, N.Y.: Arlington House, 1966).
89. G. Myrdal, *An American Dilemma: The Negro Problem and Modern Democracy* (New York: Harper and Brothers, 1944).
90. A. Hacker, *Two Nations: Black and White, Separate, Hostile, Unequal* New York: Chareles Scribner's Sons, 1992).
91. National Advisory Commission on Civil Disorders, *Report of the National Advisory Commission on Civil Disorders* (New York: Bantam Books, 1968) 235–236.

full social, economic, and political rights. The tension between the democratic guarantee of equal opportunity for all and the constant reconfiguration of racism has provoked activism since the slave revolts and the underground railroad, if not before. From the start, African American women played a major role in the battles against racism.

In a similar way, the promise of equal opportunity for women also mobilized women. As noted earlier, working-class feminism surfaced when women realized that the democratic promise did not apply to them.

THE WIDER SOCIAL CONTEXT

The first three main sections of this chapter suggest that poor and working-class women engage in collective action at the point of consumption, the point of production, and within the welfare state to achieve economic security and racial justice. However, the mobilization of poor and working-class women does not arise apart from wider social forces. Low-income women's activism has been conditioned by major social, economic, political, and historical developments as well as prior history, prevailing ideologies, the state of the economy, the level of government intervention, and the strength of social movements.

Space does not permit an elaboration of the specific ways in which contextual factors have shaped the activism of low-income women in various historical periods. It can be said, however, that these broad forces aroused or muted consciousness, heightened or lessened contradictions, and encouraged or discouraged political struggle. They underpinned the community's standard of living and the capacity of families to reconcile wages and prices with the costs and demands of subsistence. They also shape the societal expectations of women and the ways in which low-income women interpret and implement their socially defined gendered obligations. The wider context, especially prevailing political ideologies and the strength of social movements, shape the strategies available to poor and working-class women for both survival and social action.

IMPACT AND OUTCOMES

Social, economic, and political contexts contour the scale and scope of poor and working-class women's activism. At the same time, low-income women's activism often brings about personal and political change. Indeed, activism fueled by gendered obligations often leads women far beyond what traditionally has been thought of as women's proper sphere. On the personal front, some women activists acquire a more political understanding of politics, power, and society. Instead of blaming problems on individual failings or deviance, they recognize the role played by structural, cultural, and systemic forces.

On the political front collective action sparked by gendered obligations has led poor and working-class women to challenge institutional arrangements in both the private and public spheres. Activist women often move from female to feminist consciousness, from womanism to Black feminism. In some cases their political struggles evolve from addressing the immediate needs of home and community to seeking fundamental change in the wider social order. From accepting the gendered status quo they develop a broader analysis of corporate power, male domination, white supremacy, and the limits of democracy and take action to change the power structures at home, in the community, and on the job. Put in other words, the demands and actions of poor and working-class women embody the rudiments of a progressive social agenda. The victories of such popular insurgency may sometimes be narrow and short-lived. The successes, however, confirm that elites do not always have their way and that when ordinary people become organized and mobilized they can win change. Indeed, the history of activism among poor and working-class women shows that people can and do fight to defend their interests against the most powerful forces. This popular insurgency is critical, for the powers that be rarely move unless pressed from below.

Contributors

Mimi Abramovitz is a professor of social policy at the Hunter College School of Social Work in New York City. She is the author of *Regulating the Lives of Women: Social Welfare Policy from Colonial Times to the Present* (1996) and *Under Attack and Fighting Back: Women and Welfare in the United States* (1996).

Eileen Boris, Professor of Women's Studies at the University of Virginia, is the author of *Home to Work: Motherhood and the Politics of Industrial Homework in the United States* (1994), which won the 1995 Philip Taft Prize in labor history. With Nupur Chaudhuri, she edited *Voices of Women's Historians: The Personal, the Political, the Professional* (1999).

Lynn H. Fujiwara is completing her doctoral degree in sociology at the University of California at Santa Cruz. Her dissertation focuses on Asian immigrant women and welfare reform.

Eva Feder Kittay writes on issues in ethics and social and political philosophy. She co-edited (with D. T. Meyers) *Women and Moral Theory*, the first major collection of philosophical essays on feminist ethics. She is the author of *Love's Labor: Essays on Women, Dependency and Equality*, published by Routledge (1999). Professor of Philosophy at SUNY, Stony Brook, she also is the mother of a severely disabled young woman who has taught her most of what she understands about dependency needs.

Demie Kurz, a sociologist, is Co-Director of the Women's Studies Program at the University of Pennsylvania. She is the author of *For Richer, For Poorer: Mothers Confront Divorce* (1995).

Gwendolyn Mink is Professor of Politics at the University of California at Santa Cruz. She is the author of *The Wages of Motherhood: Inequality in the Welfare State, 1917–1942* (1995), which won the 1996 Victoria Schuck Award of the American Political Science Association for best book on women and politics, and of *Welfare's End* (1998).

Nancy A. Naples is Associate Professor of Sociology and Women's Studies at the University of California at Irvine. Author of *Grassroots Warriors: Activist Mothering, Community Work, and the War on Poverty* (1998), she also edited *Community Activism and Feminist Politics: Organizing Across Race, Class, and Gender* (1998).

Frances Fox Piven is Distinguished Professor of Political Science and Sociology at the Graduate Center of the City University of New York. She is coauthor (with Richard Cloward) of *Regulating the Poor* (1971, 1993), *Poor People's Movements* (1977), and, most recently, *The Breaking of the American Social Compact* (1997).

Dorothy Roberts is Professor of Law at Northwestern University. She is the author of numerous articles on gender, race, and the law and of the 1997 book *Killing the Black Body: Race, Reproduction, and the Meaning of Liberty*.

Rickie Solinger, a historian, is the author of *Wake Up Little Susie: Single Pregnancy and Race before* Roe v. Wade (1992) and *The Abortionist: A Woman Against the Law* (1994). She also is the editor of *Abortion Wars: Fifty Years of Struggle, 1950 – 2000* (1998).

INDEX

abortion: as choice, 10–11, 14, 25–26, 155, 176; constraints on, 33–34; funds for, 156; legalization of, 25, 29, 156; terminology of, 7; "therapeutic," 10

Abramovitz, Mimi, 27–28n. 60

Ackerman, Nathan, 15, 16

ACORN (Association of Community Organizations for Reform Now), 41–42

Act for Better Child Care Services (ABC bill), 157–58

Action Alliance for Children, 165

activism: class consciousness reconfigured in, 224–37; conditions for, 237–47; equality and, 246–47; family issues and, 226–29, 242–46; goal of, 216; impact and outcomes of, 247–48; kinds of, 231; notions of, 215; redefinition of, 216–20, 242; social context of, 247; social isolation's impact on, 238–40; strategies in, 220–23. See also collective action

activist women: CAP control and, 72–73; in community space, 218, 219–20, 228–32, 239–40; defense of motherwork by, 46–53; history of, 215–16; identity of, 214; as nonconformist (1950s), 13–14; political understanding of, 248; records of, 220–21; strategies of, 221–23; in welfare state space, 217–19; in workplace space, 218–19, 228–29, 239–40. See also activism; advocacy groups; collective action

ADC (Aid to Dependent Children), 38, 62n. 19, 194

adoption: forced, 164, 165–66; payment for, 30; pressure for, 10

Adoption and Safe Families Act, 165–66

advocacy groups: on battered women, 147–48; for children, 52, 61, 157–58, 165; on immigrant rights, 116–23; for older people, 61; for poor neighborhoods, 49n. 52; against PRA, 174; on suitable employment, 48–49; on welfare mothers and male employment, 51. See also activism; collective action; National Welfare Rights Organization (NWRO); political action

AFDC. See Aid to Families with Dependent Children (AFDC)

AFDC-UP program, 39–40

AFL-CIO: on child care and training, 55; ERA and, 236; labor organizing by, 234–35; on workfare, 41, 43, 44

African American families: choice and, 22; patterns of, 164. See also African American mothers

African American mothers: as child care workers, 161–62; child support and, 139; concerns about, 21; discouraging procreation by, 154–56; poverty of, 23; stereotypes of, 11, 152, 154, 158, 160; valuation of care giving by, 157–58; on welfare, 184. See also African American working mothers; poor women; single mothers

African Americans: joblessness of male, 22; middle-class, 230; migration of, 38; segregation of, 225, 229–32, 239–40; types of activism of, 231. See also civil rights movement

African American women: abortions by, 155;

African American women (*continued*)
activism of, 220, 247; club movement of, 231;
rights demanded by, 38–39; sexual "misbehavior" of, 21; standpoint theory and, 225,
229–31. *See also* activist women; African
American mothers; Black feminism; feminists
of color
African American working mothers: choices of,
19–24; domestic work forced on, 20n. 40, 21,
53–55, 160–62, 232; occupations by percentage for, 20n. 40, 21n. 45, 23
The African World (periodical), on work, 51–52
Agriculture Research, Extension, and Education
Reform Act, 122–23
Aid to Dependent Children (ADC), 38, 62n. 19,
194
Aid to Families with Dependent Children
(AFDC): activism and, 245; applications for,
38–39; Asian immigration and, 110–11, 114;
changes in, 30, 48; child care and mothers on,
158, 163; child support and, 139–40; deeming
period for, 111; demise of, 37, 40, 59, 61, 127,
142, 190; dependency in, 198; development of,
196; employment combined with, 53, 54–55;
expanded benefits of, 27–28n. 60; goal of,
46–47, 193–94; as safety net, 62, 133, 134,
148, 190–91, 211; wage level impacted by, 88–
89, 244; waivers for, 153
Aid to Needy Children (ANC), 47
Alinsky, Saul, 76
Amerasians, as refugees, 121
American Association for University Women,
174
American Federation of State, County, and Municipal Employees, 67
Americanization, in welfare, 196–97
American Revolution, women's activism in,
227–28
AmeriCorps, 68–72
Amott, Teresa, 21n. 45
Ancheta, Angelo, 123
Anthony, Susan B., 234
antipoverty programs: community control of,
72–79; funds for, 59n. 12, 143; name of, 56n.
1; women's activism and, 228; work initiatives
in, 66. *See also* community action programs
(CAPs); food stamp benefits; welfare; work-
fare initiatives; *specific programs*
Anti-Terrorism and Effective Death Penalty Act
(1996), 107
Appalachia, mining strikes in, 229
Arkansas, welfare organizing in, 41–42n. 21
Asian immigrants: hostility toward, 115–16; im-

migration reform's impact on, 116–31; as
model minority, 107–8; number of, 110–11,
115–16; poverty of, 108, 115; public assistance
and, 108–23; racial politics and, 107–8; resettlement programs for, 112–14; status of,
105n. 19; suicides of, 119–20, 123; visibility
of, 102–3; work available for, 113–15
Asian Law Caucus, 123
Asian mothers, on welfare, 184
Asian Week (newspaper), on immigrant suicide,
119–20
Asiatic Barred Zone Act (1917), 109
assimilationism, rejection of, 100
Association of Community Organizations for
Reform Now (ACORN), 41–42
Association of Head Start Grantees, 61
Australia, wage levels in, 88
authorization, empowerment as, 58n. 11

Balanced Budget Act (1997): health care under,
128n. 79; immigrant benefits under, 105–6,
121–22; welfare workers' rights under, 90–91
Baltimore (Md.), welfare in, 42, 92
Barron, Curley, 164
Bartemeier, Leo, 18
Bartky, Sandra Lee, 194n. 16
Bassuk, Ellen L., 142
Bauer, Gary, 9, 26, 28, 29, 32
behavior: benefit cuts due to, 85, 87; poor
women's choice-like, 11–12; PRA's
modification of, 152, 157; PRA's punishment
of, 27–33, 180–81, 244; sexual, 21, 93, 97–98
behaviorism, concept of, 192–93, 203
Benmayor, Rina, 58n. 11
Bernstein, Jared, 89
Billies, Michelle, 63–64
birth control. *See* contraception; reproduction;
sterilization
Black feminism, 47, 230
Black power movement, 72n. 56, 240
Bluestone, Barry, 98
"boat people," policies on, 112
Boston Globe (newspaper), cartoon in, 161
Bradley, David, 59n. 12
Brazzwell, Robert, 77
"bread and roses" slogan, 216
Brimelow, Peter, 104, 106
Brossard, James H. B., 19
Brown, Elsa Barkely, 230
Buchanan, Patrick, 100, 102, 106
Bush administration: economy under, 115;
women's rights under, 175
business. *See* employers; private business sector

Bustamante, Cruz, 127
Butler, James, 91–92

California: citizen participation in, 64; declining welfare caseload in, 1; economy of, 102; eligibility for benefits in, 126–30; family sanctions in, 163; health care in, 124, 127, 128; immigrants in, 114–15, 118–20, 122–25, 129; interunion coalitions in, 236; low-wage jobs in, 89; parental responsibility laws in, 166; Proposition 187 in, 101–4, 106; racial demographics in, 102–3; suicides in, 119–20, 123; welfare organizing in, 41–42n. 21, 47, 127; workfare initiatives, 128–31
California Department of Social Services, 114
California Food Security Monitoring Project, 122–23
California Immigrant Welfare Collaborative, 127
CalWORKs (California Work Opportunity and Responsibility to Kids), 128–31
Cambodian immigrants: context of, 112–15; public assistance and, 117–18
Canada, wage levels in, 88
Cannon, William B., 56n. 1
capitalism: inability to meet human needs, 217–18; welfare state and, 192–93, 243–44
CAPs. See community action programs (CAPs)
Card, Josephine, 75–76
care giving: assumptions of, 190; diffuse nature of, 199–200; doulia concept and, 203–6, 209–13; economic value of, 185; federal support for, 38; feminists on, 181–82; by relative, 164; social ethics of, 203–4; social justice vs., 201; social recognition of, 197–98; TANF and, 3, 164–65; as unpaid women's work, 65, 199; as wage work, 37, 185–88. See also dependency relations; housework; motherwork
Carter, Jimmy, 32
Catholic Charities, 120
Center for Survey Research (U. of Mass.), 190n. 6
Central Intelligence Agency (CIA), 122
CETA (Comprehensive Employment Training Act), 29, 69
Chan, Sucheng, 114
Charity Organization Societies, 40
Chase Manhattan Bank, 185
Chavez, Leo R., 100n. 1, 101n. 4
Chess, Stella, 18
Chicago: domestic violence in, 135; interunion coalitions in, 236
childbearing: child exclusion laws' impact on, 155–56; nonmarital, 9–11, 93, 154, 180–81; as

pathological, 28–31, 153, 176. See also reproduction; teenage mothers
child care: cost of, 3, 162–63; debate over, 157–58; established by welfare activists, 52–53; feminists on, 45, 177; funding cuts in, 30, 33, 40, 53, 162–63; labor unions on, 44, 55; lack of choice in, 172; need for, 73, 148, 163, 188; subsidies for/grants for, 50; suitability of, 172n. 5; wages for, 162, 211–12; as work, 161–62, 185–86
child exclusion laws, 153–56
children: advocacy groups for, 52, 61, 157–58, 165; benefits for immigrant, 122–23, 128; birthright citizenship for, 104; custody of, 140–41, 163–66; domestic violence and, 132; exempted from work, 193; learnfare program and, 93n. 28; maternalism's focus on, 196; needs of, 52, 199n. 34; parental responsibility laws and, 166; percentage in poverty, 31; welfare for, 43–44, 143, 165, 190. See also child support
Children's Bureau (U.S.), 44, 196
Children's Defense Fund, 52, 61
Children's March for Survival (1972), 52
child support: absence of, 139–42; assurance system in, 149; average awards for, 180n. 16; coercive aspects of, 180–81; feminist support for, 177–81; PRA's provisions on, 144, 146–47, 148–49, 171–72, 177–81
Child Welfare League, 61
Chinese-Vietnamese immigrants, 112–16
Chini, Samuel, 67
choice: concept of, 7–8; disconnecting dependency from, 24–27; expansion of issues of, 22–24; feminists on, 177, 183; lifestyle type of, 25; maintaining, 187–88; overview of, 8–13; paradoxes linked to, 33–35; pathologization of, 9–11, 13–20, 27–34; racial difference in, 20–24; of welfare vs. work, 83–87, 91
"churning," use of term, 62
CIA (Central Intelligence Agency), 122
CIO (Congress of Industrial Organizations), 234–35. See also AFL-CIO
citizen participation: contraction of, 57–59, 60–65, 72; expansion of, 56–57, 59, 79–80; forms of, 56n. 2; in War on Poverty, 56–57, 59–61. See also activism; collective action; political action
citizens: definitions of, 201–2; moral powers of, 202–3
Citizens Budget Commission (N.Y.C.), 85
citizenship: birthright, 104; definitions of, 29n. 65, 58n. 11, 100, 190, 201–3; narrowed view of,

citizenship *(continued)*
58–59; PRA's impact on, 171–73; public benefits tied to, 105–9; social, 57–58, 197–98, 202–3. *See also* naturalization; rights
City University of New York, students on welfare at, 63–64, 91
Civil Rights Act (1964), 26, 110, 235, 246. *See also* Title VII
Civil Rights Act (1991), 175
civil rights movement: AFDC benefits and, 38–39; culture of poverty theory during, 23; implications for choice and, 25; political constituencies for, 77; standpoint theory and, 225, 240, 245; women in, 220, 223, 232
Civil Rights Restoration Act (1988), 175
C.K. v. Shalala, 155–56
class: child care issues and, 52–53; dependency and, 20; domestic violence and, 136–37; feminism based in, 232–37; motherwork and, 52, 152; public policy differentiated by, 64–72, 79, 152; shift in power, 95; work ethic and, 51–52, 181. *See also* class consciousness
class action lawsuits, 62, 155–56
class consciousness: economic/social production and, 240–42; equality and, 246–47; family maintenance and, 242–46; gender and, 224, 226–37, 247; reconfiguration of, 223–26; social isolation and, 238–40. *See also* activism; collective action; political action
Clinton, William J.: on adoption, 165; on AmeriCorps, 69, 70; on empowerment zones, 77; family caps and, 153; immigration reform under, 106, 120; on race, 131; welfare reform under, 1, 32, 61, 85, 176, 185. *See also* Personal Responsibility and Work Opportunity Reconciliation Act (PRA, 1996)
Cloward, Richard, 47, 71, 74, 83, 239–40
Coalition for Labor Union Women (CLUW), 236
collective action: approach to, 215–16; conditions for, 237–47; deterents to, 221–22; empowerment as, 58n. 11; families' engagement in, 241; female consciousness and, 226–29; impact and outcomes of, 247–48; "spaces" of, 216–20, 239–40; strategies of, 221, 222–23; visibility of, 216. *See also* activism; political action
Collins, Patricia Hill, 230, 231
Communication Workers of America (CWA), 236
community: antipoverty programs controlled by, 72–79; control taken from, 57–59; labor market's link to, 226; media coverage of, 221;

women's activism in, 218, 219–20, 228–32, 239–40. *See also* community service; poor neighborhoods
community action programs (CAPs): citizen participation in, 56–57, 59–61; civil rights organizations and, 77; class differentiation in, 64–72, 79, 152; community control and decentralization of, 57, 72–74, 80; critique of, 71–72; funds for, 59, 64, 72–74; goals of, 59, 79–80; "new careers" in, 65–68, 69; political action and, 60–61, 64, 72–74; research on, 60n. 16; structure of, 75–76; support for, 64–65
community service: emphasis on, 57; encouraged for students, 64–65, 68–72, 79; requirement for, 40–41, 68
Community Services Block Grant, 59, 73
Community Work and Training Programs, 39–40
Comprehensive Child Development Act (1971), 44
Comprehensive Employment Training Act (CETA), 29, 69
congressional hearings: on AmeriCorps, 71; on child care bill, 157–58; on child support, 179; on unemployment insurance, 54; on "welfare mothers," 28, 50; on workfare, 51, 67. *See also specific acts*
Congressional Research Service, 31
Congress of Industrial Organizations (CIO), 234–35. *See also* AFL-CIO
Congress of Racial Equality (CORE), 47, 77
consciousness: definition of, 224; female, 226–29; womanist, 229–32. *See also* class consciousness
consumption: choice in, 12; gendered participation in, 226–29; women's activism and, 239, 242
contraception: access to, 34, 153, 195; as choice, 25–26; mandated, 30, 153; sterilization as, 30, 50, 154–55. *See also* reproduction
CORE (Congress of Racial Equality), 47, 77
cost-of-living protests, 218, 220
criminal justice system: domestic violence laws and, 133–34, 147, 149–50; parental responsibility laws and, 166
cult of domesticity, concept of, 159
cultural practices: concept of, 92–93; rituals of degradation in, 97–98
culture of poverty theory, 22–23. *See also* dependency
CWA (Communication Workers of America), 236

Dallas (Tex.), welfare organizing in, 41–42n. 21

Dantzler, Rick, 154

Davis, Martha F., 141

day care. *See* child care

Day Care and Child Development Council of America, 53

"deadbeat dads," use of term, 178. *See also* child support

decentralization: of CAPs, 57, 72–74, 80; as space for political action, 75

Declaration of Independence, 198n. 28

Decter, Midge, 8–9

deeming, process of, 111, 125–26, 129, 145

Delaware, suitable workfare jobs in, 48

Delta Service Corps, 69n. 45

Delta State University (Miss.), 69n. 45

democracy: contraction of, 61–65; failure of, 246–47; welfare state and, 192–93

Demonstration Cities and Metropolitan Act (1966), 78

DeParle, Jason, 85–86n. 5

dependency: advocates for, 26; bad choices leading to, 22, 28; countermeasures to, 37; definitions of, 7–8, 176, 192–93, 197–99, 203, 207; disconnecting choice from, 24–27; gendered, 8–9, 20, 23, 209; nested, 203; overview of, 8–13; paradoxes linked to, 33–35; pathology and, 8, 13–20, 27–34, 244; private vs. public, 12; as problem of morality, 84; racial difference in, 8–9, 14–19, 20–24, 27

dependency relations: accountability in, 209–10; concept of, 198, 203; context of, 206–9; principle of doulia and, 203–6, 209–13; social cooperation in, 210; social ethics of, 203–4; social goods of, 202–3; visibility of, 211–12; workers in, 198–201, 205

Depo Provera, 155

Dilseppe, D., 235–36

disabled people: benefits for immigrant, 105, 119–23, 130; poverty of, 194; universal policies and, 213; waivers for, 120–21

disease. *See* health care; pathology

disenfranchisement, concept of, 58–59

District Council 37 (New York City), 41

"diversion" programs, 1–2

divorce: choice of, 9; dependency relations and, 208. *See also* child support

divorced women: child support and, 139–42, 144, 146–47, 148–49; on male control, 137–38; paternity establishment and, 179–80; poverty of, 141; violence and, 134–35; welfare for, 243. *See also* child support; poor women; single mothers

domestic service work: immigrant women in, 118; laws absent for, 54, 160; mass exodus from, 23; poor mothers in, 152; poverty enforced in, 53–55; racialized division of, 158–63; resistance in, 232; status of, 20, 211. *See also* dependency relations

domestic violence: child support issues and, 139–42, 144, 146–47, 148–49, 179–80; economic and social impact of, 132, 137–38, 150; extent of, 132, 134–37, 190n. 6; immigrant benefits and, 126, 130; PRA provisions and, 133, 142–48, 190; prosecution for, 149–50; serious type of, 136; women's rights and, 149–50, 183

doulia: applied to welfare reform, 206, 209–13; principle of, 203–5

Economic Opportunity Act (1964): assessment mechanism in, 72; citizen participation in, 56n. 2; components of, 56–57, 64; programs funded through, 59, 66, 69; rejection of, 60–61

Economic Policy Institute, 89

economy: collapse of (1930s), 242–43, 245; racial politics linked to, 102–3. *See also* capitalism; labor market; wages

Edin, Kathryn, 86, 87

education: discrimination in, 2, 142; disregard for, 41, 63, 90, 148; goals of, 192; need for, 148; for single mothers, 183; for undocumented immigrants, 101, 103. *See also* AmeriCorps; job training; schools; students

Eisenstein, Zillah, 232

Emily's List, 174, 175

emotions, in dependency relations, 199–200, 205

employers: control by, 21; discrimination by, 26–27, 234–36, 238–40; domestic violence and, 150; hostility to women workers, 234–35; immigrant workers and, 96n. 34; outsourcing by, 94–95; political influence of, 221; social reproduction and, 240–42; tax credits for workfare, 91

employment. *See* work

empowerment, definitions of, 58n. 11, 74

Empowerment Zones and Enterprise Communities (EZEC) Program: philosophy of, 78–79; structure of, 75, 77–78

enterprise zone. *See* Empowerment Zones and Enterprise Communities (EZEC) Program

equality: assumptions about, 195; components of, 45–46, 173, 181; in family and public sphere, 208n. 57, 211; implications of,

equality (*continued*)
246–47; rhetoric of, 194n. 16, 233; support
for, 235–36; in wages, 233–34; welfare's role
in, 184–85; in workplace, 181–83, 187–88
Equal Pay Act (1963), 235
Equal Rights Amendment, 26, 49, 236
Europe: poor relief in, 93; wage levels in, 88
Evans, Faith, 48
Evans, Samuel L., 76
EZEC. *See* Empowerment Zones and Enterprise
Communities (EZEC) Program

Fainstein, Norman, 79–80
Fainstein, Susan, 79–80
Fair Housing Rights Act (1968), 110
Fair Labor Standards Act, 90–91
families: caps on, 33, 153–56, 195n. 18; complex
context of, 18; "functional disorganization" of,
16–17; immigrant, 106–7, 109–10, 116; income sources for, 53, 54–55, 86; labor market's link to, 83–84, 98–99, 226; as male responsibility, 50–51; needs of, 49–50, 211;
patriarchal, 200, 243–44; political debate on,
206–9; PRA's impact on, 163–66; social citizenship linked to autonomous, 197n. 25; social reproduction in, 240–46; structure of,
45, 97–98, 206, 243; weakened by reform, 84,
98–99, 130; welfare's link to maintenance of,
194, 211, 240–46. *See also* African American
families; children; dependency relations; domestic violence; parents; single mothers; two-
parent families
Family Assistance Plan (FAP): debate over, 46–
48, 54; failure of, 44–45, 161
family caps: feminists on, 195n. 18; implementation of, 33, 153–54; lawsuits on, 155–56
family leave policies, 188
family reunification preferences (immigration),
106–7, 109–10, 116
Family Support Act (1988), 39–40, 63, 148
Family Violence Option (FVO): feminists on,
183; "good cause" exemptions and, 146–47;
implementation of, 145–48; provisions of,
143–45
family wage, concept of, 206–7n. 54, 228–29
Farnham, Marynia, *Modern Woman*, 9
"Fast to Free Women from Poverty" Day, 49n.
52
fathers, work programs for, 39–40
female consciousness, 226–29
female-headed families. *See* African American
mothers; poor women; single mothers
The Feminine Mystique (Friedan), 45

femininity: dependency linked to, 8–9, 16;
housework linked to, 237; postwar studies of,
16–17
feminists: challenges for, 212; on child care, 45,
177; on child support, 177–81; on choice, 177,
183; on citizenship, 57–58; on family caps,
195n. 18; on Family Violence Option, 183;
gender and poverty issues for, 195; goals of,
45, 49, 223; motherwork devalued by, 45–46;
paternity establishment and, 177–81; second-
wave, 182–83; on welfare, 3–4, 171, 174–77,
184–88, 190, 206; on workfare initiatives, 43,
177, 181–84; working-class, 232–37, 247
feminists of color: equality in workplace and,
182–83; NWRO and, 47. *See also* Black feminism
The First Wives' Club (film), 160
flour riots, 228
food stamp benefits: cutbacks in, 96, 143; eligibility for, 105–6; immigration and, 110–11,
114, 117, 120–23, 126, 128, 130; minimum
wage for workfare linked to, 90n. 18
food strikes, 228
foster care, as threat, 163–66
France, poor relief in, 93
Fraser, Nancy, 192n. 8, 193, 197, 206, 211n. 63
Frazier, Franklin E., 21n. 44
Freedom Bus (NWRO), 221n. 11
freedom marches, 72n. 56
Freeman, Richard B., 98n. 39
Friedan, Betty, 45, 174
Friedman, Marilyn, 201
fuel assistance programs, 30

garment workers, strikes by, 234
Gelles, Richard, 136
gender: activism and, 216–20, 242; citizenship
defined by, 29n. 65; class consciousness and,
224, 226–37, 247; dependency and, 8–9, 20,
23, 209; in dependency relations, 200; equity
in family and public sphere, 208n. 57, 211; immigration reform and, 118, 124–26, 130–31;
labor force divided by, 187, 206, 217, 219–20,
224–25, 237–40; as perspective, 215; PRA's
use of, 190–91; spaces differentiated by, 217–
20, 239–40; welfare differences by, 207n. 55
George, Freedom, 77
Gilligan, Carol, 201
Gingrich, Newt, 90–91, 101, 164
Glass, David H., 154
Glenn, Evelyn Nakano, 212
globalization, citizenship and, 58n. 11
Glueck, Eleanor, 17, 19

Glueck, Sheldon, 17, 19
Gong-Guy, Elizabeth, 114
Goodin, Robert, 205, 205n. 51
Goodwill Industries, 63
Gordon, Linda, 192n. 8, 193, 195, 197
government: accountability and, 209–10; bu-
    reaucracy of, 72–74, 85; as responsible for
    single mothers, 172–73, 176; as target of ac-
    tivism, 242–46; violence against women and,
    133–34
Great Society programs: Asian immigration and,
    110; Johnson's goal for, 56–57; programs in,
    64–65, 78. *See also* War on Poverty; *specific
    programs*
Green, Edith, 75
Green, Gray, 68
Green Amendments, 75
Greene, Jack P., 198n. 28
Griffiths, Martha, 51
Gross, Rita, 52–53

Hacker, Andrew, 225
Hallman, Howard, 69, 72n. 56
Handler, Joel, 200
hardship, definition of, 144–45
Hargrove, Hattie, 36
Hartmann, Susan, 19
Hartsock, Nancy, 224–25
Haveman, Robert, 88
Head Start (program), 61, 64
health care: battered women and, 147; in Cali-
    fornia, 124, 127, 128; cost of, 3; demands for,
    73; immigrants and, 101, 105, 124–25, 128; pri-
    vacy vs., 178
Healthy Families program (Calif.), 128
Hegel, G. W. F., 192–93
Hein, Jeremy, 115–16
Held, Virginia, 198
Hing, Bill Ong, 110, 112, 113
Hmong immigrants: classification of, 121–22;
    context of, 112–16; public assistance and,
    117–18; suicide of, 119–20
homeless people: battered women as, 142; wel-
    fare benefits lost by, 62
Horowitz, Claudia, 71
Hotel and Restaurant Employees' and Bar-
    tenders' International Union, 236
housewives, activism of, 219–20, 227–29,
    231–32
housework: definition of, 158n. 10; femininity
    linked to, 237; social isolation of, 238–40;
    spiritual vs. menial, 158–63; wages for, 182;
    women assigned to, 159, 225; as work, 185–86.

See also care giving; domestic service work;
    motherwork
housing: demands for improved, 73; federal cuts
    in public, 29–30; rights to, 110
Hout, Michael, 88–89

Illegal Immigration and Immigrant Responsibil-
    ity Act (1996): context of, 105, 116; provisions
    of, 106–7, 124, 125–26, 145
Illinois: domestic violence in, 135; interunion
    coalitions in, 236; workfare limited in, 42
immigrants: Family Violence Option and, 145;
    hostility toward, 102–7, 115–16; origins of,
    100n. 1, 103; poverty of, 108; preference sys-
    tem for, 109n. 24; public benefits and, 96,
    101–2, 105–23; reform's impact on, 116–31;
    refugees separated from, 112, 117; right to ap-
    peal deportation, 107; sponsors for, 106–7,
    109–11, 116, 125–26; stereotypes of, 104–5,
    107; workfare initiatives and, 129–31. *See also*
    Asian immigrants; refugees/asylees; undocu-
    mented immigrants
Immigration Act (1965): Asian immigration in-
    crease under, 111; changes in, 112; enactment
    of, 109; Preference System of, 109n. 24
Immigration and Naturalization Service (INS),
    103, 106–7, 123–24
immigration reform: adjustments in, 120–23;
    context of, 101–2, 104–5, 109–16; discrimina-
    tion and, 109; gender and, 118, 124–26, 130–
    31; immigrant restrictions via, 105–9; racial
    politics of, 100–105; sponsorship deeming in,
    111, 125–26, 129, 145; states and, 126–30
income packaging, concept of, 149
independence: definition of, 191–92; deviance
    linked to, 24; masculinization and, 9, 15,
    17–18, 198n. 28; men's fear of women's, 84;
    proof of women's, 12. *See also* choice
Index of Traditional Femininity, 17
individualism: emphasis on, 12; implications of,
    189; political action and, 221–22
industrial feminism, 232–37
INS (Immigration and Naturalization Service),
    103, 106–7, 123–24
Ireland, Patricia, 174
Isaac, Rael Jean, 62n. 20

Japan: immigrants from, 110; wage levels in, 88
Jenson, Jane, 73
Jobs with Justice, 42
job training: Asian immigration and, 110; dis-
    regarded, 90; federal cuts in, 29, 31; legislation
    on, 29, 39–40, 69; limits on, 129, 148; need

job training (*continued*)
for, 68–69, 148; suitable workfare jobs and, 48–49; workfare labeled as, 92. *See also* Community Work and Training Programs; Comprehensive Employment Training Act (CETA); education
Johnson administration: Great Society programs under, 56–57, 78; Women's Bureau under, 44n. 29
Jones, Woodrow, Jr., 115
Jordan, Barbara, 102
Jordan, Vernon E., Jr., 48
justice, Rawls's theory of, 201–3
justice movement, direction for, 35. *See also* social justice
juvenile delinquency, mother's employment linked to, 15–16n. 24, 16–17, 18–19

Kammerman, Sheila, 26
Kaplan, T., 226–27, 231
Kates, C., 235–36
Katznelson, Ira, 74
Kaufman, Leslie, 71
Kaus, Mickey, 94
Keaton, Diane, 160
Kemp, Jack, 206–7n. 54
Kennedy administration: antipoverty programs under, 56n. 1; women's equality and, 235–36
Kennelly, Barbara, 177n. 11
Kensington Welfare Rights Union, 221n. 11
Keyserling, Mary Dublin, 44n. 29
King, Coretta Scott, 49n. 52
Komarovsky, Mirra, 19–20
Korean immigrants, public assistance and, 117–18
Kraham, Susan J., 141

Labor Day, 32
labor force: gender division of, 187, 206, 217, 219–20, 224–25, 237–40; low-waged, low-skilled sector in, 41, 89, 91, 95, 113–14, 162; percentage in, 98n. 39; poverty and, 194; racialized division of domestic, 158–63. *See also* labor unions; wages; work
labor market: comparable worth in, 188; dependency relations vs., 199; equality in, 181–83, 187–88; family stability and, 83–84, 98–99, 226; as feminist focus, 45, 177, 181–84; insecurity in, 94–95, 97; low-wage sector in, 41, 89, 91, 95, 113–14, 162; older people in, 95–96; production in, vs. social reproduction, 240–42; workfare's impact on, 55, 83–84, 87–92, 191–93

labor unions: activist women in, 219, 222, 224, 229, 232, 234–36; on AmeriCorps, 70–71; on child care, 44, 55; ERA and, 236; strikes by, 219, 228, 229, 234; weakness of, 236–37; for women, 234; women's departments of, 235, 236; on women's work, 43–44; workfare jobs and, 41–44, 48–49, 55, 66–68, 91–92. *See also* working-class women
Ladies Home Journal (periodical), on working mothers, 14
Landrum, Philip, 54
Lane, Vera, 69
language, public benefits and, 119–21
Laotian immigrants: classification of, 121–22; context of, 112–16; public assistance and, 117–18
Latino immigrants: hostility toward, 107; public assistance and, 184; visibility of, 102–3
laws: on labor, 54, 90–91, 160, 234; on parental responsibility, 166; role of, 184; on women, 237. *See also* class action lawsuits; legal representation; rights
learnfare program, 93n. 28
legal representation: AFDC benefits and, 38–39; federal cuts in free, 30
Legal Services Corporation, 62, 62n. 20, 64, 80
Lein, Laura, 86, 87
Lewis, Mike, 64
Lewis, Oscar, 22–23
liberalism: government funds and, 60–61, 209–10; inadequacy of, 196–97n. 23; on political vs. family, 45–46
Lindsay, John, 72n. 56
"living wage" ordinance, 42
local level: activism at, 223; media's dismissal of, 221; role of, 184. *See also* community; poor neighborhoods
Long, Russell, 54, 161
Los Angeles (Calif.), welfare in, 1, 41–42n. 21, 47
low-income women. *See* poor women
loyalty oath, 120–21
Lundberg, Ferdinand, *Modern Woman*, 9
Lundgren, Dan, 104

Maccoby, Eleanor, 18
Mahoney, Martha, 140
Maney, Greg, 68
Manhattan, CAPs in, 74
Manpower Development and Training Act (1962), 69
marriage: encouragement of, 172, 243–44; men's control of women in, 137–38. *See also* child support; divorce; widows

Marshall, T. H., 58
Maryland, workfare jobs in, 42, 92
Massachusetts: domestic violence in, 135; interunion coalitions in, 236; public aid in, 190n. 6
Massachusetts Transitional Aid to Families with Dependent Children (TAFDC), 190n. 6
maternalism: slavery and, 152; welfare justified in, 196–97. *See also* motherhood; mothers; motherwork
Mathias, Bill, 77
Matthaei, Julie, 21n. 45
Matusow, Allen J., 76
McCall's (periodical), on working mothers, 18, 19
McCarran-Walter Act (1952), 109–10
McCormack Institute (U. of Mass.), 190n. 6
McCrate, Elaine, 88
McEntee, Gerald W., 67
Mead, Lawrence, 28, 29, 30, 31
Mealy, Fred, 77
meat boycotts, 228
media: changing attitudes in, 20–22; on choice to work, 14–16; local level absent in, 221; on NWRO, 221n. 11; on social spending, 97; on workfare, 86–87
medicaid: contraception through, 153; cutbacks in, 143. *See also* health care
Medi-Cal (Calif.), 124, 127, 128
men: abusive, 84, 126, 130, 136–38; independence and, 198n. 28; irresponsibility of, 176–79; paternity establishment and, 146, 148–49, 171–72, 177–81; responsibilities of, 50–51; restraining orders against, 141. *See also* child support; domestic violence
Meredith Mississippi Freedom March (1966), 72n. 56
Michigan, welfare recipients in, 46
micromobilizers, concept of, 223
middle-class women: childbearing and, 153–54; on child support enforcement, 178–81; as choice makers, 11–12; motherhood and, 157–58; PRA's impact on, 176; women of color's dependency work and, 212; work requirements and, 181–84
migration, citizenship and, 58n. 11. *See also* immigrants
Millet, Kate, 190
Milwaukee (Wis.), homelessness in, 62
Milwaukee County Welfare Rights Organization, 51
Milwaukee Task Force on Emergency Shelter and Relocation Services, 62

Mineola County Department of Social Services (N.Y.), 36
mining, strikes in, 229
Mink, Gwendolyn, 98, 196
Mink, Patsy, 183
Minnesota, workfare limited in, 42
Mishel, Lawrence, 89
Mississippi: service corps in, 69n. 45; work program in, 164
Model Cities Program, 78
Modern Woman (Lundberg and Farnham), 9
Montgomery bus boycott, 228, 232
Moody-Adams, Michele, 196–97n. 23
Moon, Anson, 115
Moon, Donald, 192
Moore, Bessie, 49
Moore, Geneva, 36
Moore, Hilmar G., 30
Moore, Mildred, 232
morality: cultural practice and, 93–94, 97–98; dependency and, 84; in dependency relations, 199–200, 205; emphasis on, 83, 87; feminist, of care, 196–97; learnfare program and, 93n. 28; supervision in, 157. *See also* choice
motherhood: ban on poor, 152–67; as choice, 34; complex context of, 18; components of, 98; definition of, 24–27; dependency linked to, 23; pathology linked to, 15; representation of, 13–14; women assigned to, 159, 225. *See also* motherwork; reproduction
mothers: differentiation of, 37–38, 157–58; full family sanctions on, 163; ignored in maternalism, 196; married vs. unmarried, 30; redefinition of, 24–26; rights of, 50, 152, 157–58, 163–66, 171–73, 176. *See also* African American mothers; single mothers; teenage mothers; "welfare mothers"; white working mothers; working mothers
mothers' pensions, 37–38, 194, 196
motherwork: defined as work, 37, 49, 55; devaluation of, 45–46, 55, 157–63, 172, 181, 191; rights of, 184; social class and, 52, 152; as social reproduction, 240–46; tasks of, 193–94; value of, 46–53, 55, 156–58, 182, 183, 185–88. *See also* care giving; dependency relations; housework
Moynihan, Daniel Patrick, 44–45, 76–77
Moynihan Report, 21–22
Ms. (periodical), on work, 52
Municipal Hospital Workers Union Local 420, 92
Murray, Charles, 29

Murray, Patty, 183
Myrdal, Gunnar, 246

NARAL (National Abortion Rights League), 174
National Advisory Commission on Civil Disorders, 246
National and Community Service Trust Act (1993), 69
National Association for the Advancement of Colored People (NAACP): Legal Defense and Education Fund Inc., 61; Youth Council, 77
National Committee on Household Employment, 54
National Committee on Household Workers, 53
National Community Action Foundation, 59n. 12
National Conference of State Legislatures, 2
National Consumers' League, 44n. 29
National Council of La Raza, 61
National Council of Senior Citizens, 61
National Crime Victimization Survey, 136
National Governors Association, 1, 161
National Organization for Women (NOW): on child care, 53; on family caps, 195n. 18; on Family Violence Option, 183; founding of, 236; on welfare, 174, 175; Welfare Mothers March and, 49n. 52
National Urban League, 48
National Welfare Rights Organization (NWRO): on abuse of administrative power, 62–63; on child care, 53; on citizenship, 43; control of, 50; goals of, 37, 47, 51–52; as model, 205n. 52; on work, 46–49, 51–52, 54–55
National Welfare Rights Union (NWRU), 221n. 11
National Working Mothers Day, 53
nation-state: citizenship in, 58n. 11; identity in, 100, 104–5; women's role in, 65
Native American mothers, on welfare, 184
naturalization: assistance in, 120–21; benefits tied to, 122–23, 127; requirements of, 119–20
Neighborhood Action Program (Manhattan), 74
neighborhood improvement projects, 220
New Careers concept, 65–68, 69
New Jersey: domestic violence in, 135; family cap in, 155–56; welfare organizing in, 41–42n. 21
New Mexico, welfare organizing in, 41–42n. 21
"New Nativism," use of term, 100
New York City: CAPs in, 60, 74–75; community control in, 72–73; union jobs lost in, 91–92; welfare organizing in, 41–42, 71–72; workfare jobs in, 91–92, 94

New York State: immigrant suicides in, 119; low-wage jobs in, 89; workfare requirements in, 48
New York State Department of Social Services v. Dublino, 39
New York Times Magazine (periodical), on working women, 15
New York Times (newspaper): on motherhood, 25; on workfare, 63; on working women, 16
New York Workers' Rights Board, 42
New York Work Rules, 39
Nine-to-Five (union), 236
Nixon administration: Model Cities funding under, 78n. 74; welfare reform under, 44–45, 47
Norplant, 30, 153, 155
NOW. See National Organization for Women (NOW)
NWRO. See National Welfare Rights Organization (NWRO)
NWRU (National Welfare Rights Union), 221n. 11

Occupational Safety and Health Administration (OSHA), 90
Office of Community Affairs, 59n. 12
Office of Refugee Resettlement (ORR), 112–14
Okin, Susan, 201
older people: advocacy group for, 61; benefits for immigrant, 105, 119–20, 122–23, 128, 130; in labor market, 95–96; language difficulties of immigrant, 119–21; poverty of, 194; social security for, 245
Omnibus Budget Reconciliation Act (1993), 77
Orleck, Annelise, 227
Orloff, Ann Shola, 197n. 25, 207n. 55, 208
OSHA (Occupational Safety and Health Administration), 90

"paper plate campaign," 122
parents: handbooks for, 8; parental responsibility laws and, 166; rights of, 163–66. See also fathers; mothers
Pastore, John, 46
Pateman, Carol, 29n. 65
pathology: childbearing linked to, 28–31, 153, 176; choice linked to, 9–11, 13–20; dependency and, 8, 13–20, 27–34, 244; linked to choice to work, 10–11, 13–16
Payne, C. M., 214n. 1
Peace Corps, 69
Pearce, Diana, 195n. 17
Pearl, Arthur, 65–66
Pennsylvania. See Philadelphia (Pa.)

personal responsibility, use of term, 172–73
Personal Responsibility and Work Opportunity Reconciliation Act (PRA, 1996): amendments to, 143–44, 175; children and, 162–66; components of, 171, 177; debate on, 40, 171; domestic violence issues and, 133, 142–48, 190; enactment of, 33, 61, 214; evaluation of, 1–4; family caps in, 33, 153–56, 195n. 18; funding system of, 73; gendered nature of, 190–91; immigration and, 96, 103–5, 116, 117; implications of, 152; labor market impacted by, 83–84, 87–92; limits in, 85, 89, 98n. 38, 143–44; paternity establishment and, 146, 148–49, 171–72, 177–81; racial politics of, 100–105, 180–81; requirements of, 40–41; rights eliminated by, 171–73, 176, 179–81; safety net eliminated by, 63–64, 148–50. See also Family Violence Option (FVO); Temporary Assistance for Needy Families (TANF) program; workfare initiatives
Pfaelzer, Mariana, 103–4
Philadelphia Anti-Poverty Committee, 76
Philadelphia (Pa.): boycott in, 77; CAPs in, 60, 75–79; divorced women in, 134–35n. 7
Piven, Frances Fox, 47, 71, 74, 239–40
Plyler v. Doe, 101, 103
Polanyi, Karl, 89–90
Politan, Nicholas H., 155–56
political action: contexts of, 75–76; decentralization and, 73–74; poor neighborhoods and, 49n. 52, 56–57, 60–61, 64, 75–77; training in, 79–80; types of, 221–23. See also activism; class consciousness; collective action
political consciousness. See class consciousness
political participation. See activism; citizen participation; political action
politics: approach to, 215–16; collective action discouraged in, 221; debates on family in, 206–9; feminists and welfare reform, 174–77; principles of care and, 196–97, 201; of punishing poor mothers, 27–33, 180–81, 244; racial, 100–105, 107–8, 180–81, 183–84
Poor Law Commission, 93
poor neighborhoods: CAP control and, 72–74; disinvestment in, 57–59, 72–74; "new careers" in, 65–68, 69; political action and, 49n. 52, 56–57, 60–61, 64, 75–77
Poor People's Campaign, 49n. 52
Poor People's Summit (Philadelphia), 221n. 11
poor relief, history of, 93
poor women: activism of, 47, 59–61, 216; "bad choices" of, 11–1222–23, 27–34, 67, 83; child support and, 139–42, 144, 146–47, 148–49; citizen participation by, 59–61; definition of,

32; dependency of, 8, 11; dependency work of, 212; domestic violence against, 132–51; "forced work" opposed by, 37; income sources for, 53, 54–55, 86; invisibility of, 216; as mothers, 152–67, 182–84; needs of, 142, 148–50; punishment of, 27–33, 180–81, 244; rights of, 163–66; safety net for, 62, 63, 133, 134, 148, 190–91, 211; "spaces" inhabited by, 217–20, 239–40; standpoint of, 226; stereotypes of, 143, 194–95; welfare as rationale choice for, 87; work experience of, 137–38. See also activist women; class consciousness; domestic violence; single mothers
poor women of color: choices of, 19–24; hostility toward, 97–98; poverty of, 141–42
Pope, Elizabeth, 19
poverty: countermeasures to, 191–93; definitions of, 193–95, 207n. 56; domestic violence linked to, 135–37; feminization of, 142, 190; gender and, 195; increase in, 31–33, 102, 108, 115, 194; persistence of, 2–3, 207; racialization of, 142. See also culture of poverty theory
PRA. See Personal Responsibility and Work Opportunity Reconciliation Act (PRA, 1996)
pregnancy. See childbearing
Presidential Commission on the Status of Women, 235
privacy: elimination of, 172, 178; racial differentiation of, 181
private business sector: profits in, 95–97; social spending opposed by, 97n. 36; workfare jobs in, 92, 162. See also employers
private sphere: domestic violence and, 133; women assigned to, 159. See also care giving; housework; motherwork
privatization, shift toward, 43, 63, 70, 73, 80, 145–46
Proposition 187 (Calif.), 101–4, 106
psychology: on dependency vs. choice, 13–20; individualism and, 189. See also pathology
public household, concept of, 196–97n. 23
public policy. See social policy
public sector, workfare jobs in, 48–49, 91–92
public sphere: dependency relations in, 204–5; maternalism in, 196–97

Quadagno, Jill, 45, 77

race: dependency and, 8–9, 14–19, 20–24, 27; in division of domestic labor, 158–63; family caps and, 154–56; on national agenda, 131; politics of, 100–105, 107–8, 180–81, 183–84; segregation by, 225, 229–32, 239–40; sexual "misbehavior" and, 21

racial uplift, movement for, 231
racism: effects of, 2, 230; persistence of, 246–47; in PRA's assumptions, 180–81; as target of activist women, 220
Rawls, John, 201–3
Reagan, Ronald: on "sob sisters," 31–32; on welfare "queens," 39
Reagan administration: attitudes toward working women in, 26–27; "cycle of dependency" in, 29–30; economy under, 115; poor mothers punished under, 28–33; WIN under, 67
reciprocation: accountability and, 209–10; concept of, 204–5, 206; social cooperation in, 210
Refugee Act (1980), 112, 113
Refugee Assistance Act (1975), 113
refugees/asylees: benefits for, 105, 117, 121–23; definition of, 105n. 19; hostility toward, 115–16; origins of, 103, 121; Vietnam War's impact on, 111–12, 115–16, 121; work available for, 113–15
rent strikes, 220
reproduction: activism and, 240–42; child exclusion laws' impact on, 155–56; contradictions in policy on, 33–35; discouraging poor women's, 153–56; options in, 25–26; rights of, 12, 30–31, 153–56, 184, 190, 195; social, vs. economic production, 240–42; social, welfare's role in, 242–46. See also childbearing; child support
residualism, concept of, 192–93, 203
resistance, individual strategies of, 221–22
responsibility, collective vs. personal, 205n. 51
restructuring, use of term, 94–95
Reyes, Nina, 61
Riessman, Frank, 65–66
rights: to autonomous family formation, 208, 211; domestic violence and, 149–50, 183; to economic and physical security, 149–50; fathers', 178; housing, 110; immigrants', 107; mothers', 50, 152, 157–58, 163–66, 171–73, 176; PRA's elimination of, 171–73, 176, 179–81, 183; reproduction, 12, 30–31, 153–56, 184, 190, 195; social goods and, 202–3; to welfare, 173, 184–88; of women, 233–34; workfare initiatives as threat to, 163–66, 172–73. See also equality
Riposa, Gerry, 78–79
Robinson, Ann, 72–73
Robnett, B., 223
Rochester [N.Y.] Action for Welfare Rights, 48
Roe v. Wade, 25, 156
Romm, Mary, 10, 34

Rose, Nancy, 66, 69
Rose, Stephen, 59–61, 98
Ross, Harriet, 27–28n. 60
Roybal-Allard, Lucille, 183
Rudé, George, 222

Sacramento Bee (newspaper), on immigrant suicide, 119
safety, workfare and, 48–49, 90, 91
Salt Lake City (Utah), workfare jobs in, 92
Sanders, Beulah, 49, 51
Sarvasy, Wendy, 57–58
Saturday Evening Post (periodical), on working women, 15
"Save Our State" campaign (Proposition 187 in Calif.), 101–4, 106
Sawhill, Isabel, 27–28n. 60
Scheman, Naomi, 189
Scheuer Amendments (to EOA), 66
Schiff, Tamara, 70–71
Schmitt, John, 89
schools: control of, 73; learnfare program and, 93n. 28; role in urban conflict, 74. See also education; students
Schram, Sanford, 62
Schroeder, Patricia, 31
Schultze, Charles L., 56n. 1
Sen, Amartya, 208
separation assault, use of term, 135, 140
Service Employees International Union, 236
sexuality: making choices in, 12; "misbehavior" and, 21, 93, 97–98
SF Weekly (periodical), on language, 119
Shaw, E. Clay, Jr., 102
Shear, Jeff, 60–61
shelter system. See homeless people
Sheppard-Towner Act, 196
Siim, Birte, 57–58
single mothers: child support for, 139–42, 144, 146–47, 148–49; citizenship and rights of, 171–73, 176; core problem for, 3, 29; dependency pathologized for, 27–34; education funds for, 183; exempted from wage work, 193–94, 205; number of, 25–26, 32; paternity establishment and, 146, 148–49, 171–72, 177–81; poverty of, 141, 207n. 56; punishment of, 27–33, 180–81, 244; right to welfare, 184–88; use of term, 24–25; welfare for, 43–44, 180n. 16, 243. See also dependency relations; divorced women; poor women
slavery: conditions of, 230; "Mammy" in, 159–60; maternalism and, 152
Smith, O'Delight, 230

SNCC (Student Nonviolent Coordinating
    Committee), 77
social citizenship, concept of, 57–58, 197–98,
    202–3
social class. *See* class
social cooperation, concept of, 210
social goods, concept of, 201–3, 206
social housekeeping, concept of, 196, 203–4
social insurance: effects of, 192–93; targets of,
    194–95
social isolation, activism from, 238–40
social justice: care giving vs., 201; social goods
    and, 201–3; welfare system and, 166–67,
    184–88; workfare initiatives and, 88
social policy: care ethic in, 203–4; class differ-
    entiation in, 64–72, 79, 152; contradictions
    in, 33–35; decentralization in, 57, 72–74, 80;
    dependency advocates on, 26; for extending
    social citizenship, 197–98; job insecurity
    linked to, 95, 97; maternalism in, 196–97;
    motherwork devalued in, 55. *See also* citizen
    participation; immigration reform; welfare
    reform
Social Security Act (1935), amendments to, 36–
    37, 110, 194
Social Security program: cost of living formula
    in, 95–96n. 33; eligibility changes in, 95–96,
    116–23; growth of, 245
social services: Asian immigrants and, 111–16;
    community control of, 71–72; federal cut-
    backs in, 30–31; need for, 49–50; political ac-
    tion and, 61, 64; for undocumented immi-
    grants, 101, 103, 105, 123–25, 127. *See also*
    community action programs (CAPs)
society: social reproduction in, 240–46; struc-
    ture of, 224–26. *See also* dependency relations
Solmon, Lewis, 70–71
Speenhamland plan, 89–90
standpoint theory, 224–26, 229–32, 240, 245
Stanton, Elizabeth Cady, 234
states: benefit amounts by, 38; block grant ap-
    proach and, 73–74, 85; child care and, 163,
    164, 172n. 5; control shifted to, 57–59, 63, 85,
    143; "diversion" programs of, 1–2; domestic
    violence and, 144, 146–48, 150; family caps
    in, 153–56; federal requirements for, 40, 85,
    144–45; immigration and, 103–4, 123–24,
    126–30. *See also specific states*
Steinem, Gloria, 174
stereotypes: of Black mothers, 11, 152, 154, 158,
    160; of Black women, 231; of immigrants,
    104–5, 107; of poor women, 143, 194–95
sterilization, 30, 50, 154–55

Strand, Paul, 115
Straus, Murray, 136
Student Nonviolent Coordinating Committee
    (SNCC), 77
students: community service encouraged for,
    64–65, 68–72, 79; on welfare, 63–64, 91
suicides, of Asian immigrants, 119–20, 123
Summer of Service, 71
Sundquist, James L., 56n. 1
Supplemental Security Income (SSI): eligibility
    for, 105–6; immigration and, 110–11, 114,
    117–23, 126, 128
survivors' insurance, 38, 186
Swarns, Rachel, 68

TANF. *See* Temporary Assistance for Needy
    Families (TANF) program
Tashima, Nathaniel, 115
Tate, James, 76
Teach-In on Welfare, 190n. 5
teenage mothers: contradictory policy on, 34;
    opposition to, 26; PRA's impact on, 165; pun-
    ishment for, 94
teenagers: delinquency of, 15–16n. 24, 16–17,
    18–19; welfare requirements for, 40, 93n. 28,
    165
Teghtsoonian, Katherine, 157–58
television, representation of mothers on, 13–14
Temporary Assistance for Needy Families
    (TANF) program: assumptions about poor
    women in, 134; care giving and, 3, 164–65;
    child support and, 140, 144, 146–47, 148–49;
    eligibility for, 106, 117, 128–29; funds for,
    126–27; immigration and, 129–30; regula-
    tions of, 40, 127, 143, 145; workfare jobs un-
    der, 161–62
Tepperman, Jean, 165
Texas: privatization attempts in, 43; sterilization
    in, 30; welfare organizing in, 41–42n. 21
textile mill workers: consciousness of, 233–34;
    slogan of, 216
Thai immigrants, public assistance and, 118
Thomas, Rev. Norman P., 46
Thompson, E. P., 241
Thompson, Linda, 150
Tiahrt, Todd, 71
Tillmon, Johnnie: background of, 190n. 5; on
    motherwork, 49; on NWRO goals, 51–52; on
    poverty, 190; on "welfare mothers," 7; on
    work ethic, 47; on workfare, 48
Title IV, mothers' pensions under, 37
Title IX, court decision on, 175
Title VII: enforcement of, 46; ignored, 26–27

Title XX: federal cuts in, 30; refugee services under, 114
Tocqueville, Alexis de, 246
Torruellas, Rosa M., 58n. 11
trade unions. *See* labor unions
Tronto, Joan, 199
Tulane University, conference at, 25
Turner, Jason, 85–86n. 5
two-parent families: conservative support for, 206–7; economic problem with, 207–8; ethical problem with, 208–9; number of, 32; poverty of, 207n. 56; PRA's encouragement of, 171–72, 177

UAW (United Auto Workers), 49n. 52, 235–36
Uba, Laura, 115
UE (United Electrical Workers), 235
underemployment: educational level and, 89; persistence of, 2–3
undocumented immigrants: countermeasures to, 106; reform's impact on, 123–25; social services for, 101, 103, 105, 123–25, 127; stereotypes of, 104–5
unemployment: Asian immigrants and, 115; factors in women's, 27, 29n. 67, 89; low wages and, 94; persistence of, 2, 207
unemployment insurance: debate on, 54; reform of, 188; workfare and, 90–91
Union Women's Alliance to Gain Equality, 236
United Auto Workers (UAW), 49n. 52, 235–36
United Electrical Workers (UE), 235
United Kingdom: poor relief in, 93; wage levels in, 88
United Nations, 221n. 11
United Parcel Service (UPS), 94
United States: rhetoric vs. reality in, 246–47; wage levels in, 88; women's activism in, 227. *See also specific states*
U.S. Civil Rights Commission, 29n. 67
U.S. Commission on Immigration Reform, 102
U.S. Congress, 175–77, 179. *See also* congressional hearings
U.S. Constitution, 198n. 28
U.S. Department of Health and Human Services: family caps and, 155–56; on Family Violence Option, 145; Office of Community Affairs, 59n. 12; Office of Refugee Resettlement, 112–14
U.S. Department of Labor, 90–91
U.S. Supreme Court, 155–56, 173
United Union Women, 236
universal policies, concept of, 209, 212–13
Uprising of 20,000, 234

UPS (United Parcel Service), 94
Utah, workfare jobs in, 92

Van Dang, Tuan, 119
veteran, definition of, 121–22
victim blaming, 194n. 16
Vietnamese immigrants: context of, 112–16; public assistance and, 117–18
Vietnam War, immigration and, 111–12, 115–16, 121
violence, gang, 166. *See also* domestic violence
Violence Against Women Act (1994), 126, 133–34, 145
Vocational Education Act, 29
Volk, Joe, 62
volunteerism, shift toward, 70
voting: African American, 110; women's, 234–35
Voting Rights Act (1965), 110

wages: accountability and, 209–10; below-poverty, 2–3, 32; call for equality of, 233–34; for child care, 162, 211–12; declining real, 33, 41, 88–92, 94–97; "family," 206–7n. 54, 228–29; for housework, 182; income packaging and, 149; minimum, 42, 67, 90–91, 188; as seductive, 19; social, 245; society's valuation of, 47–48; welfare benefits vs., 27–28n. 60, 84–85; welfare's impact on, 88–92, 244; in workfare initiatives, 42–43, 47–49, 55, 64, 67. *See also* motherwork, value of
Walker, Alexis J., 150
Walker, Alice, 230
War on Poverty: activist women in, 218; Asian immigration and, 110; CAPs under, 59, 76–77; citizen participation in, 56–61; critique of, 71–72; goals of, 56–57, 79–80; legacy of, 80; low-income women and, 59–61; programs in, 64–65, 78
Wasserman (cartoonist), 161
welfare: abuse of administrative power in, 62–63; accountability and, 209–10; contradictions in, 33–35; deeming period and, 111, 125–26, 129, 145; definition of, 32, 37, 187; dependency linked to, 12–13, 176; expansion of, 25–26, 27–28n. 60, 243, 245; family maintenance and, 194, 211, 240–46; feminists on, 3–4, 171, 174–77, 184–88, 190, 206; gender differences in, 207n. 55; historical perspective on, 37–43, 217–19; immigration policy and, 102, 108–16; as impetus for activism, 243–46; justifications of, 191–97, 203–5; labor market's link to, 55, 83–84, 87–92, 191–93; material and cultural practices of, 92–94; opposition to, 64–65;

privatization of, 43, 63, 70, 73, 80, 145–46; racialization of, 2; right to, 184–88; as social control, 176–77; terminology of, 7; universal policies in, 212–13; as women's issue, 51–52, 189–91; as women's "space," 217–19; work combined with, 53, 54–55, 86. *See also* dependency

welfare fraud investigations, 85, 94

"welfare mothers": "bad choices" of, 27–33; blaming, 27; stereotypes of, 11, 152, 154, 177

Welfare Mothers (group), 63

Welfare Mothers March (1968), 49n. 52

welfare recipients: characteristics of, 46, 184; choice eliminated for, 91; cut from benefits, 62, 85; divorced women as, 134–35n. 7; domestic work forced on, 53–55; needs of, 49–50, 211; number of, 1, 84n. 2, 87; stereotypes of, 11; as workers, 53, 54–55, 86; "worthy," 46, 244

welfare reform: as assault on poor mothers, 152–67; consensus on, 174; context for, 104–5; doulia applied to, 203–6, 209–13; families weakened by, 84, 98–99, 130; family caps in, 33, 153–56, 195n. 18; feminists on, 3–4, 184–88; focus of, 37, 67; impact of, 1–3, 88–92, 214; job insecurity linked to, 95, 97; model for current, 73; morality in, 93–94, 97–98; motherwork ignored in, 156–58; politics of, 174–77; potential in, 244–46; as punishment for poor mothers, 27–33, 180–81, 244; racial divisions enforced in, 158–63; racial politics of, 100–105, 180–81, 183–84; subtext of, 189–91, 245–46. *See also* Personal Responsibility and Work Opportunity Reconciliation Act (PRA, 1996); workfare initiatives

welfare rights movement (1960s), 215, 218, 220, 222, 228, 244–45

Welfare Warriors (group), 63n. 26

Wellstone/Murray Amendment (to PRA), 143

WEP (Work Experience Program, N.Y.), 36, 41–42

white women: community activism of, 220; dependency of, 8–9, 14–19, 27; equality for, 182–83; on family needs, 49–50; as feminists for PRA, 174–76; as majority on welfare, 39; as norm, 45; sexual "misbehavior" of, 21; spiritual housework assigned to, 159–61; in welfare state development, 196; women of color's dependency work and, 212. *See also* middle-class women; poor women

white working mothers: changing attitudes toward, 13; children of, 15–20; hostility toward, 14–16, 18–19, 23–24; number of, 12n. 14, 14;

pathology linked to postwar, 10–11; postwar studies of, 16–17

WIC (Women, Infants, and Children), 101

widows: single mothers and, 37–38, 157, 186; "worthy," 46

Wiley, George, 47, 50–51

Wilson, Pete, 104, 124, 127

WIN. *See* Work Incentive Program (WIN)

Wisconsin: homelessness in, 62; immigrant suicides in, 119; learnfare program in, 93n. 28; welfare organizing in, 41–42n. 21, 51; workfare in, 63, 68, 85

Wisconsin Works (W-2), 63, 68

Wolfgang, Myra, 236

Wollstonecraft, Mary, 233–34

womanism, concept of, 229–32

women: battered immigrant, 126, 130; dependency relations among, 211–12; differences among, 51–52, 152, 159, 181–83; invisibility of, 216; marginalization of, 238–40; roles idealized for, 13–14, 32; social expectations for, 237–38; triple roles of, 65; welfare as issue of, 51–52, 189–91; in welfare state development, 196–97. *See also* African American women; choice; dependency; domestic violence; white women; women of color

Women, Infants, and Children (WIC), 101

women of color: menial housework assigned to, 159–61; PRA's impact on, 182–84. *See also* African American women

Women's Committee of One Hundred, 174, 175n. 7, 191

women's movement, 25, 34, 223, 225. *See also* feminists

Women's Trade Union League (WTUL), 232, 234

women's work: motivation for, 16, 228–29; postwar transition in, 19; racial division in, 159–63. *See also* care giving; housework; motherwork; work

Woolsey, Lynn, 179

work: availability of, 68–69, 84, 113–15; capacity for, 193; centralization's impact on, 238–39; as choice, 10–12, 14–16, 34; definitions of, 37, 41, 49, 55, 63, 161–62, 185–86; discrimination in, 2, 26–27, 54–55, 142, 234–36, 238–40; feminists on, 45, 177, 181–84; as male responsibility, 50–51, 237; in motherhood definition, 24–27; as source of equality, 181–83; welfare combined with, 53, 54–55, 86; welfare rights organizations on suitable, 48–49; women's activism and, 218–19, 228–29, 239–40. *See also* job training;

work (*continued*)
motherwork; underemployment; unemployment; wages; working-class women
work ethic: class and, 51–52, 181; contradictions in, 47–48, 51–52; enforced traditional, 45, 50
Work Experience Program (WEP, N.Y.), 36, 41–42
workfare initiatives: AFDC-UP, 39–40; AmeriCorps vs., 69–72; critique of, 43–46, 67–68, 130, 152, 172–73, 200; debate over, 193; domestic work in, 53–55; feminist support for, 43, 177, 181–84; history of, 36–37, 89–90, 193–94, 244; labor market effects of, 55, 83–84, 87–92, 191–93; labor unions and, 41–44, 48–49, 55, 66–68, 91–92; motherwork ignored in, 156–58; occupations in, 48–49, 79, 91–92; opposition to forced, 47–48; privatization of, 63; racial divisions enforced in, 158–63; records on, 91n. 22; regulations in, 39–41, 64; rights threatened by, 163–66, 172–73; as slavery/indenture, 36–37, 42–43, 48, 53, 55, 63n. 26, 92, 184; wages in, 42–43, 47–49, 55, 64, 67; workers defined in, 90–91. *See also* community service; Personal Responsibility and Work Opportunity Reconciliation Act (PRA, 1996)

Work Incentive Program (WIN): child care standards under, 52–53; effects of, 55; establishment of, 36–37; focus of, 39; forced participation in, 48, 51, 67
working-class women: feminism of, 232–37, 247; holidays for, 32, 53; menial housework assigned to, 159–61; "spaces" inhabited by, 217–20, 239–40; standpoint of, 226. *See also* activism; class consciousness; poor women
working mothers: labor union's rejection of, 43–44; as norm, 32; number of, 25–26, 55, 194; opposition to, 26–27; subsidies for, 156
Working Mother's Day, 32
working women: ambivalence about, 26; as nonconformist (1950s), 13–14; on "welfare mothers," 50. *See also* working-class women; working mothers
working women of color, choices of, 20–24. *See also* African American working mothers; working-class women
World War II, women workers and, 14, 235

Yang, Chia, 119–20
Young Militants, 77

Zack, Naomi, 195